THE
SIGNALS
ARE
TALKING

THE
SIGNALS
ARE
TALKING

Why Today's Fringe Is
Tomorrow's Mainstream

AMY WEBB

PublicAffairs
New York

Published in the United States by PublicAffairs™, an imprint of Perseus Books, LLC, a subsidiary of Hachette Book Group, Inc.

PublicAffairs books are available at special discounts for bulk purchases in the U.S. by corporations, institutions, and other organizations. For more information, please contact the Special Markets Department at Perseus Books, 2300 Chestnut Street, Suite 200, Philadelphia, PA 19103, call (800) 810-4145, ext. 5000, or e-mail special.markets@perseusbooks.com.

Book design by Jeff Williams

Library of Congress Cataloging-in-Publication Data

Names: Webb, Amy, 1974– author.
Title: The signals are talking : why today's fringe is tomorrow's mainstream
  / Amy Webb.
Description: First edition. | New York : PublicAffairs, [2016] | Includes
  bibliographical references and index.
Identifiers: LCCN 2016028425 (print) | LCCN 2016039541 (ebook) | ISBN
  9781610396660 (hardcover) | ISBN 9781610396677 (ebook)
Subjects: LCSH: Business forecasting. | Strategic planning. | Technological
  innovations.
Classification: LCC HD30.27 .W39 2016 (print) | LCC HD30.27 (ebook) | DDC
  658.4/0355—dc23
LC record available at https://lccn.loc.gov/2016028425

First Edition

10 9 8 7 6 5 4 3 2 1

To my daughter, Petra, and to her classmates:
We have entrusted the future to you. Be bold and bright.

CONTENTS

INTRODUCTION

"Hello, Are You Lost?"

THE FUTURE DOESN'T simply arrive fully formed overnight, but emerges step by step. It first appears at seemingly random points around the fringe of society, never in the mainstream. Without context, those points can appear disparate, unrelated, and hard to connect meaningfully. But over time they fit into patterns and come into focus as a full-blown trend: a convergence of multiple points that reveal a direction or tendency, a force that combines some human need and new enabling technology that will shape the future.

It's something I discovered living in Japan, way back in the twentieth century.

•

Akihabara District, Tokyo, 1997. The bottom of my jeans were already drenched as I made my way from the subway through the downpour and past a cacophony of cartoon voices and computer-generated swirls of electronica. The sheer amount of information and noise made it hard to concentrate.

I had a map written in Japanese, but that wasn't the problem. The waterlogged paper made it impossible to read the few characters left that hadn't blurred entirely. I found myself under some elevated railroad tracks and standing in front of a nondescript door, but the hacker friend I expected to meet was nowhere in sight. Maybe I was in the wrong place.

I shoved my hands deep into my coat pockets and squeezed past a series of twisting alleys all lined with rows and rows of circuits, motherboards, cables, wire cutters, and tiny plastic parts of all shapes and sizes. More information. More noise. There were "no smoking" signs everywhere, but that didn't stop the group of men walking ahead of me.

Eventually, I stopped at a tiny electronics shack and tried to read the map again.

"Hello," I heard a tentative voice. "Are you lost?"

He was, it turned out, a computer geek, albeit one who had a couple of decades on most of the folks who make up this species. Tattered back issues of *Pasokon Ge-mu* and "*Oh! X*" magazines were piled up next to disassembled PC towers. I explained that I was trying to find my friend, a regular in Akihabara who was building a new kind of game that could be played on a mobile phone. The corners of his mouth crinkled upward as he motioned me over toward a counter in the back of the store.

On the glass were two small mobile phones. He gave me one and told me to wait. He took the other in his hands and started tapping on the alphanumeric keypad. A moment later, I saw a message flash on my screen. こんにちは—"hello" in Japanese. I'd used mobile-to-mobile messaging before, but tried to muster a "gee-whiz" look so as not to offend him.

Then, he sent me another message. This time, the text was blue and underlined. It looked like a web address, but that wasn't possible. It was 1997, and back in America, the most exciting mobile technology was a compact 1G flip phone that had a retractable antenna. This was something entirely different.

"Try," he said. I pressed a button and the phone started downloading something.

"Wait . . . is this a ringtone?" I asked. "Am I on the internet?"

On the screen, I moved the cursor down to the link and pressed "enter." As I did, all the noise and all that information diffused into decipherable nodes of data. I could hear the signals talking.

This phone in my hand was an experiment on the fringe, a clever hack. I shifted my thought to networks of phones all connecting to the internet, to websites, to the Shinkansen train schedule . . .

Another signal. If we could receive information, we would necessarily give out our information, too—passively and directly. We would buy train tickets, right from our phones. Network operators would know details about us, what we clicked on, what we downloaded. Service providers would earn revenue based on our usage. They would have incentives to provide more bandwidth and faster speeds . . .

Another signal. I started thinking about all the other early research I'd been hearing about. Japan was on the brink of a much faster mobile network that would allow for more people to connect at once. Increased capacity also meant higher speeds, and for the first time, the ability to send files to other devices . . .

Another signal. Digital cameras were getting smaller. An engineering professor at Dartmouth was at work on an active pixel image sensor, something so tiny it could be embedded into a pen. Two Japanese companies, Sharp and Kyocera, were trying to put image sensors into their phones. Teenagers had become obsessed with *puri-kurabu* photo vending machines—they regularly visited with friends, posing for photos of themselves. They'd use an interactive screen to decorate the photos with different backdrops and doodles before printing them out as stickers.

I listened as the signals connected me to adjacent nodes. I knew of others who were experimenting with tangentially related projects. A startup in New York City had successfully wrested electronic mail—"email," for short—from university researchers and turned it commercial. For the first time, everyday people were getting online, transfixed by this new medium and excited about sending fast, short messages between computers within just a few seconds. Commercial email networks were starting to boom, unable to meet demand. At the same time, consumer behavior had started to shift. People expected and received faster communication. They created digital identities with vanity email addresses. They had access to a "reply-all" command—a futuristic megaphone that broadcast their messages to large, engaged audiences.

And then there was the group of mad scientists out in Sunnyvale, California—engineers who'd created the first car-based GPS in the early 1980s. Nothing remotely similar had existed until that point, so they had to borrow an ancient Polynesian term to name the thing they'd built. They called it the Etak Navigator[1] (Polynesian for "a set of moving navigational points"); it was so far ahead of its time that its value meant little, if anything, to the average consumer. I remembered reading an old issue of *Inc.* magazine, where the founder of Etak explained his bigger vision: "Let's say you're in your car, and you want to go to dinner. You've got this box on the dash. You punch in 'Japanese,' then 'cheap,' then 'good sushi.' The box takes over and guides you to a place."[2]

The Etak never made its way into our cars, but standing there, holding this black mobile phone in the middle of Akihabara, I could imagine a future version of myself using an adapted form of that fringe technology. I'd punch in "good sushi" and text my hacker friend the GPS coordinates of where to meet me. Rather than carrying around a camera so that I could take photos, get them developed, and send them through the mail back to the United States, I'd make a video phone call to my parents and share my sushi dinner with them, in real time.

Suddenly, I realized I wasn't lost at all. I heard the signals talking, and they were telling me how this experimental phone from the fringe would eventually enter our mainstream to dramatically transform all facets of human life in the future. I was holding a physical manifestation representing breathtaking change: it would reshape how we operate our businesses, how we work, learn, and relate to each other. It would democratize our access to knowledge. It would manipulate our attention spans and shift the neural pathways in our brains. It would speed life up and usher in a universal expectation of immediate access to information and, inevitably, a culture of on-demand goods, services, and content.

"*Mirai kara kita ne.*" It's from the future, said the old computer geek.

"No," I told him. "Not from the future."

Because right now, standing in his tiny electronics stall in Akihabara, we were in the present. Just as the phone hadn't traveled back in time from some futuristic date to 1997, neither was our pre-mapped destiny already written in the stars. It was up to us to listen to the signals talking, and to map out the future for ourselves.

•

Waterloo, Ontario, 2007. Mike Lazaridis, the cofounder of BlackBerry, was working out on his treadmill at home, staring up at the television. Forgettable commercials cycled through every fifteen minutes. Then one caught his attention. Set against a minimalist black background was a hand holding a mobile phone, one that had no buttons. A male voiceover began: "This is how you turn it on," and with a simple swipe the phone was unlocked, revealing a dozen candy-colored, sleek icons. "This is your music," the voice continued, as the phone turned horizontally and album covers appeared, which could be flipped through with the simple flick of a finger. "This is the web," the voice said, and the *New York Times* instantaneously loaded inside of a web browser, mimicking exactly what it looked like on a computer screen. "And this is a call on your iPhone," the voice said at last, before Apple's iconic logo faded in.[3]

Lazaridis, a global pioneer in mobile communications, hadn't seen the iPhone coming. And yet here was this new trend in mobile technology—a computer-like phone, with no buttons—that was now entering the mainstream. He found out about the iPhone via a commercial, just like everyone else.[4]

That summer, Lazaridis got his hands on an iPhone and pried it open. He was shocked by what he saw—it was as if Apple had stuffed a Mac computer into this tiny, handheld mobile device.

Two decades earlier, Lazaridis and a fellow engineering student, Douglas Fregin, had founded a computer-science consulting company, which they called Research in Motion, or RIM. Their breakthrough product was a new kind of mobile phone, which offered workers the ability to send and receive emails securely while they were out of the office. They called it the BlackBerry.[5]

BlackBerry quickly became a status symbol as much as an essential productivity tool. "If you had a BlackBerry you were an important person, as at that time a lot of people didn't have a smartphone," said Kevin Michaluk, founder of the CrackBerry.com news site. Vincent Washington, who was a senior business development manager, said that new product meetings would often remind him of that infamous briefcase from *Pulp Fiction*. Lazaridis would walk in with his own special briefcase, and "there would be this golden glow of devices." Brendan Kenalty, who was in charge of RIM's customer base management, often found himself chided for his job title. Why on earth would anyone need a loyalty and retention strategy for a BlackBerry?[6]

Lazaridis was curious, but dismissive. With a device that had become so addictive and indispensable—it did earn the nickname "CrackBerry," after all—RIM had become one of the largest and most valuable companies in the world, valued at $26 billion.[7] It controlled an estimated 70 percent of the mobile market share and counted 7 million BlackBerry users.[8]

Lazaridis already had a successful suite of products, so he and his team weren't watching the fringe. They weren't paying attention as a new trend emerged—smartphones that would become all-purpose mobile computing devices, with the power of a PC right in our pockets. Rather than carrying a BlackBerry for business and an iPod or a laptop for personal use, consumers would naturally gravitate toward one device that could meet all the demands of their everyday needs and work tasks.

Initially, it wasn't clear that this single-device trend—and especially a phone with such a radically different design—would stick. In addition to disparaging the iPhone's short battery life and weak security relative to the BlackBerry, Lazaridis mocked its lack of a physical keyboard: "Try typing a web key on a touch screen on an iPhone, that's a real challenge. You cannot see what you type."[9]

At its launch, comparisons to the BlackBerry were inevitable, and they were harsh for the iPhone. Adding a calendar event or updating a contact had to be synched manually on an iPhone. There was no push email, and the inbox system was confusing. The Safari browser offered a stunning interface, but it was extremely slow, even with text-only pages. Apple's iTunes store may have offered far more apps, but could they be trusted? They'd been made by outside developers, not certified partners as was the case with BlackBerry.

These arguments further distracted RIM from recalibrating its strategy and from monitoring the fringes of society, even as it was becoming clear that the iPhone was ushering in a new era of mobile connectivity. Rather than quickly adapting its beloved product for a new generation of mobile users, RIM continued tweaking and incrementally improving its existing BlackBerrys and their operating systems. But that first iPhone was in many ways a red herring. Apple swiftly made improvements to the phone and the operating system. Soon it became clear that the iPhone was never intended to compete against the BlackBerry. Apple had an entirely different vision for the future of smartphones—it saw the trend in single devices for all of life, not just business—and it would leapfrog RIM as a result.

Cisco and SAP adopted iPhones. Apple and IBM entered into a long-term partnership to develop one hundred new apps. As RIM executives struggled to understand how they'd been blindsided by this new trend, the company was forced to launch a desperate marketing campaign that paid iPhone users up to $550 to switch back to a classic BlackBerry. In 2012, Lazaridis and his co-CEO Jim Balsillie stepped down. By the end of 2014, RIM's market share had collapsed to 1 percent.[10]

BlackBerry executives failed to make the necessary leaps like the ones I'd made a decade earlier in Akihabara. I was immersed in the fringe, looking at new experimentation and research, spotting patterns and working out possible scenarios for the future. They kept their heads down, fixated on their successful product. "Success is a lousy teacher," wrote Microsoft cofounder Bill Gates. "It seduces smart people into thinking they can't lose."[11]

Success rendered RIM helpless in the end. What about the rest of us? Are we helpless as well, because the future is full of surprise competitors and moonshot devices? Polaroid, Zenith, Blockbuster, Circuit City, and Motorola struggled because the future surprised them, too. Rather than helping to create their new reality, executives were instead asking themselves, "How did we miss that?"

README.TXT

This book contains a method for seeing the future. It's an organized approach that, if followed, will advance your understanding of the world as it is changing. Reading it, you will learn how to think like a futurist, and to forecast emerging trends as they shift from the fringe to the mainstream, and how to make better decisions about the future, today.

If you are in any position of leadership—whether you're the CEO of a large corporation, a member of a nonprofit board, a mid-level human resources manager, a media executive, an investor, a chief marketing officer, a government administrator, a school superintendent, or the head of your household—you must strategically monitor trends and plan for the future. Failing to do so will put your organization and your future earnings at risk, but there are greater forces at work. If humans do not make a greater effort to understand the implications of our actions today, we are in danger of jeopardizing our own humanity.

I am a futurist, and I research emerging technology and forecast trends for a living. The term "futurology" comes from the Latin (*futurum*, or future) and the Greek suffix *–logia* (the science of), and it was coined by a German professor named Ossip Flechtheim in 1943,[12] who, along with author H. G. Wells several decades earlier,[13] proposed "futurism" as a new academic discipline. It's an interdisciplinary field combining mathematics, engineering, art, technology, economics, design, history, geography, biology, theology, physics, and philosophy. As a futurist, my job is not to spread prophecies, but rather to collect data, identify emerging trends, develop strategies, and calculate the probabilities of various scenarios occurring in the future. Forecasts are used to help leaders, teams, and individuals make better, more informed decisions, even as their organizations face great disruption.

Technology is the unilateral source of nearly all of the significant things that have changed the world in the past five hundred years, including movable type, the sextant, the moldboard plow, the cotton gin, the steam engine, oil refining, pasteurization, the assembly line, photography, the telegraph, nuclear fission, the internet, and the personal computer. At some point, these were all mere fringe science and technology experiments.

This is not a book about technology trends per se, as a book of today's trends would be outdated and useless even before it came off the press. That's how fast the world is changing. A book that only offers a series of trends would force you to apply someone else's vision of the future to your own organization, industry, or market. Technology trends themselves—smartwatches, virtual reality, the Internet of Things—make for good media headlines, but they don't solve for the ongoing questions facing every organization: What technology is on the horizon? How will it impact our customers or constituents? How will our competitors harness the trend? Where does the trend create potential new partnerships or collaborators for us? How does this trend impact our industry and all of its parts? Who are the drivers of change in this trend? How will the wants, needs, and expectations of our customers change as a result of this trend?

To answer these questions, you need more than someone else's prognostications. You need a guided process to evaluate and adapt the pronouncements made by researchers, other businesspeople, and thought leaders within their professional spaces. You need a way to see the future for yourself.

The Signals Are Talking is a systematic way of evaluating new ideas being developed on the fringe that, at first blush, may seem too "out there" to affect you. But in every possible construct, our future is completely intertwined with technology, and as I discovered in Tokyo's Akihabara District[14] in 1997, nothing in technology is ever really too esoteric that it doesn't deserve a few moments of attention. There is no possible scenario where technology does not play a significant role in the years, decades, and centuries to come. Therefore, the trends we must track and the actions we put into place necessarily involve technology in some way.

The method in this book is made up of six steps. You can think of it as a set of instructions for the future—though this is no ordinary instruction manual. First, you must visit what I call the "unusual suspects" at the fringe. From there, you will uncover hidden patterns, connecting experimentation at the fringe to our fundamental human needs and desires. The patterns will reveal to you a possible trend, one you'll then need to investigate, interrogate, and prove. Next, you'll calculate the trend's ETA and direction: Where is it heading, how quickly, and with what momentum? However, identifying a trend isn't enough—as RIM discovered in 2008, when it attempted to launch its self-described "iPhone killer." You must develop probable, plausible, and possible scenarios in order to create a salient strategy in the present. There is one final step: pressure-testing the strategy against the trend to make sure the action you're taking is the right one.

The instructions are illustrated with stories that range from Sony being brought to its knees by hackers, even though company executives could have easily foreseen its future troubles, to the scientific community being shocked, and then outraged, when it learned that Dr. Ian Wilmut and his team had cloned a sheep named Dolly.

These and other stories may be familiar to you. But when we use the instructions to decipher the signals, what you see will start to seem quite strange. Your perception of present-day reality will, I hope, be challenged. You may even feel disoriented. But I feel confident that you will never interpret the world around you in quite the same way again.

Turn the page and listen closely. The signals are talking.

CHAPTER ONE

The Instructions

A Futurist's Playbook for Every Organization

WHAT WAS ONCE top-secret military technology has left the domain of government and is now sitting in my living room, with its batteries recharging. I've used it to take photos of my daughter's kindergarten class field trips. It came in handy when I noticed a possible leak in our roof. I flew it after a big winter storm to survey whether my neighborhood streets had been cleared. Realizing they hadn't, I streamed aerial footage to my neighborhood association and asked that they send a plow.

It's a drone, and a rather unremarkable one at that. Just like many of the other consumer models available for purchase, it has four propellers and will fly autonomously along my preset waypoints.

In 2015, two drones operated by civilians trying to capture video inadvertently prevented firefighters from putting out a rapidly spreading California wildfire.[1] As a result, the fire crossed over onto a freeway and destroyed a dozen vehicles. There were several incidents of drones flying around airports to shoot photos and video, too: in one case reported to the Federal Aviation Administration (FAA),[2] a drone just missed the nose of a JetBlue flight. In another, a drone got in the way of a Delta flight trying to land.[3]

By the end of 2015, the FAA was estimating that a million drones would be sold and given as holiday presents that year[4]—but neither the FAA nor any other government agency had decided on regulations for how everyday Americans could use them. Close encounters with airplanes prompted conversations about whether or not the airspace should be regulated, which forced drone manufacturers and the aviation industry into uncomfortable conversations, since each has an economic stake in the future of unmanned vehicles (UMVs).

Drones were a fringe technology barreling toward the mainstream, and a lack of planning and foresight pitted dozens of organizations against each other. One proposal from Amazon called for a new kind of drone highway system in the sky, separating commercial UMVs from drones belonging to hobbyists, journalists, and the like. Hobbyists like me would be restricted to flying below an altitude of two hundred feet, while commercial delivery drones—including the fleet Amazon is planning to launch—would gain access to a zone between two hundred and four hundred feet overhead. The rest of the airspace would belong to planes.[5]

It certainly sounded like a reasonable plan, but it lacked context: namely, emerging trends from adjacent fields. No one involved in the proposals and debate considered how restricting the airspace might impact us in ways that have nothing to do with midair collisions. They dealt with an issue in the present-day, but didn't go through the process of forecasting likely developments that would intersect with this plan in the future.

Let me walk you through how a futurist would address this problem. Since there are many issues involved, let's analyze just one plausible scenario that connects a series of unrelated dots. It will, I believe, reveal why stopping to focus on flying altitudes alone, rather than mapping out the full trajectory of drones as a trend, would result in unintended changes in geopolitics and widespread environmental damage in the future.

If commercial drone lanes operate in an altitude range of two hundred to four hundred feet, a new twenty-five-story apartment building might require a special right-of-way easement, which could be costly and tedious to pursue. So it might be easier for architects to start building laterally. But who wants to walk the length of a football field just to get to a morning meeting? As it happens, ThyssenKrupp, a German engineering firm, has invented self-propelled elevators that can travel both horizontally and vertically.[6] Rather than taking an elevator up twenty floors, you could take it across the expanse. With these conditions in place, a new kind of building, which I'll call a "landscraper," will start to occupy all that empty land covering much of the United States. Environmentalists will protest, arguing that soil displacement will flood local rivers and streams with sediment, killing off the plants that feed the fish, which in turn feed terrestrial wildlife. But if the drone-lane proposal is accepted, we would wind up with busy overhead highways. The only open space would be horizontal.

The result: a necessary shift in how our cities are built and maintained. The change would be felt less in places like New York City, where there is scant open land available, and more in less populated areas between the East and West coasts. Landscrapers would be developed in smaller cities across the Plains and Midwest, helping to catalyze new centers of business and innovation (where Google has started to lay fiber networks). Our thriving urban centers of the future will be San Antonio, Kansas City, and Oklahoma City. Established tax bases, congressional districts, and educational resources would be disrupted. Without proper advance city planning, these new hubs will suffer from traffic jams and a lack of sustainable basic civic resources, such as housing—issues that have already become significant problems in communities like Austin, Texas, and San Jose, Sunnyvale, and Santa Clara, California.

American farmers will be happy to sell their land, destroying big agricultural corporations like Monsanto, Dupont, and Land O'Lakes. Without American farms, we'll find ourselves forced to become less than self-sufficient in food resources and more reliant on agricultural imports, changing the geopolitical power dynamic between the United States and countries such as China, Mexico, India, and Canada, which would become our primary fruit and vegetable providers.

All because in 2015, we thought it would be cool to fly an unmanned vehicle up into the air to take some pictures for our blogs and social feeds.

This future scenario won't simply arrive, fully formed, as I've just described and as a futurist would forecast. Rather, it will evolve slowly over a period of years, and as various pieces fall into place, we would continue to track the trends and recalibrate our strategy. At first, all these developments will seem novel, unconnected, and random, like odd experiments or impossible theories hatched on the fringe of society. Without context, those points can appear disparate, unrelated, and hard to connect meaningfully. (Invisible drone highways in the sky? Landscrapers?) But over time, they will fit into patterns and come into focus: a convergence of multiple points that reveal a direction or tendency, a force that combines some human need and new enabling technology that will shape the future.

Futurists are skilled at listening to and interpreting the signals talking. It's a learnable skill, and a process anyone can master. Futurists look for early patterns—pre-trends, if you will—as the scattered points on the fringe converge and begin moving toward the mainstream. They know most patterns will come to nothing, and so they watch and wait and test the patterns to find those few that will evolve into genuine trends. Each trend is a looking glass into the future, a way to see over time's horizon. The advantage of forecasting the future in this way is obvious. Organizations that can see trends early enough to take action have first-mover influence. But they can also help to inform and shape the broader context, conversing and collaborating with those in other fields to plan ahead.

No one should plan for a future she cannot see. Yet that is exactly what's happening every day in our boardrooms and legislative office buildings. Too often, leaders ignore the signals, wait too long to take action, or plan for only one scenario. Not only will first-movers create new strategies, thought leadership, hacks, or exploits to align with the trend, they are likely developing third and fourth iterations already. As a trend develops and advances, a vast network is being formed, connecting researchers to manufacturers, venture capital money to startups, and consumers with strange new technologies—such as a drone with such a sophisticated onboard computer that it can be sent on reconnaissance missions well past our line of sight. As is often the case with new technologies, those in leadership positions wait until they must to confront the future, which by now has already passed them by.

The paradox of the present is to blame: we are too fearful about the intricacies of technology, safety, and the needs of the various government agencies and equipment manufacturers to think more broadly about how technology like drones might emerge from the fringe to become our future mainstream.

I may be wrong, but I suspect that few, if any, leaders in organizations working on the future of drones today are following a futurist's playbook, giving thought to traffic congestion in San Antonio, farmers in the Midwest, or our potential dependence on Chinese corn in the world we are creating for tomorrow.

LIZARD BRAINS

We must dedicate time and effort to planning for the future. However, our fear and rejection of the unknown has been an ongoing thread throughout human history. The fact that we continue to struggle with this problem, from generation to generation, suggests either that Friedrich Nietzsche was right, and that we're living the exact same life now that we've lived an infinite number of times in the past,[7] or that we've internalized a belief that the future is something that happens *to us*, rather than something that we, in fact, *create*.

Our resistance to change is hardwired in the oldest, reptilian portion of our brains, which is located down by the brainstem and cerebellum. It's that section that's responsible for our automated vital functions, such as our heart rate and body temperature. It also controls our "fight-or-flight" response, which has preserved and protected humans throughout our evolution. When that system gets overwhelmed with a complex new concept or is forced to make a decision about an unfamiliar topic, it protests by causing us psychological distress, fear, and anxiety. Adrenaline floods our bodies so that we're physically ready to fight or flee if we need to. Like breathing, our resistance to new technology happens automatically, without thought.

In 1970, social thinker Alvin Toffler theorized about a "future shock" in his groundbreaking book of the same name,[8] arguing that the emerging computers and the race to space would cause disorientation and fragmentation within our society. British physicist and Nobel Prize winner Sir George Thomson posited that the nearest parallel of technological changes taking place in the late 1960s to early 1970s wasn't the Industrial Revolution, but instead the "invention of agriculture in the Neolithic age."[9] At that same time, John Diebold, the American automation pioneer, warned that "the effects of the technological revolution we are now living through will be deeper than any social change we have experienced before."[10]

Adapting to big, sweeping disruption or taking risks on unproven technology causes that part of our lower brains to kick into gear. It's more comfortable for us to make incremental changes—we trick ourselves into feeling as though we've challenged the status quo in preparation for the future, without all that reptilian distress.

Our reptilian brains sometimes tempt us into denying that change is afoot in any meaningful way. Many prominent thinkers would disagree that this is the first time in human history when real, fundamental change is taking place within a single generation, and the driving force is technology. For example, economist Robert Gordon argued in *The Rise and Fall of American Growth* that our greatest innovations occurred between 1870 and 1970, and that that era's level of American ingenuity and productivity cannot be repeated.[11] Those one hundred years ushered in life-altering change that was immediately observable and uncomplicated: the discovery of penicillin eradicated many bacterial infections; Henry Ford's assembly-line production brought automobiles to the masses; submarines took warfare below the oceans; robotic equipment replaced humans in factories; radio delivered the news in every American's living room.

And yet, compared to that time period, the advancements of today are orders of magnitude more nuanced and complex, and without intentional effort, they are difficult to see. Take, for example, the quantum computer. This is an entirely new kind of system capable of solving problems that are computationally too difficult for our existing machines. The computer at your home or office can only process binary information expressed as 1s and 0s. In quantum computing, those 1s and 0s actually exist in two states (qubits) at once, allowing computations to be made in parallel. If you build two qubits, they hold four values simultaneously: 00, 01, 10, and 11.[12]

When a programmer needs to debug a system, she can write code that copies and extracts the values from the correct 1s and 0s. It's straightforward. In a quantum system, those 1s and 0s form different combinations, and the very act of trying to observe that data as it is in transit changes its nature. Yes, quantum machines are computers—but they're not like any computer you've seen before. Not in the way they look, or in how they operate, or in the functions they can perform.

You may never see a quantum computer, and even if you do, it will appear rather unremarkable—in the present day, it looks like a big enclosed server rack. The only remarkable aesthetic change in the farther future is that it will shrink in physical size. But you will benefit from the technology nonetheless: quantum computing will be used for encrypting your personal data and your credit card number when you're shopping, in figuring out how to extract pollution from the air, and in designing new personalized drugs and predicting the spread of future public health epidemics.

A generation ago, a single computer took up an entire room—and Pluto was still a planet floating in a theoretical icy belt system beyond the orbit of Neptune. Today, you have access to more computing power in your little smartphone than all of the National Aeronautics and Space Administration (NASA) did when it sent Neil Armstrong, Buzz Aldrin, and Michael Collins to the moon. Your smartphone seems pedestrian because you are only exposed to the final product—you don't see the underlying technology that powers it, and how that tech is evolving independent of the device itself. Yes, we send Tweets to reality TV shows. We Instagram no-makeup selfies. We allow our phones to track and monitor our levels of fitness, our whereabouts, our vital signs. And then we share our personal information with whoever's interested, even with complete strangers whom we will never meet.

Just as many people discounted that early internet-connected phone I described in the Introduction, you may be tempted to argue that our smartphones are toys that cannot be compared to putting humans on the moon—not technological breakthroughs. However, the very technology that's in your phone is being used to fundamentally alter the operations of most businesses, to perform life-saving medical tests in remote areas, and to change our political ideas and worldviews.

One of the reasons you don't recognize this moment in time as an era of great transformation is because it's hard to recognize change. Another reason: novelty has become the new normal. The pace of change has accelerated, as we are exposed to and adopt new technologies with greater enthusiasm and voracity each year. Consider the washing machine, a groundbreaking new technological innovation when it was introduced in the early 1900s. It took nearly three decades for more than 50 percent of Americans to buy them for their homes.[13] In 1951, CBS broadcast the "Premiere," the first show in color,[14] and within fifteen years the majority of households had abandoned their black-and-white sets.[15] Between 2007, when the first-generation iPhone was released, and 2015, more than 75 percent of Americans bought some kind of smartphone.[16] In fact, 7 percent of us have now abandoned our landlines and traditional broadband services altogether.[17]

The year Toffler's *Future Shock* was published, about 7,000 new products entered America's supermarket shelves. Fifty-five percent of them hadn't existed a decade previously.[18] In 2014, 22,252 projects were successfully funded on Kickstarter.[19] One of them came from a guy with an idea for a computerized watch, the Pebble. He raised $10 million from 69,000 individual backers and forced big, established companies like Apple and Samsung to hurry up and get their own products to market.[20]

We've even had to invent a new term for all the tech startups crossing the billion-dollar valuation threshold: "unicorns," because investments on that scale had previously been just a myth. By mid-2015 there were 123 unicorns, with a total cumulative valuation of $469 billion.[21] To put that incomprehensible number into perspective, Uber's $51 billion valuation was equal at that time to the gross domestic product (GDP) of Croatia.[22]

The gravitational pull toward what's new, what's now, and what's next has left us in a constant state of fight-or-flight. Paradoxically, we both worry about and look forward to the latest gadgets and tools. Overwhelmed with the sheer amount of new shiny objects, we don't take the necessary step back to connect all the dots and to ask: How does one technology influence the other? What's really going on? Are we missing a bigger and more important trend? What trajectory are we on, and does it make sense? These are questions futurists think about all the time. But when it comes to organizations, it's only after a fringe technology moves into the mainstream that we suddenly raise concerns, attempt to join in, or realize it's too late—and that an industry has been upended.

Because we lack this necessary dialogue on future forecasting, when it comes to technology-driven change, organizations are philosophically schizophrenic, arguing for and against contradictory positions. We may have initially lambasted Edward Snowden, who in 2013 leaked classified documents about cybersecurity and digital surveillance through the press, but with some distance has come appreciation. Political leaders, news organizations, and everyday people at one point called for Snowden's arrest (and worse). Then we changed our minds. In a January 2014 editorial, the *New York Times* editorial board wrote: "Considering the enormous value of the information he has revealed, and the abuses he has exposed, Mr. Snowden deserves better than a life of permanent exile, fear and flight. He may have committed a crime to do so, but he has done his country a great service. . . . In retrospect, Mr. Snowden was clearly justified in believing that the only way to blow the whistle on this kind of intelligence-gathering was to expose it to the public and let the resulting furor do the work his superiors would not."[23]

We don't suffer from the "future shock" that Toffler warned us about as much as we suffer from ongoing disorientation. We are bewildered at the implications of technology because technology is becoming more pervasive in our everyday lives. From biohacking our genomes to robots that can repair themselves, it's becoming more and more difficult to make informed decisions about the future.

But decisions must be made, and either subconsciously or with dedicated effort, each one of us is making thousands of them every single day, including two hundred on food alone.[24] Which app should you build? Which new innovation should you try? Which startup should you back? In which direction should you pivot? Those are in addition to the more quotidian decisions, like which movie to watch on Netflix, what song to stream on Spotify, what dinner entrée to order from Seamless, or which of one of the 2,767 versions of the board game Monopoly to order from Amazon.[25]

We've made a devil's pact, swapping convenience and efficiency for an ever-increasing tyranny of information and choice. Technology has forced us to either make poor decisions or make none at all, and it is causing or will eventually lead to cataclysmic, unwelcome disruption. During this period of intense technological change, we focus too narrowly on value chains rather than thinking about how what we're doing fits into the bigger ecosystem.

THE PARADOX OF THE PRESENT

As we marvel at the prospects of genomic editing, self-driving cars, and humanoid companions, we have to keep in mind that our present-day reality binds us to a certain amount of perceptual bias. Fight-or-flight may have kept our prehistoric ancestors from getting eaten by a saber-toothed tiger, but over time it has stunted our unique ability to daydream about and plan for a better future.

Without a guided process, we fall victim to the paradox of the present. We have a hard time seeing the future because we lack a shared point of reference rooted in our present circumstances. How could you explain to a Sicilian living through the plague in the Middle Ages that in just a few hundred years, not only would we have invented a simple shot to cure us of many diseases, but robots and lasers would help doctors perform open heart surgery? How could you have explained to Henry Ford, as he sent his first Model T through an assembly line, that his grandchildren would see the advent of self-driving, computerized, battery-powered cars? Do you think that in 1986, as Toyota's fifty-millionth car came off the line,[26] company chairman Eiji Toyoda would have believed that within a few decades the four biggest car companies wouldn't be Toyota, Honda, General Motors, and Mazda, but instead Tesla, Google, Apple, and Uber? How could you articulate the concept of quantum computing—that the same information could both exist and not exist within a computer simultaneously—to Ada Lovelace, when she wrote the first algorithm ever carried out by a machine?

Without instructions as a guide, we face the same perceptual bias as all of the generations who came before us; we have a difficult time seeing how not only the far future will unfold but the near future as well. Organizations, communities, and we as individuals must cope with hundreds of first-time situations driven by technology at a pace unmatched in any other time in history. We experience these micro-moments on a near-daily basis: new mobile apps, new wearable fitness devices, new hacks, new ways to harass others on social media, new directives in how to "binge watch" the latest show on Netflix.

Novelty is the new normal, making it difficult for us to understand the bigger picture. We now inhabit a world where most of the information that has ever existed is less than ten years old. From the beginnings of human civilization until 2003, five exabytes of data were created. We are now creating five exabytes of data *every two days*.[27] In fact, in the minute it took you to read that last sentence, 2.8 million pieces of content were shared on Facebook alone.[28] On Instagram, 250,000 new photos were posted.[29]

A lack of information isn't what is preventing us from seeing the future. Searching for *drone* on the visible web (the searchable, indexed part) returns 142 million results.[30] There are hundreds of thousands of forum posts, spreadsheets, and comments about it on the hidden web, too—the deeper layers of the internet that do not show up on searches for a variety of reasons (they require a password, they can only be accessed using special software, they're peer-to-peer networks, or they lack the code necessary for a search engine crawler to discover them). The *Washington Post* published 717 stories about drones during 2015 alone.[31] The Brookings Institution published 65 white papers, op-eds, and blog posts about drones during that same time period.[32] Barraged with ever more information, we must now interpret all this new knowledge and data we're being fed and figure out how to make all of it useful. Exposure to more information tends to confuse rather than inform us. Thousands of drones are being flown all around the country. Lawmakers have access to plenty of information, and yet they don't have a plan for the future.

Information overload hampers our ability to understand novelty when we see it. This tendency is especially pronounced when it comes to technology, where exciting new products launch daily. Joost, a much-hyped video service called a "YouTube killer" by tech reporters, raised $45 million in venture capital before launch.[33] Color, a photo-sharing app created by two charismatic, popular denizens of Silicon Valley, raised $41 million as a prelaunch tech startup.[34] AdKeeper raised $43 million before launch, billing itself as a new kind of digital coupon clipping service.[35]

In all three cases, the founders promised something unique. But novelty is a distraction, not a clear trend worth tracking. Joost's investors lost all their money—the timing for streaming video wasn't right in 2006. Color was a confusing product that consumers didn't understand

and that tech bloggers hated. AdKeeper's pitch sounded interesting, but in practice no one wanted to save the banner ads they saw online. That's $129 million in investment that evaporated, and I've only given you three examples.

The paradox of the present impairs our judgment when we're looking for far- and near-future technologies. If we're not mistaking trendy apps for bona fide trends, then the paradox tricks us into mistaking a wave of disruption as a once-in-a-lifetime occurrence, so we dismiss that disruption as a novel circumstance—when it's anything but.

PERILS OF THE PARADOX: SONY'S DAEMONS

Sony, the giant media and electronics company, is all too familiar with the paradox of the present. Sometime in early February 2014, hackers obtained the credentials for two corporate user accounts at Sony Pictures Entertainment. Courtney Schaberg, a vice president of legal compliance at Sony, sent an email to the company's chief counsel and other executives about the breach, writing that the unauthorized user may have uploaded malware. "The two accounts have been disabled," she wrote, adding that a colleague was looking into the matter. In a follow-up email, Schaberg said that the hackers had infiltrated Spirit-WORLD, a kind of central nervous system for Sony's distribution of media files as well as billings, bookings, and the like.[36]

Rather than planning in a meaningful way for the future—like searching for zero day vulnerabilities (software holes that Sony hadn't discovered yet), or listening to hacker community chatter about emerging malware and exploits—the executives instead brushed off the incident. They weren't paying attention to what the signals were telling them—that hackers were increasingly focusing their attention on corporations. Epsilon, the largest email marketing service company in the world, had also been hacked, exposing the account information of 2,500 customer email lists for businesses ranging from Wal-Mart to Capital One.[37] Hackers had compromised 70 of the in-store PIN pads at arts-and-crafts chain Michaels, stealing credit and debit card information, which was later used to forge ATM cards that got used throughout California and Nevada.[38] Citibank revealed that hackers had compromised 200,000 credit card accounts.[39]

While all these breaches were serious, the underground hacking community had always regarded Sony as one of the biggest targets. Sony first raised the ire of the tech community when in 2005 the company's music division took an aggressive stance on its CDs. Sony embedded two pieces of protection on its CDs, which prevented them from being copied—but which also secretly installed rootkits onto a computer without the user's knowledge or permission. (A rootkit is a special kind of software that is used to gain control of a computer system without being detected.) In a sense, Sony itself was acting like a hacker, deploying its own malicious code and getting lots of detailed information, such as listening habits, sent back to the company. Because the software would run continuously, it caused a strain on the computer's CPU, which ultimately made the whole machine work slower. The average person couldn't easily uninstall the rootkits, which was problematic, especially given that within just two years Sony had sold more than 20 million infected CDs.[40]

Ultimately, there were big media stories and lawsuits. The Federal Trade Commission (FTC) got involved, finding Sony in violation of US law, forcing the company to clearly label protected discs, and prohibiting it from installing any software without a consumer's prior consent.[41]

Any futurist would have heard the signals talking, as there were clear harbingers of what was yet to come. The hacker community, which equated Sony's actions to collusion within the industry to control what we're allowed to do with our computers, was incensed. Across internet bulletin boards and listservs, there were calls to infiltrate Sony's servers. A few years later, a hacker collective known as fail0verflow found the security codes for the PlayStation 3 and posted a very basic, rudimentary hack online. Next, George Hotz, a high school student who went by the username "GeoHot" and had gained notoriety for jailbreaking his iPhone, announced that he'd found the PS3 root key, which allowed anyone to jailbreak the console of PlayStation 3 to run both homemade and pirated software. Hotz not only posted the details on his website, he made a YouTube video explainer.[42]

Needless to say, this didn't go over well at Sony, which threatened to sue anyone for posting or distributing the code and demanded that a federal judge order Google and Twitter to hand over the IP addresses and any other data available for anyone involved. Sony successfully won a temporary restraining order, forcing Hotz to surrender his computers to the company.[43] It won the right to unmask the IP addresses of everyone who had visited Hotz's website. Sony followed up by releasing a mandatory firmware update that would prevent the PS3 from executing any unauthorized code.[44]

That response only baited the hacker community, which was now ready for war. That firmware update was cracked within hours by KaKaRoToKS, a well-known hacker activist. Someone launched HasSonyBeenHacked.com, which enthusiastically tracked each and every new exploit. The hacker collective Anonymous mobilized its network, urging hackers to go after Sony in retaliation for the PS3 lawsuit and for trying to throw Hotz in jail, posting online: "Your corrupt business practices are indicative of a corporate philosophy that would deny consumers the right to use products they have paid for and rightfully own, in the manner of their choosing. . . . Having trodden upon Anonymous' rights, you must now be trodden on."[45]

Again, no action by Sony. Remarkably, inside the company, executives treated these incidents as novel, one-off attacks. They were focused on their successful products, but they hadn't included tracking and acting on trends in cybersecurity.

In the months that followed, hackers got into Sony's PlayStation network, stealing the usernames, addresses, birth dates, passwords, password security answers, profile data, credit card numbers, and purchase/billing history for 75 million people—which wound up costing the company $171 million.[46] There were twenty-one known major attacks within the next six months.[47]

By 2014, hackers had lost interest in hacking the PlayStation. But they hadn't lost interest in Sony. Gaming is just one part of Sony's global business. The corporate giant also operates divisions in electronics, music, network services, and financial services. Its products range from image sensors and semiconductors to digital cameras and LCD televisions—and, of course, movies.

Despite the numerous attacks, it is clear that Sony hadn't made plans to come to grips with the problem. On November 24, 2014, nine months after Schaberg, the VP of legal compliance, sent her message about the SpiritWORLD infiltration, a disturbing image took over all of the employee computer screens at Sony Pictures Entertainment: a realistic-looking red-tinted human skeleton with claws for hands that seemed to be reaching out of the monitor. Text overlaying the image said: "We've obtained all your internal data including your secrets and top secrets. If you don't obey us, we'll release data shown below to the world." There were five links, which went to zipped files, and an 11:00 p.m. deadline in a yellow font. The hacker group called itself #GOP, or "Guardians of Peace."[48] They remotely wiped the hard drives, shut down email, and stole troves of private company data.[49]

Those links routed to directories containing highly sensitive internal data, including passwords, credit card numbers, social security numbers, and contracts for Hollywood celebrities, such as Sylvester Stallone and Judd Apatow. They included the same for Sony Pictures employees—along with their salary information. The hackers had not only released the information, they had preserved the file structure and original nomenclature, which revealed that Sony had been storing documents under plainly labeled filenames like "YouTube login passwords. xlsx," "Important Passwords-TAAS, Outlook, Novell.txt," "Password/ Social Password Log.xlsx," "SPI Employees Levels_401(k) sort_pass wordv2.xls," and a catch-all "UserNames&Passwords.xls."[50]

Security experts were stunned by what they saw. Passwords in plaintext. Unencrypted Excel spreadsheets. Open company fileshares from which terabytes of data could be exfiltrated by anyone who knew how to click to open a basic computer file.

Sony had been trapped in the paradox of the present, continually assuming that each new exploit was novel and unique. By not taking a long view and planning for the future, the company had allowed a tawdry, humiliating look into the inner workings of Sony Pictures and Hollywood. A long string of emails between producer Scott Rudin and Sony Pictures' former co-chairman Amy Pascal included one where Rudin called Angelina Jolie a "spoiled brat" who was "a camp event and a celebrity and that's all"; "the last thing anybody needs," he wrote, "is to make a giant bomb with her that any fool could see coming."[51] There were also emails between Sony and Motion Picture Association of America (MPAA) attorneys. One message included an attachment for an October 8, 2014, agenda in which the parties were set to discuss "scalability and cost of site blocking" and how to migrate blocking to mobile apps at the MPAA office in Sherman Oaks, California.[52] Sony, along with the MPAA and five other studios—Universal, Fox, Paramount, Warner Brothers, and Disney—were secretly working on legal and technical maneuvers that would allow Internet Service Providers (ISPs) like Comcast to block access to any website hosting pirated Sony Pictures content.

The more the hackers dug into the files, the more the circle of damage widened. The hackers used the websites Pastebin and GitHub to share daily communiqués, and they also operated a daily email blast to members of the news media. Soon, they revealed their primary demand: they wanted Sony to cancel its planned release of *The Interview*, a comedy about two hapless Americans sent to assassinate North Korean leader Kim Jong Un.

This attack provides a clear example of how, in our modern age, one technological invention or misstep in a perceived silo actually affects myriad other industries and individuals. Ultimately, Sony Pictures' failure to track the future of cybersecurity resulted in legislation creating a legal framework for federal agencies and companies to collect and use your personal data, even if you aren't being investigated for a crime. Here's how a futurist would connect the dots:

Canceling a wide release of a film also meant pulling an estimated $10 million to $12 million marketing spend with other companies.[53] Outside of Hollywood, the hackers were threatening acts of physical terrorism at American movie theaters, which lost millions of dollars in potential box-office revenue.

Sony > theater businesses > the entertainment economy.

Money was an issue, but the devastating 2012 mass shooting inside an Aurora, Colorado, movie theater showing *The Dark Knight* was still on everyone's mind. Security experts reviewing the leaked files could not confirm that the hackers were from North Korea, but there was enough evidence to take the threat seriously. Who would risk another horrifying attack on innocent moviegoers? Although the Department of Homeland Security said there was "no credible intelligence to indicate an active plot against movie theaters within the United States,"[54] Sony complied with demands, halting distribution of the movie.[55]

Lawmakers, including President Barack Obama, urged Sony to show the movie anyway. In a December 19 press conference, Obama said that the studio had made a "mistake" in canceling its planned release. "We cannot have a society in which some dictator in some place can start imposing censorship in the United States. . . . I wish [Sony had] spoken to me first. I would have told them: Do not get into a pattern in which you're are intimidated."[56]

Sony > theater businesses > the entertainment economy > freedom of speech activists > North Korean geopolitical relations with the United States and US allies.

Politicians used Sony's breach as leverage to once again try to pass controversial cybersecurity legislation. Representative Peter King (R-NY) reignited debate over the Terrorism Risk Insurance Act, which would reimburse insurers for terrorism-related losses, corporate or otherwise. Senator Dianne Feinstein (D-CA) said she would work to pass a cybersecurity bill as quickly as possible. Senator John McCain (R-AZ) said he would pursue the Secure IT Act, a competitor to the highly contentious Cyber Intelligence Sharing and Protection Act.[57]

McCain made good on his promise. In March 2015, the Senate Intelligence Committee held a closed meeting on S.754, the Cybersecurity Information Sharing Act of 2015, and voted 14–1 to advance the legislation.[58] The House companion legislation, the Protecting Cyber Networks Act, passed on a bipartisan vote of 307–116.[59] The Electronic Frontier Foundation called it an "invasive surveillance bill that must be stopped," arguing that it "gives companies broad immunity to spy on—and even launch countermeasures against—potentially innocent users."[60]

Sony > theater businesses > the entertainment economy > freedom of speech activists > North Korean geopolitical relations with the United States and US allies > passage of controversial cybersecurity legislation that had been defeated years ago.

In the end, Sony changed course, announcing that it would release its film to independent movie theaters willing to carry it. Google offered to release it via YouTube and Play, its on-demand platform, and Sony agreed. During its opening weekend, *The Interview* grossed $15 million online and $3 million in theaters.[61] (Sony spent $44 million producing the film.[62])

But Sony's financial loss on that film was just the tip of the iceberg, since its lack of foresight trapped the company in a seemingly endless paradox of the present. Nearly a decade earlier, the executive director of information security at Sony Pictures had met with an auditor who had just completed a review of the company's security practices. That was in

2005, just after the first big hack in retaliation for the CD malware. In an interview published just after that meeting, the auditor had revealed some of Sony's security flaws, such as poor passwords and unencrypted files. In the resulting story in the November 2005 issue of *CIO* magazine, he said that it was a "valid business decision to accept the risk" of a security breach, and that it wasn't worth the money or effort to plan for the future of cyberattacks directed at Sony.[63]

A former Sony staff member anonymously told a security reporter at the website Fusion that "the real problem lies in the fact that there was no real investment in or real understanding of what information security is."[64] Other former employees were quick to tell media sources that Sony believed each of its attacks to be a novel, once-in-a-lifetime breach rather than part of a bigger, more disturbing trend in cybervandalism. Risk assessments were done regularly, in order to identify vulnerabilities, but staff said that those reports were not always acted on.[65]

Sony. Drones. BlackBerry. These are just three examples of how the paradox of the present obstructs our thinking about and planning for the future. To break through the paradox, you must become chronologically ambidextrous, and be able to focus on the needs of your immediate and very-near future while simultaneously allowing yourself to think critically about a time far into the future. In order to do that, you need a futurist's playbook.

FUTURE FORECASTING IS A PROCESS

Only 1 percent of humans are truly ambidextrous, with equal amount of ease using either their left or right hand. Researchers believe that many people who think they are ambidextrous are actually lefties who have had to adapt to a right-handed world.[66] With practice, you can train yourself to use both hands asynchronously and with fluidity. In fact, if you're a piano player, this is a skill you've already mastered to some degree. Composers Sergei Rachmaninoff and Thelonious Monk both created music that defy human dexterity—and yet, with enough practice, a skilled musician can learn to play their classical and jazz piano pieces with technical proficiency.

Forecasting the future requires a certain amount of mental ambidexterity. Just as a piano player must control her left and right hands as she glides around the keyboard playing Monk, you need to learn how to think in two ways at once—both monitoring what's happening in the present and thinking through how the present relates to the future. Forecasting involves a series of six steps, which I'll get to shortly. For now, you need to know that the steps are governed by the following rules:

1.   The future is not predetermined, but rather woven together by numerous threads that are themselves being woven in the present.

2.   We can observe probable future threads in the present, as they are being woven.

3.   We can impact our possible and probable futures in the present.

To most people, time feels linear, with a beginning, a middle, and an end. However, the events happening during a particular time are neither predestined nor bound to follow a set path. Instead, individual events are influenced by known and, more problematically, unknown variables.

In physics, the Heisenberg uncertainty principle states that you can never know both the exact position and the exact speed of an object— essentially, everything influences everything else.[67] (For example, to know the velocity of a quark, we have to measure it, and the very act of measuring it can affect it in some way.) If we subscribe to the laws of the universe, we must agree from the outset that there is no one, predetermined future, but rather a possibility of many futures, each depending on a variety of factors.

Future forecasts are probabilistic in nature, in that we can determine the likelihood and direction of how technology will evolve. It is therefore possible to see elements of the future being woven in the present, as long as we know how to see the entire fabric at once, not just a small, finite piece of it.

Picture a millhand working in a massive factory that looks like an enclosed football field, with a series of lines hung across every yard line. On one side of the line are buckets of raw cotton, which are being fed through big rollers and slightly twisted onto a bobbin. A worker runs up and down his part of the row watching for breakdowns, snags, or jams. In another room, there are workers mounting that yarn onto an enormous frame, where threads are woven between wires on a rotating beam. Eventually, beams would be affixed to a loom, where, line by line, elaborate cloths and textiles are woven with an infinite variety of patterns.

If one of the workers in the factory looks at a one-inch-square swatch of cloth, the colors may look interesting, but he would have a difficult time seeing what those threads, together, signify. He would need a system in order to help him see both the detail of the thread and the entire loom, where patterns reveal a complete picture. In fact, the millhands could reconstruct exactly what's there—by methodically reviewing inch by inch and recognizing patterns. Indeed, the millworkers by necessity remain narrowly focused on their present tasks, because their immediate responsibility is making sure that day-to-day benchmarks—a certain amount of yarn or cloth woven per worker, a minimum amount of time or product lost—are being met.

Even the most technically savvy among us are often unwitting millhands, as managing the operation of a modern organization has become a complicated, formidable task. We are all engaged in some form of strategic thinking and development, like creating annual budgets or three-year strategic operational plans, work that is essential in order to confront the strategic environment. But taking a step back, looking at the patterns in order to understand the cloth as it's being woven— and intervening in order to change the course of events—is more time consuming and difficult. This is forecasting: simultaneously recognizing patterns in the present, and thinking about how those changes will impact the future. You must flip the paradigm, so that you can be actively engaged in building what happens next. Or at least so that you're not as surprised by what others develop.

Joseph Voros, a theoretical physicist and professor at Swinburne University of Technology, offered my favorite explanation of future forecasting, calling it "an element of strategic thinking, which informs strategy-making," enriching the "context within which strategy is developed, planned and executed."[68]

The forecasting method I have developed—one, of course, influenced by other futurists but different in analysis and scope—is a six-part process that I have refined during a decade of research as part of my work at the Future Today Institute.[69] The first part involves finding a trend, while the last two steps inform what action you should take. These are the instructions:

1. **Find the Fringe:** Cast a wide enough net to harness information from the fringe. This involves creating a map showing nodes and the relationships between them, and rounding up what you will later refer to as "the unusual suspects."

2. **Use CIPHER:** Uncover hidden patterns by categorizing data from the fringe. Patterns indicate a trend, so you'll do an exhaustive search for Contradictions, Inflections, Practices, Hacks, Extremes, and Rarities.

3. **Ask the Right Questions:** Determine whether a pattern really is a trend. You will be tempted to stop looking once you've spotted a pattern, but you will soon learn that creating counterarguments is an essential part of the forecasting process, even though most forecasters never force themselves to poke holes into every single assumption and assertion they make.

4. **Calculate the ETA:** Interpret the trend and ensure that the timing is right. This isn't just about finding a typical S-curve and the point of inflection. As technology trends move along their trajectory, there are two forces in play—internal developments within tech companies, and external developments within the government, adjacent businesses, and the like—and both must be calculated.

5. **Create Scenarios and Strategies:** Build scenarios to create probable, plausible, and possible futures and accompanying strategies. This step requires thinking about both the timeline of a technology's development and your emotional reactions to all of the outcomes. You'll give each scenario a score, and based on your analysis, you will create a corresponding strategy for taking action.

6. **Pressure-Test Your Action:** But what if the action you choose to take on a trend is the wrong one? In this final step, you must make sure the strategy you take on a trend will deliver the desired outcome, and that requires asking difficult questions about both the present and the future.

These six steps help to identify the future of *x*, where you might define *x* as: driving, governing, banking, health care, journalism, national security, shopping, insurance, orchestras, K-12 education, law enforcement, movies, investing, or any number of other fields. That's because technology is permanently intertwined with everything we do, and researching tech trends should be embedded into the everyday operations of a twenty-first-century organization.

CHANCE AND CHAOS

A chance event can alter the future of anything, from a baseball game to the traffic on your commute home. It can also dramatically affect a textile. Indeed, anyone who has ever spent time knitting will tell you that one small deviation can completely transform the outcome of a scarf. Knitting creates tiny "v's," which interlock and build upon each other in rows. One dropped v won't be immediately noticed, until a long tear appears. Additional v's will embed themselves, causing the scarf to change shape. Things get even more complicated with multiple thread colors. By sheer chance—perhaps a distraction, or a miscount, or even an intentional omission in order to experiment—the future of the scarf is forever altered by just one little v. We have a general sense of what outcome is likely—some kind of fabric that hopefully can be used as a scarf—but for even the most seasoned knitters there is some probability that deviations will result in a final product that may not match the initial idea.

Forecasting the future is subject to chance and chaos. Every action can cause effects across entire complex systems. The emergence of one new technology may raise the probability of any number of occurrences, because it might change our economic circumstances, social dynamics, financial opportunities, political access, or any number of other factors. Environmentalist John Muir once explained this phenomenon: "When we try to pick out anything by itself, we find it is hitched to everything else in the universe."[70] In our modern age, technology is inextricably and especially woven into the fabric of our organizations, our societies, and our everyday lives.

Sometimes, what may seem like a bunch of wayward or random v's is actually part of a larger pattern that's evolving. Chaos theory tells us that any complex system is dynamic, and that a multitude of results are possible. Therefore, rather than attempting to predict a singular outcome, we instead project a set of possible, probable, and preferred scenarios, using trends as anchors.

History informs us that scientists in Scotland successfully cloned a sheep named Dolly, born in 1997, and that the scientific community cried foul only after the news had been published.[71] In the end, their objections didn't stop the researchers from continuing their work. What history doesn't tell us is what might have happened if public outcry over their research had led to the UK Parliament enacting emergency legislation, arresting the scientists and forever banning embryonic cloning. It doesn't tell us what might have happened if, rather than responding with anger, the scientific community had instead immediately started in on a secondary round of research to clone specific tissues, like Dolly's right lung. It doesn't tell us what might have happened if Dolly had only lived a month. Or what might have happened if a massive earthquake, decimating the west coast of Scotland, had occurred the day that announcement was made.

Some may argue that given the rate and expansive scope of technological innovation and our cultural and political response to it, it is impossible to forecast the future. "How can I, or anyone else, possibly anticipate the future, given how quickly everything seems to be changing?" you might wonder.

This is why forecasting the future requires thinking in contradictory ways. We must accept that the future is not predetermined—that we can both know what's past the horizon and intervene to shape it—while simultaneously acknowledging that any number of variables, at any time, can influence an outcome. We must solve the paradox of the present by practicing ambidextrous thinking. Using the instructions, which are governed by the three rules, we can focus on finding interconnected relationships between one or more technologies and thinking systemically, rather than becoming fixated on a single, promising new gadget or app.

Seeing the future is possible, even though the rate of technological advancement has begun to outpace the speed at which people are accustomed to working and making decisions. Forecasting what's ahead is a matter of recognizing emerging trends and then taking the right action at the appropriate time. Look no further than Nintendo, IBM, Diebold, Wells Fargo, and 3M. These companies are more than one hundred years old. More than once, emerging technologies and fickle consumer behavior have threatened to destroy their businesses, and yet they all continue to thrive today. For example, IBM was founded in 1911 as the Computing-Tabulating-Recording Company, and it manufactured time-keeping systems, scales, and punched-card machines. In 1924, the company adopted a new name—International Business Machines, or IBM—and reinvented itself as a service that could keep track of vital statistics and, in later decades, other data, such as Social Security numbers. By the 1960s, IBM was making computers for big government agencies and corporations. Two decades later, it partnered with a new software upstart called Microsoft and manufactured personal computers. IBM clones permeated the market, so it pivoted to becoming a services company, investing in advanced software. In 1997, IBM's Deep Blue beat world chess champion Garry Kasparov, who resigned after just nineteen moves. In 2015, IBM's artificially intelligent computing platform Watson was assisting doctors at the Mayo Clinic and at the Memorial Sloan Kettering Cancer Center with complex diagnoses.[72]

Everything new now seems novel, because the changes heading our way will seem too extraordinary to become part of our daily lives. And yet, I have a drone in my living room. Landscrapers, hackers taking down one of the world's largest companies, embryonic cloning, artificially intelligent computers assisting doctors—these technological events will not only become commonplace, they will provide the essential basis for our human-machine evolution.

The question we are going to explore throughout this book is this: *How do we make the soon-to-be-normal feel less novel?* The instructions will help us find the answer. But first, we ought to distinguish between what is a real trend—and what's merely a shiny object.

CHAPTER TWO

When Cars Fly

Understanding the Difference Between Trend and Trendy

WHEN YOU WERE a kid, you probably imagined yourself not just riding in the family car of the future, but flying in, say, the Jetsons' hovercar or Luke Skywalker's Landspeeder, or a Spinner soaring in congested lanes above the dark streets in *Blade Runner*. For me, it was the DMC-12 DeLorean with its dashboard computer, flux capacitor, and gull-wing doors. I daydreamed about that car all the time. Its parts were old and rusty, but it flew through the space-time continuum, not just through the air.[1]

Dreams like these are part of a centuries-old quest for autonomous transportation, and flying cars have been a persistent, trendy theme within our popular culture on and off for more than a hundred years. Since John Emory Harriman filed the first patent for an aerocar in 1910, we've been alternatively excited and disappointed by a steady stream of prototypes and promises. Waldo Waterman's Arrowbile was the first to leave the street for the sky in 1937. Three years later, Henry Ford remarked confidently, "Mark my word: a combination airplane and motorcar is coming." Aviation publicist Harry Bruno clarified, saying that cars of the future would look like tiny "copters"; when school let out, they would "fill the sky as the bicycles of our youth filled the prewar roads." In 1949 *Life* magazine featured the Airphibian, an aerocar that could fly from a backyard airstrip to LaGuardia Airport and then transform into a convertible-like vehicle capable of driving to Times Square.[2]

The dream of flying cars continued into the twenty-first century and up to the present day as people built new prototypes with vertical take-off and landing capabilities, super-strong carbon fiber bodies, ducted fan propulsion, and cheaper flight-stabilizing computer systems.

Although these futuristic aerocars *look* completely different from their twentieth-century prototypes, there hasn't, materials aside, been any innovation in design since Harriman filed that first patent.

Flying cars are now a synonym for failure: a perceived lack of innovation or an inability to accurately forecast the future. No one has been more vocal about this than venture capitalist Peter Thiel, who cofounded PayPal with Elon Musk and was Facebook's first outside investor. Thiel has stood before countless audiences arguing that we no longer live in a technologically accelerating world, and that there haven't been any true, futuristic innovations since the 1960s. In fact, his firm's slogan, "We wanted flying cars; instead we got 140 characters,"[3] is a slight to both innovators and to Twitter.

But rather than a poster child for technological failure, flying cars—or the lack thereof—illustrate why spotting trends is so difficult. Flying cars are trendy, shiny objects; the concept emerges every ten years with regularity. Henry Ford's innovations in car manufacturing were followed by Buick's Autoplane and the Bryan Autoplane concepts in the 1950s,[4] the Wagner Aerocar in the 1960s,[5] the AVE Mizar (which combined a Ford Pinto with the rear end of a Cessna plane) in the 1970s,[6] Boeing's Sky Commuter prototype in the 1980s,[7] and so on. Meanwhile, there is a real trend worth following, but it wasn't cars that can fly. Rather, each decade brought significant advances in automobile technology that resulted in humans having to devote less and less of our attention to physical driving tasks. As those advances took place, we failed to realize how important they would eventually become for bringing about a whole different paradigm shift. Compounding the problem were the paradox of the present—the bias of paying most attention to the last few signals you've seen, read, or heard—and the difficulty the human brain has in describing something new using terms and ideas we don't yet understand. Rather than tracking the trend in autonomous transportation, which has to do with infrastructure, artificial intelligence, and a lot of computer systems you can't really see, we naturally looked for what was novel within a familiar frame of reference. And so we established cars—but with wings! up in the air!—as the signal to follow. Distracted by what is temporarily trendy, we find ourselves continually disappointed.

Though they're difficult to identify correctly, trends are vitally important, because they are the necessary signposts that must be recognized early for you to be a participant in shaping the future. And, flying cars aside, there are game-changing innovations in some stage of development taking place right now across many different fields that will transform not just travel but human longevity, communications, education, governance, and more. In fact, flying cars don't represent failure; they illustrate how the promise of exciting new technologies sometimes obscure real change that's actually underfoot.

•

Flying cars are not the only example of how we misread the future. Another, also concerning the trend of autonomous transportation, comes from the late 1800s. US cities were struggling with the pressures of America's fast-growing population, much of it due to a heavy wave of new immigration. Chicago, for example, had great architecture and music, but it also had serious drainage problems, largely due to these population pressures. Too many people and animals crowded its unpaved streets. As the population increased, a larger number of horses were needed for transportation, and people had to slog through horse manure and squalor to get around by foot. Walking was not that much faster than the slow-moving public transit system, which was powered by horse-drawn "omnibuses" that seated only twenty people at a time.[8]

The very first gasoline-powered cars were by then being given their first tests in Springfield, Massachusetts, and Germany, but they were experiments out on the fringe. The common frame of reference for people thinking about transportation was that image of people on foot, trying desperately to walk through those crowded streets. They, too, were hampered by the paradox of the present.

Alfred Speer, a New Jersey inventor and wine merchant, wanted to solve the hassle of getting around. His idea was drawn from the immediate vantage point outside his shop: there was an omnipresent mob of people moving every which way around the sidewalks and streets. What if, instead of walking, they were organized into a neat file as they commuted around the city? Speer's idea was an invention to automatically move people around, without actually requiring them to do any walking themselves: a sidewalk that moved.[9] Moving sidewalks promised to organize Chicago's throngs of people as they commuted around the city. It would mean clearer roadway access for horse-drawn carriages. Streets would become cleaner by default, reducing the strain on merchants, who were charged with maintaining their little plots of land. Moving sidewalks would lessen the burden on all Chicagoans, automating a difficult part of daily life.

Speer received a patent for his invention in 1871, and it was built for the 1893 World's Fair in Chicago. It spanned the length of a 3,500-foot pier, was made out of wooden planks, and moved people at the speed of two miles per hour. There was a secondary platform—an express lane with benches—that was twice as fast. At five cents per ride, Speer's wooden sidewalk could transport 31,680 people an hour.[10]

Speer's invention caught on, because it solved a fundamental human need—to move around a city safely and quickly—and because it made life easier for everyday people. Enthusiastic engineers and city planners started building on Speer's original invention and improving it. The *trottoir roulant*, launched in Paris at the Exposition Universelle of 1900, had three tracks and moved slightly faster than Speer's sidewalk.[11] All along its two-mile track, the trottoir amazed passengers and irritated nearby merchants, since the clanging of its machinery was so noisy.[12] There were soon plans to build an elevated moving sidewalk in Manhattan that could travel nineteen miles per hour in order to relieve foot-traffic congestion down below. There was yet another plan to create a moving walkway in a loop system over the Brooklyn Bridge. Entrepreneurs proposed similar moving sidewalks in Boston, Detroit, Los Angeles, Atlanta, and Washington, DC.[13] By 1905, everyone thought that the future of transportation was a sidewalk in perpetual motion.

Of course, none of those later projects came into being. For one thing, Chicago winters can be harsh—and there were no contingency plans for how to operate (much less ride) a moving sidewalk during high winds and lake-effect snow. The original wooden models were extremely loud and rickety, and they suffered from ongoing mechanical problems. Rather than rejoicing, merchants complained that the sidewalks were a disruption.

The moving sidewalk was an exciting new technology, as was the newly invented "safety bicycle," which allowed for better steering and greater speed and was deemed suitable for a woman to ride.[14] And yet out on the fringe, a handful of engineers had started to experiment with gasoline and internal combustion engines. In this world, which, remember, was entering the golden age of bicycles, most people couldn't conceive of riding in a 1,200-pound metal box that could whiz down the street at forty miles per hour.

It is hard for us today to appreciate the excitement that moving sidewalks generated in the late nineteenth and early twentieth centuries. We effortlessly wheel our carry-on luggage from the ticket counter at the airport to the gate without even thinking about the fact that our "moving sidewalks" aren't actually sidewalks at all. It's invisible infrastructure to us now.

You may have assumed that when Chicago abandoned its moving sidewalks and when the Airphibian failed to go commercial, those trends were dead. In fact, moving sidewalks and flying cars were never trends in and of themselves. Rather, they were manifestations of something different: a trend in autonomous travel. We have been trying to automate transportation for the past one hundred years, inventing everything from streetcars pulled by horses to advanced machines that essentially move without much of our direct input or supervision at all.

WHAT IS A TREND, EXACTLY?

Technology has made it difficult to distinguish between a trend and something that is simply trendy, and that is because much of it is complicated and confusing. Or it is invisible. It's easy to fixate on what's trendy—the latest app, the newest gadget, the hottest social network—but more difficult to track how technology is shaping our organizations, government, education, economy, and culture. At any moment, there are hundreds of small shifts taking place in technology—developments on the fringe—that will impact our lives in the future. A trend, therefore, is a new manifestation of sustained change within an industry, the public sector, or society, or in the way that we behave toward one another. A trend is a starting point that helps us to simultaneously meet the demands of the present while planning for the future. In a sense, trends are the analogy our minds need to help us think about and understand change.

All trends intersect with other aspects of daily life, and they share a set of conspicuous, universal features. Here is how those features—present in all trends—relate to the trend of autonomous transportation:

A trend is driven by a basic human need, one that is catalyzed by new technology. As society evolves, we require progressively advanced technologies to serve our busy lifestyles. We need to spend less time traveling from place to place. With increasingly busier schedules, we are traveling more, which makes our roads, trains, and airports more and more crowded. Better transportation and technology results in more meetings, events, and opportunities, which cycles back to a need for additional travel. We experience "road rage" and a lack of freedom to use our time as we choose. Or we try to multitask as we drive, answering email messages, participating in teleconferences, or clicking through mobile apps.

•

A trend is timely, but it persists. Transportation has always been about fulfilling our need for efficiency, speed, and automation. Could the army of King Ennatumh, one of the ancient Sumerian rulers, have defeated his enemies and conquered the city of Umma without having invented the chariot? Possibly, but having access to a wheeled cart meant faster attacks on the battlefield, and it also spared their soldiers and horses from the exhaustion caused by carrying heavy loads. For thousands of years, we have been trying to lighten our loads and move around more quickly.

•

A trend evolves as it emerges. We didn't progress in a straight line from wheeled carts to self-driving Google cars. Technological innovations lead to new ways of thinking, and, as a result, new kinds of vehicles. Each iteration includes learning from past successes and failures. In the 1950s, General Motors and RCA developed an automated highway prototype using radio control for speed and steering.[15] A steel cable was paved into the asphalt to keep self-driving cars on the road. The autonomous-vehicle trend evolved over the next six decades, and Google eventually put a fleet of self-driving cars onto the roads of Mountain View, California, and Austin, Texas. Google uses an algorithm-powered driver's education course: the cars "learn" to sense and avoid things, like a teenager riding on a skateboard, that they haven't been explicitly taught to recognize. A decade from now—in the late 2020s—will we all own and drive Google cars that are just like the ones being tested now? Probably not. But we will no doubt be driving cars that require significantly less of our attention and direct supervision behind the wheel as a result of Google's research.

•

A trend can materialize as a series of unconnectable dots that begin out on the fringe and move to the mainstream. With the benefit of hindsight, here are several dots from the year 2004 that, at first glance, don't seem to connect:

- The Defense Advanced Research Projects Agency (DARPA), the arm of the US Department of Defense that's responsible for creating the future of military technology, launched a Grand Challenge for fifteen self-driving military vehicles, which had to navigate 142 miles of desert road between California and Nevada.[16]

- That same year, the R&D department at DaimlerChrysler was studying the future of telematics—that is, the system of sending, receiving, and storing information related to vehicles and telecommunications devices (like a GPS)—and intelligent transportation systems.[17]

- *Motor Trend*'s Car of the Year was the brand-new Toyota Prius, praised by reviewers for its newfangled computerized dashboard. The magazine said that "the cockpit may look like it came from a NASA clean room, but the Prius is as easy to use as a TV. Press 'Power' to bring the vehicle to life, select 'D' with the joystick, press on the electronic 'drive-by-wire' throttle pedal, and you're off."[18]

- Google acquired the digital mapping company Keyhole.[19]

- Developers at Google were working on an early version of an advanced mobile operating system called Android that would be aware of the owner's location.[20]

- Another operating system, this one for cars, was built by QNX and soon acquired by Harman International Industries, which wanted to expand the technology for use in infotainment and navigation units.[21]

How do these dots connect? Technology begets technology. Just as the *trottoir roulant* built on Speer's invention, DARPA learned from the original experiment by General Motors and RCA in autonomous cars, adding telemetry and computerized controls. Separately, car manufacturers like Toyota were building electronic and "drive by wire" technologies to replace mechanical linkages. Eventually, Google could incorporate all of this work, combine advanced navigation into a new kind of operating system, and develop and test its first fleet of self-driving cars. It's easy to connect the dots in hindsight, but with the right foresight you can identify simultaneous developments on the fringe and recognize patterns as they materialize into trends.

SORTING OUT REAL TRENDS FROM RED HERRINGS

Using autonomous transportation as the trend, how could we build alternate narratives—the probable, the plausible, and the possible—for the future?

Scenario #1: Probable. A hybrid system of semi- and fully autonomous transport utilizing a grid system covering the 3.9 million miles of public roads in the United States.[22] You might drive your car from your house to a connected highway and surrender control as sensors in your car link to other cars in the moving network. From there, your car would drive itself, monitoring and maintaining safe distances. Three minutes before your exit, the navigation system would ask you to prepare to drive again, and you would take over the controls once you've turned off the highway.

These mostly autonomous cars won't achieve vertical lift. That's because the elements that make cars safe to drive either don't matter in the air or become a hindrance. For example, a three-ton car would require 3,000 pounds of thrust from the engine just to get off the road, and the majority of our paved roads would buckle under the pressure. Now, what if we add additional weight? Today, when we make a big trip to the grocery store or pack a lot of suitcases for vacation, a car easily handles whatever we put into it. That would not be the case with a flying version—before takeoff, either the driver-pilot or a highly advanced computer system would need to carefully calculate and balance the weight load. You could argue that one hundred years from now, we will have innovated a workaround for this problem. But does a flying car solve an inherent human need?

Though that still begs the question: Why bother with a flying *car* at all? There have been important changes to transportation since the Sumerians first built horse-drawn carriages and Leonardo da Vinci borrowed from a bird's anatomy to sketch his flying machine, but more often than not they have been incremental.

•

Scenario #2: Plausible. The airspace overhead, as noted earlier, will eventually be regulated to allow for recreational and commercial drone flight. In the next one hundred years, we could have a layer on top of those zones, in the 2,000- to 3,500-foot range, designated for semi-autonomous human transport. I'll call that lane a skyway, and the vehicle a disc. Just like autonomous drones, which are programmed using GPS coordinates and powered by a collision avoidance system, three sizes of discs—single occupant, up to four occupants, and up to eight occupants—could transport us from points A to B using the shortest, safest route available. As with our cars in the future, we might subscribe to a skyway service rather than owning a disc of our own. Skyway access points would probably require a short ride up 140 stories to a disc pad, which would occupy the roofs of existing buildings. An artificially intelligent operating system would load our tastes and preferences, automatically adjusting the climate control, seats, ambient lighting, and music to our liking. We could use skyways for longer-distance travel, and highways for shorter distances within or between cities.

But still, what does the flying disc problem really solve? For those who currently commute, if a sensor network eradicated traffic so that they could reclaim that time for another purpose, would a flying disc really matter? Would skyways of the future prove safer than the highways we already have? For those who use public transit, would a disc traveling as the crow flies justify spending a lot of money on a new kind of vehicle and the infrastructure to operate it? Would the average person come to rely on it as a necessity?

•

Scenario #3: Possible. What if we could move around without any vehicles at all? A few years ago, Dutch physicists at Delft University of Technology's Kavli Institute of Nanoscience successfully completed experiments in something called "quantum entanglement."[23] Einstein had once dismissed the concept because, as he put it, "physics should represent a reality in time and space, free from spooky actions at a distance."[24] Up until recently, quantum entanglement was only a strange theory in quantum mechanics. But a physicist at IBM, during an annual meeting of the American Physical Society in March 1993, confirmed that it was possible.[25] Electrons orbit an atom much like the Earth orbits the sun. Just as the Earth spins on an axis, so do electrons. When they become entangled—when they're made to smash up against each other—and then separated again, the spin reverses. In essence, the two electrons are converted into mirror images. What the Kavli researchers discovered was a way to change the spin of two particles separated at a distance. The results in their study showed a replication rate of 100 percent.[26]

You've probably already heard about quantum entanglement by its sci-fi name: teleportation (as in "Beam me up, Scotty"[27]). Just as it would have been inconceivable for those early moving-sidewalk engineers to imagine a future that included space travel, in our present-day context we can't fathom actually beaming ourselves up. For one thing, we would need to build a machine capable of sending the data for all 7 billion billion billion atoms that make up the average human body (that's 7 followed by 27 zeros) the same way the Kavli scientists have for single particles. Naturally, our minds wander to bugs, hacks, and firmware updates, each of which could throw an error into your system, such as smashed cells that would render you a blob of goo on the other end of your journey. You would have to get over any squeamishness about whether the replicated person on the other end would even really *be* you. Technically, the person who comes out on the other side would be a replica—a copy, essentially—of what you were when you went into the teleporting machine. On the destination side would be your atoms, rearranged in exactly (hopefully exactly) the same way they were at the beginning of your teleportation.

But again, that's using the frame of reference we know without digging deeper or factoring in the notion that technology itself causes the acceleration of technology in weird and wonderful new ways. Perhaps two hundred years from now, we won't physically travel at all. Instead, we'll leave our physical bodies behind and instead teleport our minds into human blanks elsewhere. Just as we rent and share cars to get around today, we'll pick up a body near our destination. Visual presets will overlay our physical characteristics on the blank so that others recognize us.

·

These are only three scenarios for the future of transportation, and none include a car with wings. This gets to the heart of why, when thinking about the future, it's important to see around the corners of established thought, and why we cannot dismiss what appear to be only incremental changes. While there are a few people working on flying cars, many more researchers on the fringe are building on earlier innovations as they create alternative hypotheses, models, and plans.

Autonomous transport—not flying cars or moving sidewalks—as we've seen, is the trend to follow. But what does that mean? Especially given that we've been thinking about moving sidewalks and flying cars for a century or more?

A trend doesn't materialize overnight, and it shouldn't be conflated with something that's new and "trendy," as it's more than the latest shiny object. A freshly anointed unicorn like Uber valued at $1 billion or more may be part of the trend, but on its own, it's just one data point to consider. In the years to come, you will no doubt hear about several flying-car startups readying vehicles for market. They're exciting, but they're a red herring. We've never needed a flying car. We've just needed a system of transportation that corresponds with the needs of our current lifestyles. In the United States, that will mean getting around while devoting less of our attention to driving, so we can dedicate ourselves to other tasks.

Fundamentally, a trend leverages our basic human needs and desires in a meaningful way and aligns human nature with emerging technologies and breakthrough inventions. We need to think about how a trend might develop into the farther future: Will scenario #2, flying discs, complement a busier and more tech-infused lifestyle significantly better than scenario #1, automated cars and highways? Probably not.

If we're intent on forecasting the future of transportation, and we know that autonomy is a trend, then we need to abandon the comfortable analogy with which we're already familiar. In other words, why are we still trying to build cars that fly—an idea that sounded exciting in an era when airline travel wasn't yet available to everyone, when cars were still too expensive for the average household, and when meetings only happened face-to-face?

We will someday have the freedom to move around, unencumbered by traffic or other people, in an automatically moving vehicle. Our transportation of the future will arrive; it just won't look anything like what we saw on TV and in the movies.

HOW SOON IS THE FUTURE?

"The future" is a meaningless distinction, especially when it's used to make projections or decisions. The future is simultaneously three hundred years, one decade, twelve months, two days, or forty-seven seconds from this very moment. As soon as you start talking about the future of something, everyone will undoubtedly want to know how soon the future will get here.

It is helpful to organize the evolution of trends along six general time zones, which I will define in just a moment. They are not arbitrary;

they follow the pattern of acceleration across various sectors of an eco-system, which includes academic, scientific, and DIY researchers; tinkerers and hackers building and breaking systems; grant makers and investors; government regulators; equipment manufacturers; supply chain managers; marketers and advertisers; early adopters; and every-day consumers.

Progress in science and technology accelerates in part because of the technology itself. Moore's Law is the best-known expression of this phenomenon. Gordon Moore, the cofounder of Intel, wrote in 1965 that the number of components on integrated circuits would double every two years as the size of transistors shrank.[28] This simple, elegant projection became the golden rule for the electronics industry, enabling Intel to make faster, smaller, and cheaper transistors and tech innovators to plan ahead for computer processing power that would double in capacity every year.

As a trend moves through time zones, progress increases exponentially, in part because of Moore's Law, and in part because of an even more broadly applicable law: the very acceleration of change causes the rate of technological change to accelerate. For example, we can organize our thinking about the autonomous travel trend along the following six time zones:

Now: within the next twelve months. Within a year of the date this book is released (that is, roughly by the end of 2017), cars will be equipped with software updates and new sensors that perform more functions for the driver, such as parking and adaptive cruise control.

Near-term: one to five years. By 2022, most cars will be equipped with cross-path cameras to sense nearby objects, and they will have adaptive cruise control for driving in stop-and-go traffic.

Mid-range: five to ten years. By 2027, advanced GPS and LiDAR (light detection and ranging) technology will transmit your vehicle's location and recognize other vehicles sharing the road. This technology will begin to enable cars to drive themselves.

Long-range: ten to twenty years. By 2037, the highway system will have been upgraded to work in symbiosis with semi-autonomous vehicles. Human drivers will take over on smaller streets. On mandated autonomous highway lanes, people will be free to read, watch videos, or conduct work.

Far-range: twenty to thirty years. By 2047, we will no longer own cars and cities will no longer operate buses. Instead, automated vehicles will be subsidized through taxes and offered at no cost. Those with the means to do so will subscribe to a transportation service, which operates pods that are fully automated. Pods will transport us to destinations as required.

Distant: more than thirty years. By 2057, pods will be connected to a series of high-speed maglev trains, which have started to supplant commercial air routes on the east and west coasts of the United States.

These time zones are deliberate, and my assignment of them to the autonomous-travel trend isn't a stab in the dark. Rather, they are based on what I currently know about how technology is advancing.

It is important to keep time zones in mind when thinking about trends. When envisioning the future, we can't draw a straight line starting from today to some distant time. Instead, we must account for the fact that the rate of progress is influenced by what's happening right now *as well as what will likely occur in the future*. If we consider the trajectory of autonomous transport, we can see that there wasn't a lot of progress between 1950 and 1980. Between 1980 and 2005, cars were influenced by the adjacent industry of computing, so we saw subtle—but important—shifts away from manually operated to automatic vehicles. There has been tremendous innovation between 2006 and today, from touchscreen dashboard systems to fully electric vehicles to prototypes of driverless cars. That's because trends are influenced by the compounding acceleration of change in technology.

We are continually interrelating the past, present, and future time zones within the context of our personal experiences, the groups we belong to, and the projects we work on. If you aren't thinking in terms of time zones, you cannot effectively plan for the future.

TREND INFLUENCERS:
THE TEN SOURCES OF CHANGE

Because trends and time zones are a different way of seeing and interpreting our current reality, they provide a useful framework for organizing our thinking, especially when we're hunting for the unknown and trying to find answers to questions we do not yet even know how to ask. The task of following shifts in technology should not be under the purview of a company's R&D team alone; nor should it only excite enthusiastic, tech-savvy Millennials. Changes in technology affect all of us, regardless of our personal or professional calling. Everyone within an organization should be aware of trends.

Technology trends not only impact emerging platforms, code, devices, and digital workflows, but also influence societal change. We can see how seemingly small tech trends and forces in other sectors can result in great consequences by revisiting the Sony hacking scandal.

Earlier, I explained how Sony suffered its first major breach in 2005. In the decade leading up to the 2014 attack involving Sony Pictures, there were a number of adjacent trends and social changes to note:

- Internet users were starting to gather in unusual places online. A relatively new imageboard website called 4chan, which was essentially a message board where photos could be posted for discussion, had launched recently, and its audience was growing. Another message board, called Reddit, launched as a sort of marketplace for ideas. Its design wasn't intuitive or immediately easy to use, so only those fluent with online communities—a lot of them were hackers—signed on to talk and share links. It was all anonymous, and a significant portion of the posts had to do with gaming.

- Hackers, typically sole actors, were starting to collaborate on bigger projects. A distributed group of activist hackers (or "hacktivists") calling themselves "Anonymous" were starting to organize on 4chan.

- US citizens had grown distrustful of the government, questioning the White House's official position about weapons of mass destruction in Iraq and giving then president George W. Bush a 60 percent disapproval rating.[29] Hurricanes Katrina and Rita devastated communities around the Gulf Coast, eliminating hundreds of thousands of jobs.[30] There was widespread, harsh criticism of the government's response, which was riddled with mismanagement of resources, politicking, and miscommunication. Bush's final approval rating by the time he left office would fall to just 22 percent, the lowest rating for a president in seventy years.[31]

- The US subprime mortgage crisis had caused a nationwide banking emergency; millions of people had lost their savings, their jobs, and their homes.

- Occupy Wall Street, supported in part by Anonymous, gathered in Zuccotti Park and began the Occupy Wall Street movement.[32]

- Everyday people were angry and had started directing their ire at the government, large banks, and corporations. Hackers were angry as well, and they now had a coalition of supporters behind them.

Sony could have seen trouble brewing, if not from internal IT audits, then from a growing shift in how the heaviest users of its gaming consoles were behaving online and their mushrooming anger toward the government and corporations. To wit: there have been dedicated, anti-Sony subreddits (or channels) on Reddit with posts dating back to 2009.[33]

Technology does not evolve on its own, in a vacuum. Even the most forward-thinking innovators are still grounded in reality, tethered to other areas of society. Trends are subjected to and shaped by external forces. Just as it's useful to organize our thinking along a chronological path through time zones, it's important to categorize the various dimensions of our everyday life, with technology as the primary interconnector:

1. *Wealth distribution:* Even as technology becomes more accessible, a ubiquitous, persistent digital divide will impact our future wealth distribution. The highest-paying jobs in America are the ones for engineers, computer and information systems managers, and doctors and surgeons, and all of those occupations rely on technology.[34] In fact, technology is even disrupting the livelihoods within those groups. A provision within the Affordable Care Act, which was signed into law by President Obama in March 2010,[35] requires that all health-care providers use electronic medical records (EMRs).[36] That may sound simple enough, but consider the following: In order to create an EMR, by law a doctor must attach a special code to the diagnoses she makes from the most recent version of the World Health Organization's International Statistical Classification of Diseases and Related Health Problems (otherwise known as the ICD-10). There are currently 68,000 possible codes.[37] Because the system is so complicated, doctors must use an approved EMR management system in order to meet the standards of the law. This requires computers, installation, and a significant layer of encryption. EMR management system interfaces—the screen that the doctor uses when she sees her patients—aren't standardized, and they are wildly complicated. In order to handle all those codes, the interface tends to be a very long decision tree with hundreds of radial buttons. The companies that make these EMR management systems have to keep their own systems updated, so they are constantly tinkering with

where all the buttons and windows are. This means that doctors, who went to medical school to treat people—not for tech support—must continually subject themselves to a very high level of computer training to do something that for centuries required only a notebook and a pen. You might argue that doctors, who are at the upper echelons of the pay scale, don't deserve our pity—but the point I'm making is that technology impacts wages and wealth across the entire spectrum.

2. *Education:* After decades of falling behind other nations on our science and math scores, American schools have redoubled their STEM (Science, Technology, Engineering, and Math) curricula. The US Department of Education cited "an inadequate pipeline of teachers skilled in those subjects," and in 2011 a federal program was created to address the gap.[38] Technology doesn't just affect students—teachers and administrators must now use electronic recordkeeping systems for tests and grading.

3. *Government:* There are no fewer than forty-five different US government organizations and agencies managing dozens of cybersecurity initiatives right now. Those include the National Reconnaissance Office, the Department of Homeland Security, the White House, and Congress, among others. Fifteen executive departments—from the Department of Health and Human Services to the Department of Transportation—lead policy creation and manage programs that affect daily life in America.[39] Locally, state and municipal governments rely on technology to deliver services and to govern. There isn't a facet of our modern-day government that does not intersect with science and technology trends.

4. *Politics:* Our elections are now powered by coders and engineers, who are using data, predictive analytics, algorithms, and protocols to get out the vote. They build micro-targeting models in order to appeal to each constituent individually, and they mine our data using special

software to find potential supporters. Those who want to sway political opinions use the same tools and techniques no matter whom they are targeting, whether it is voters or lawmakers, and they include lobbying groups, trade associations, and the like—even other governments. Citizen activists are banding together and using online petitions and social media to make sure their voices are heard.

5. *Public health:* Cognitive computing platforms are helping public health researchers predict and map the health of our neighborhoods and communities. Predictive models are able to track the potential spread of new biological threats, while emerging science technologies will soon enable us to eradicate the spread of certain diseases, such as malaria.

6. *Demography:* Understanding how our population is shifting—our birth and death rates, income, population density, migration, incidence of disease, and other dynamics—is core to managing everything from big business to city governments. Many countries, including Japan, Italy, and Germany, will soon face rapid demographic shifts. In Japan, one in four people are now age sixty-five or older—there aren't enough people working to support both retirees and children.[40] Science and technology will eventually stand in for the lack of people: robots will assist with elder care, transportation and other services will become more automated, and tracking systems will help too few health-care providers keep tabs on their growing list of patients.

7. *Economy:* Science and technology trends intersect with all of the major economic indicators, whether that's durable goods, retail trade, or residential construction. Automated systems will begin to disrupt the workforce—yes, robots will take some of our jobs. But new jobs will also be created in the process. High-frequency trading firms have changed how Wall Street operates, and that has had an impact on our markets.

8. *Environment:* Technology is both harming and improving our planet. Our techno-trash and e-waste are piling up both in landfills and across our oceans. Our cars may be increasingly eco-friendly, but the factories where they are manufactured still pollute our atmosphere. And yet there are innovative new technologies to help solve these problems, such as bioluminescent trees, which could someday replace our streetlamps at night. Researchers are already thinking about terraforming Mars with 3D printed microbes from Earth. There is an entire field of synthetic biology that aims to make life programmable: in 2010, biotechnologist Craig Venter created Synthia, a synthetic cell—essentially, the world's first living organism to have a computer as its mother. Venter believes the innovation will eventually help to transform our environmental waste into clean fuel and allow us to make vaccines more easily, among other things.[41]

9. *Journalism:* How do we learn about the world around us? Newsgathering, publishing, and broadcasting are inextricably tied to the internet, our computers, our mobile devices, algorithms, and the cloud. Emerging technology platforms control not only what news you see, but when and why you see it. Emerging platforms and tools have enabled journalists to be better watchdogs and to effect greater change.

10. *Media:* Our individual and collective use of social networks, chat services, digital video channels, photo-sharing services, and so on have forever changed how we interact with each other. There are boundless opportunities to produce our own content, to band together with like-minded people, and to share our thoughts and ideas in real time. We influence each other on Snapchat and Instagram, but we also have the power to change national conversations outside the traditional news channels. Look no further than the Center for Medical Progress, an antiabortion group, and its widely publicized undercover videos. Activists recorded Planned Parenthood officials, edited their statements, and then crafted a series of wildly inaccurate stories about fetal tissue trade.

The videos went viral across YouTube, Facebook, and Twitter, eventually sparking lawmakers to propose that Planned Parenthood lose its federal funding.[42]

If we want to forecast the future of anything, we need to plot out these intersecting vectors of change—their direction and magnitude—as they relate to new developments in emerging technology. The first Sony hack may have been the result of a compromised codebase and an enterprising hacker. But *people* play Sony's games, buy its hardware, and watch its movies. Therefore, anyone seriously concerned about cybersecurity at Sony should have also considered how developments in media, the economy, government, politics, and wealth distribution would play a future role in people's attitudes, behaviors, and actions toward the company.

Like Sony, you might be tempted to decouple trends in technology from the ten modern sources of change listed above, but in our information age they are very much intertwined. Consider how these seemingly disparate developments in Japanese demographics have become the catalyst for breathtaking advances in robotics:

Modern Sources of Change: Demography, Public Health, Wealth Distribution, Government.

Context: One-quarter of Japan's population is now sixty-five or older, and no amount of policymaking will suddenly cause a mass of working-age people to materialize. No economic regulations will solve for the expansive hole in tax revenue. No social welfare policy will result in enough highly trained home health-care workers becoming available to serve this enormous group of people overnight.

Technology Trend: Robot-assisted living.

Implication: Within a generation, there will not be enough people to make Japanese society work as it does today. Anyone interested in the future of robotics would be wise to look not to Silicon Valley, but instead to universities and R&D labs in Japan, where there is extensive research underway. Out of necessity, robots—mechanical systems, artificial intelligence, and automated services—will act as productive, efficient stand-ins for a Generation X that simply wasn't big enough.

Or how understanding the future of terrorism necessitates following trends in digital media:

Modern Sources of Change: Media, Government, Education.

Context: Terrorist groups are using social media channels to recruit new members in plain sight. Soldiers are outfitted with guns and smartphones and trained to shoot both bullets and video. They maintain and operate active Twitter, Facebook, YouTube, Instagram, and Tumblr accounts.

Technology Trend: Hackerrorists. Hactivists, while often destructive, are hacking for what they perceive to be in the public interest. Hacker-terrorists, "hackerrorists," will use the online world in order to evoke real-world acts of terrorism.

Implication: Hackerrorists are digital media experts. They're quick to adopt new social networks and create a presence in them, and like a hydra, when one social media provider suspends service to a terrorist group, countless new accounts immediately pop up. Hackerrorists are also adept at using "dark nets," niche online spaces promising anonymity and the kinds of encryption tools that hackers favor. Fighting terrorism in the future will mean creating highly sophisticated, algorithmically personalized digital propaganda. Law enforcement will need to hunt down terrorists in the dark web to disrupt and disarm them. Governments will have a complicated encryption battle to fight, since the various groups won't exactly be using a standardized set of tools.

A GOOD TREND IS HARD TO FIND

If we know what a trend is, that trends connect to the ten modern sources of change within society and share a set of common characteristics, then why are they so hard to spot? I'll answer that question by asking another: Why can you instantly envision what the "Jetsons' car" is? You still know it was a flying car even if you weren't alive to watch the Jetsons in 1963 and don't remember that the car's base was green, that it was controlled by a single joystick, that it had modular red bucket seats capable of moving around the cabin, or that it folded up into George's briefcase before he—wait for it—hopped onto a futuristic moving sidewalk that whisked him into the office.

Now, if I were to ask you to imagine a new kind of micro-electro-mechanical sensor for stability control that will connect to an upgrade in a car's operating system for . . . there's probably no need for me to go on, right? How can even the most significant innovation in a microchip or sensor even begin to compete with that visceral image we all have of the Jetsons' car?

Sometimes, trends are really boring, so we don't pay any attention to them. If we want to plan for the future of transportation, we would need more than an artist's sketch and a memorable story. In order to figure out the future of how we will move around—a Google car? flying discs? teleportation?—we would need to consider at least some of those ten modern sources of change, which aren't quite as captivating as a Jetsons' cartoon car:

Government: Are new laws regarding drones being drafted today that might intentionally or implicitly change how we will operate vehicles on roads or in the sky?

Politics: Are companies in adjacent industries lobbying elected officials for anything unusual, such as a larger budget for the Highway Trust Fund? Are they advocating for investment in sensor technologies?

Economy: Will unpredictable gas prices amid a tepid job market have weaned us away from driving in the near future? Will the largest auto manufacturers need to develop new profit centers in response?

Media: Auto manufacturers are integrating mobile phones into the driver experience. Some manufacturers offer platforms that enable drivers to connect their social media accounts to a car's dashboard. Will consumers demand even more digital functionality and information as they grow accustomed to these newer systems? Will they care less about driving and more about connecting with media while in a vehicle?

Public Health: In 2014, more than 3,000 people were killed and 431,000 were injured because of distracted drivers.[43] We are increasingly dependent on our devices. Will car crashes increase such that distracted driving is considered a public health epidemic?

Demography: Research has shown that Millennials place much less importance than earlier generations did on getting a driver's license and owning cars. In 1983, 46 percent of sixteen-year-olds in the United States got their driver's licenses. By 2014, that percentage had dropped to just 24.[44] Researchers blame factors such as e-commerce, which decreases the need to drive in order to shop, and social media, which enables people to gather together in digital environments. Millennials who do have licenses are increasingly participating in sharing platforms like Zipcar and Citibike. By the time autonomous technology has advanced sufficiently for widespread use on highways, will Millennials have caused a permanent shift in society's attitude toward car ownership?

We misidentify trends (or miss them altogether) when we focus exclusively on technology, when the other factors in play are seemingly unrelated, or when the adjacent sources of change aren't part of a compelling narrative. Forecasting the future doesn't always yield headline-worthy results, even if certain trends promise to change how we live on this planet. Early on in *The Graduate*, the character played by Dustin Hoffman is offered an insightful glimpse into the future, when Mr. McGuire says just one word to him: "plastics."[45]

In 1967, plastics were actually a pretty exciting subject, if you recognized the signals. The audience winced at McGuire's misguided passion about industrialization, conformity, and mass-market goods. But the near future of plastics made personal computers a reality and turned free-spirited Baby Boomers into wealthy, Wall Street Yuppies by the time they were forty. Plastics also spawned the plastic water bottle craze that eventually created the Great Pacific Garbage Patch, an ocean wasteland predicted in a 1988 paper published by the National Oceanic and Atmospheric Administration[46] and later discovered by Charles J. Moore in 1999.[47] Sailing home from a race, Moore encountered an impassible stretch of plastics: bottles, toothbrushes, and millions upon millions of unidentifiable plastic fragments. A lack of planning in 1967 still impacts us fifty years later: in the 2010s, no scientist, environmentalist, or governmental agency has been able to establish a global policy for dealing with humanity's massive, and still growing, plastic footprint.

Often, future game-changing trends enter society without attracting media attention or interest from the general public during the early years of development out on the fringe. Just as it took more than a decade for the Great Pacific Garbage Patch to become visible, another important techno-social phenomenon—global adoption of the mobile phone—wasn't noticed by most people for sixty years.

Phones became "mobile" in 1947, when AT&T researcher Douglas "D. H." Ring discovered a new method of linking phones to a car's antenna.[48] There weren't many subscribers to the service, but for nearly four decades, the car phone service was available in a few cities around the United States. In the 1960s, AT&T perfected that original technology via cellular towers that could hand off calls as a driver moved around. The first commercially available mobile phone not tethered to a car was sold in 1984.[49] Just ten years ago, you or someone you know was probably still using a flip phone with an antenna and, quite possibly, a matching leather sleeve. Checking your voice mail meant dialing *86, waiting for a prompt, pressing the # key, waiting for another prompt, then entering your PIN code and pressing # again. Taking a photo required using the keypad to get to the home screen, pressing "a," then "h," to get to another screen, and pressing another series of keys to take, name, and store the photo. Convenience trumped the complicated menu system. Mobile phones engendered an always-on lifestyle and entered our collective conscious.

If you're like most people today, you rely on your flat-screened smartphone to send work emails, shop at the grocery store, or order a car from a subscription service like Uber or Lyft. This change is breathtaking, but it doesn't feel like it to us today. That's because we're living in the midst of that change. To evolve from a car phone to basic flip phones took six decades. And yet within the next ten years, our mobile devices will have the computational power of a human brain—the least exciting of their features will be their ability to make a phone call. Which is still relatively short, but bear in mind Moore's Law and the compounding effect of technological advances. All of those incremental achievements in cellular networking, user interfaces, and processors tend to get overlooked until they add up to something big and recognizable, like the iPhone.

It can be difficult to see trends, and especially challenging when all of the changes leading up to a trend's formation are relatively uninteresting, or when they threaten to upend our established, cherished beliefs. That is certainly what happened with Sony. Yet concentrating your efforts on tracking trends in just one area, without taking into consideration adjacent areas, will lead you to follow shiny objects, rather than to consider how the ten sources of change are contributing to a bigger shift. The future isn't just some nebulous point in the far-off distance, and so we must think about trends as they relate to different time zones.

Because trends align with our evolving human nature and leverage our basic needs, they help us to foresee and forecast change in the future.

So how do you find trends? Before I introduce the first of our six instructions, it's worth showing you what happens when organizations track trends correctly, as you will see with one well-known company that's still thriving more than 125 years after its founding. You will also learn the grim fate of a breathtaking organization that, like BlackBerry, failed to acknowledge the change that was happening.

CHAPTER THREE

Survive and Thrive, or Die

How Trends Affect Companies

TRENDS CAN BE slow to develop, and we don't often understand (or we misunderstand) their long-term potential. Trends help us to understand change, which is an essential part of every organization's mandate—or, at least, of any organization hoping to survive more than a decade or two. That's the moral we can take away from the story of two organizations, one that is well over a century old, and another whose star shone in the firmament for a couple of decades, but ultimately flamed out when it failed to listen to the signals.

•

Those who intentionally plan for what's next—even very large, sprawling organizations—can more easily forecast what's on the horizon and manifest their own preferred futures. That was certainly the case with a game company founded in Kyoto, Japan, in 1889. You know it today as Nintendo.

Nintendo, which brought us Super Mario Brothers, the Game Boy, and the Wii, started out as Nintendo Koppai, a small playing-card company based in Kyoto. Founded by businessman Fusajiro Yamauchi, Nintendo Koppai produced *hanafuda* cards, which were similar to today's common set of fifty-two playing cards, except that rather than numbers and suits, *hanafuda* were printed with one of twelve sets of beautiful flowers.[1]

By 1953, Yamauchi's grandson, Hiroshi Yamauchi, had become fascinated with an emerging trend, in fact, the same one from that iconic scene between Mr. McGuire and Benjamin in *The Graduate*: plastics. Nintendo's paper card business was profitable, but it was far too limited.

Hiroshi Yamauchi had been meeting with the unusual suspects at the fringe and connecting the dots: The advent of plastics for commercial use, combined with new manufacturing capabilities, meant that the gaming space would inevitably become crowded. The price of televisions was dropping, and children's cartoons featuring the Looney Tunes and the Mickey Mouse Club were capturing widespread attention. Walt Disney was getting ready to open his eponymous theme park, Disneyland. Traditional cards, checkers, and chess games would no doubt be replaced by mass-produced board and card games with new strategies, storylines, and even characters.

As he assumed the position of Nintendo president in place of his grandfather, Yamauchi made several bold moves in planning for the future. First, he produced *hanafuda* cards in plastic.[2] His contemporaries at the time no doubt questioned his logic. Plastic cards were far more durable than paper. Wouldn't Nintendo's sales shrink, since, unlike delicate paper cards, a plastic deck could ostensibly be used forever? With these new operations in place, he took a trip to the United States and met with Disney executives. In 1959, which was still very early on in Disney's development, he made a deal to print Disney characters on Nintendo cards. This collaboration opened the playing-card market, which had mostly been targeted to gambling adults, up to children.[3]

Yamauchi kept listening to the signals and connecting dots. Soon, there were books with explanations for how to play Nintendo's new Disney card games. Millions of packs of cards had been sold. By the 1970s, Nintendo had completely saturated the playing-card market, however, and the company, which had gone public, saw its stock price plummet. Looking for new efficiencies, Yamauchi toured Nintendo's factories and met with employees. One engineer had been tinkering with a mechanical arm of sorts—it was an expandable set of crisscrossed plastic, with scissor-like handles on one end and tongs on the other. Nintendo developed the arm into the Ultra Hand.[4] It marked the introduction of a new kind of toy, one that was both fun and functional. It sold millions of units and paved the way for new products and more experimentation.

In the 1970s, early videocassette machines were making their way into households. Meanwhile, computer programmers had been tinkering with electronic games, which had primarily been a simulation of real-world board games. Again, considering future scenarios, Nintendo asked its engineers to think through other ways in which video consoles might one day be used, both in the home and in places like restaurants and arcades. What about a television screen at eye level, where someone could stand and play while others watched?

Nintendo made another bold move and in 1973 created the Laser Clay Shooting System, a game intended for everyone to play, not just computer programmers. The following year, it developed another new technology—an image projection system—and manufactured the hardware for it. Nintendo started selling video-game machines, as well as the games to play on them, throughout Japan, the United States, and Europe. By 1979, Yamauchi's son-in-law Minoru Arakawa had moved to New York City to create a base for what would soon become a multinational corporation.[5]

Nintendo was still very much a company that made games, just as it had in 1889. But it was also a company that invested in tracking emerging trends throughout gaming and adjacent industries. As a result, Nintendo developed products that set the course for the future. Soon came game titles like Donkey Kong, Super Mario Bros., and my personal favorite, The Legend of Zelda. It created advanced home console systems like the NES (Nintendo Entertainment System). In 1988, Nintendo's R&D department was at work on a number of other new projects that melded advances in personal computing and wearable technologies with games. As a result, Nintendo created a hands-free controller vest with a mouthpiece that allowed quadriplegics to play video games. The following year, Nintendo debuted the world's first portable, handheld game system—the Game Boy—that had interchangeable game cartridges and had introduced a little game called Tetris.[6]

There were plenty of competitors along the way (Atari, for example) as well as hardware and software bugs that at times proved challenging, if not potentially disastrous. And yet, the company continued to innovate. At the end of 2006, Nintendo launched the Wii, a motion-sensing game system that was accessible to everyone, regardless of age or computer experience. It was connected to the internet, and the controller was a lightweight, wireless handheld wand. To play a game of bowling, you simply held onto the wand and moved your arm, just as you would in a real bowling alley. To golf, you'd swing your arms and hips just as you would out on the course.[7]

Nintendo survived—and, for the most part, thrived—for more than 125 years because it listened to the signals, spotted early trends, and blazed a new trail for the entire gaming industry. Many of the play control features we now take for granted—not just on rival gaming platforms but also in other places, including our phones and computers—are directly attributable to Nintendo's foresight.

As of 2016, Nintendo was one of the most successful video-game companies in the world, and it was still the leading playing-card manufacturer in Japan. Nintendo is a company that might have been crushed by new technologies, changing customer tastes, and upstarts in the entertainment space, but for one simple fact: it leveraged trends.

The same was not true of a company that, had it been listening to the signals and tracking trends, might still exist today. That company was the Digital Equipment Corporation (DEC), and it completely missed the advent of personal computers.

•

It's difficult to imagine it today, but two generations ago, computing was only a fringe experiment—and a rudimentary one at that. The earliest computer engineers were total outliers tinkering on the fringe. The first machines took up the size of a large room—but if we follow the work of those early engineers up through the advent of the personal computer, we will be able to see a trend unfold. And what happened to one of America's most exciting companies when it refused to see how that fringe research could go mainstream.

In 1937, Bell Labs research mathematician George Stibitz sat at his kitchen table, thinking about the electromechanical relays found inside telephone switching systems. Could they be used for other purposes? If they could transmit voice, what about something else, like text? Stibitz decided to start tinkering. Using electromechanical relays, along with some flashlight bulbs and a switch he fashioned out of a tobacco tin, Stibitz built a working prototype for a new kind of machine that could calculate numbers using binary addition.[8]

Stibitz kept reworking his machine, adding more telephone relays and crossbar switches. Eventually, it could calculate a long division problem, correctly finding the quotient of two eight-place numbers in just thirty seconds. Stibitz soon found himself with a research program and a team to further test and build on his work.

In September 1940, at the American Mathematical Society conference at Dartmouth College, Stibitz discussed his Complex Number Computer (CNC), the world's first electronic digital computer.[9] (Then, "digital" referred to the ten numbers 0 through 9 that were used to make calculations.) Stibitz used a telegraph to send a difficult calculation—one that could not be solved by a person without enough time to do the work by hand—from the meeting in Dartmouth to his CNC back in Lower Manhattan. About a minute later, the Teletype line returned a message showing the correct answer. Conference-goers were stunned, having just witnessed this act of computing—as well as the first time a computer had ever been used remotely. For the next three hours, they called out equations, trying (without success) to stump the Complex Number Computer.[10]

The demonstration sparked great interest in computers, prompting students and researchers at the Massachusetts Institute of Technology (MIT) and the University of Pennsylvania to experiment with new designs. Crunching a few numbers was a clever trick; however, they had a more important goal, envisioning a computer capable of doing advanced mathematics remotely using a series of machines distributed over a network.

War has a habit of marshaling scientific advancements forward. As it happened, while Stibitz was at Dartmouth showing off his invention, the Luftwaffe had been given orders to target British civilians, bombing St. Paul's Cathedral and Buckingham Palace in London in the beginning of the Blitz. Then, America's entry into World War II in December 1941 mobilized funding for research into war-related technology, including computerization. There were a host of problems to tackle. One had to do with the inaccuracy of the US Army's artillery, which required constant recalibration. The gunners needed to track hundreds of variables, such as wind speeds, humidity, and the kind of gunpowder supplied. There wasn't time to calculate all of the conditions—and there were too few artillery shells to waste on guessing.

To solve these and other emerging problems, the War Department decided to fund research on an electronic computer—the Electronic Numerical Integrator and Computer (ENIAC)—in April 1943. Of all the experiments that came before it, the ENIAC was the first that could multitask, as our computers do today: it was programmable, it could complete any calculation, and it was very fast.[11] Another computer, the Colossus Mark 1, became operational later that year, and it was used to help decrypt German radio teleprinter messages.[12]

One of the earliest programmers, Grace Hopper, had worked on the Colossus Mark 1 as a naval reserve officer. (In 1985, Hopper would be promoted to rear admiral.) After the war, she and her team at the Remington Rand corporation had built the first compiler for computer languages, which allowed computers to use language, not just numbers. It was such an unimaginable feat of engineering that initially, nobody inside academia or the military-industrial complex believed that it had been built.[13]

In the 1950s, Hopper's compiler became the basis for the universal standard for computer languages, COBOL (an acronym for Common Business-Oriented Language). Meanwhile, computers were proving useful to the US Census Bureau, the US Atomic Energy Commission, and the broadcasting network CBS, which used a UNIVAC (for

Universal Automatic Computer) to predict a landslide for Dwight D. Eisenhower in the 1952 presidential election.[14]

It should have been clear that the first era of computing, marked by machines that could calculate numbers, was giving way to a second era of programmable computers. These were faster, lighter systems that had enough memory to hold instruction sets. Programs could now be stored locally and, importantly, written in English rather than complicated machine code. Moore's 1965 thesis, that the number of components on integrated circuits would double every year, was proving accurate. Computers were becoming more and more powerful and capable of myriad tasks, not just arithmetic.

But for the next twenty years, the business world remained skeptical because it couldn't see this second phase of computing as anything more than a fringe research project. In order to sell one of its computers, the new manufacturer IBM would often send its chairman, Thomas Watson Jr., to convince department managers that investing in one of its costly computers was worth the expenditure. Even as computers shrank from the size of rooms to desktops, few could imagine a day in which someone might use a computer outside of work. The paradox of the present blinded CEOs to the sweeping changes taking place before their eyes across the ten sources of change, which included women entering the workforce. Our economy was globalizing, with many companies opting to do business overseas. Universities were starting to offer degrees in computer science. Students at MIT and Harvard had even built rival computerized dating services.[15]

Computer scientist J. C. R. Licklider, the head of the Behavioral Sciences and Command and Control programs at DARPA, envisioned another dimension to this second phase of computing. It was a system of computers—maybe four or eight—linked together, using a homogeneous programming language. People might use the system to retrieve a set of data to work on and then share, so that others could use it to further their own research. In a memo, Licklider described "linkages" between a user's programs and those she borrowed. This idea became the basis for ARPANET, the Advanced Research Projects Agency Network, which would soon bridge together programmers at the University of California at Los Angeles (UCLA), the Stanford Research Institute, the University of California at Santa Barbara (UCSB), and the University of Utah.[16]

Meanwhile, MIT engineers Ken Olsen and Harlan Anderson imagined a smaller computer meant to be used by just one person. They founded the Digital Equipment Corporation (DEC) and went to production on what they called "minicomputers" in the late 1960s.[17] They could be used by research labs, government agencies, and businesses that depended on heavy computer use by multiple staff at once. This startup quickly grew to become a market leader, and by the 1980s, DEC would employ 120,000 people, reach $14 billion in sales, and become one of the most profitable companies in the United States.[18]

There were already people on the fringe starting to think about a third era of computing, one that enabled professional researchers and scientists to share data and collaborate on projects. Futurist Olaf Helmer, writing in his seminal 1967 "Prospects of Technological Progress" paper for the RAND Corporation, said that such a "world-wide network of specialists, each equipped with a console tied to one central computer and to electronic data banks," would someday "interact with one another via the computer network" for the purpose of scientific research.[19] But almost no one, including Helmer, foresaw the real trend: a third era taking a radically different shape as *personal* computing. They couldn't see how that very same technology might be desirable for everyday people to send messages to each other, to read the news and to record history. The failure spelled disaster for many businesses, including DEC.

In 1977, Olsen, who had become DEC's president, said that there was "no reason for any individual to have a computer in their home," and that "the personal computer will fall flat on its face."[20] Olsen was shackled by his immediate frame of reference. He had built a wildly successful company predicated on small, programmable computers built specifically for businesses and researchers. However, outside his view of the present, there was a revolution underfoot:

Education: ARPANET was fully operational, connecting fifty-seven Interface Message Processors, which served as gateways connecting a growing network of computers—and more importantly, computer programmers. Programmers created Transmission Control Protocol and Internet Protocol, otherwise known as TCP/IP, making it possible to remote-access the network.[21]

Economy: The marketplace was being invaded by upstarts. Atari and Commodore had personal computer models to show. Two young enthusiasts named Steve Wozniak and Steve Jobs had built a small computer in their Los Altos, California, garage. Adam Osborne, who had been a pioneer in writing easy-to-read technical manuals for computers, built the world's first commercially available portable computer. Not only did it weigh a mere twenty-four pounds, but it could be used anywhere there was a wall outlet.[22]

Media: Programmers had built games for computers, including Galactic Empire and Galactic Trader. Disney used computer-generated graphics for the movie *Tron*. Ward Christensen and Randy Suess launched a digital bulletin board system that could be used to post messages.

By the 1990s, we had transitioned away from the era of personal computing to a fourth era: the internet, which was democratizing how information was shared. Everyday people were getting online to help build this new frontier, which impacted every industry sector.

Remarkably, the same negative forecasts that seemed to follow the previous eras of computing were prominent yet again. The internet trend wouldn't last, people said. It was an unnecessary frivolity. In 1995, Robert Metcalfe, co-inventor of Ethernet, argued that the internet would "soon go spectacularly supernova and in 1996 catastrophically collapse."[23] That same year, *Newsweek* published a column by renowned author and computer geek Clifford Stoll, who wrote: "They speak of electronic town meetings and virtual communities. Commerce and business will shift from offices and malls to networks and modems. And the freedom of digital networks will make government more democratic. Baloney. The truth is no online database will replace your daily newspaper, no CD-ROM can take the place of a competent teacher and no computer network will change the way government works."[24]

Today, the internet is ubiquitous save for extremely remote areas. But even that's changing, as companies like Google and Facebook have launched enormous space balloons to help deliver connectivity from beyond the clouds. The most common computer used around the world offers far more than word processing, calculating programs, and an internet connection. It weighs under four ounces, doesn't need to be plugged into a wall, and is inching closer to passing the Turing test by showing enough intelligence for its interface to seem indistinguishable from a human's. In fact, you probably have one in your pocket right now: the smartphone.

This fourth era is nothing at all like what those earlier computing experts had predicted. Everyday people, not just programmers, are able to configure smartphones to their liking, adding and removing apps as they design their own digital experiences. Those experiences are shaping our behaviors as we shift from owning software to leasing it, co-creating content rather than subscribing to it, and manufacturing peripherals that fit our personal needs via online platforms or 3D printers in our homes.

GETTING IT WRONG

Why did so many brilliant people get the personal computing trend wrong? How could they have failed to predict that the internet would take off, and that modern computers would become so deeply integrated into our daily lives?

We tend to underplay the significance of something when it is not significant to our immediate frame of reference. In the mid-1990s, Clifford Stoll said that the internet couldn't survive in part because of a "wasteland of unfiltered data" where there was no way to search for information easily. Because Stoll was an early super-user, his vision was naturally limited to the Internet v1.0's significant shortcomings. Robert Metcalfe was similarly biased by his own expertise. He was questioning capacity—How could the internet continue to grow without suffering outages? A lack of coordination and cooperation between the first Internet Service Providers had already led to big network problems. Without any changes in sight, Metcalfe saw outages rather than advancements.

Conversely, there were plenty of techno-utopians who placed far too *much* emphasis on the internet and computing, since it was their focal point. John Perry Barlow, cofounder of the new Electronic Frontier Foundation, proclaimed that there were no laws in cyberspace, that it was free of government rule.[25] Media theorists Richard Barbrook and Andy Cameron postulated that the internet would make possible a perfect "cybercommunist" society, where all were equal, all software would be free, and technology would emancipate those who were disenfranchised by the free market.[26]

Smart thinkers get trends wrong because of present-day bias and because they fail to think outside their usual frame of reference. Sometimes, they misunderstand trends because they discount new technological innovations when they sound too fantastical to ever find practical use. In the 1960s, science fiction writers were telling stories about omniscient computers, such as the HAL 9000 in *2001: A Space Odyssey*, or The Thinker, a supercomputer in *Logan's Run*. They weren't purely imaginary. If researchers had temporarily put aside process—tabling questions about how exactly these computers would be built—they could have plotted out the trajectory of personal computing and internet connectivity and envisioned similar scenarios.

Put another way, what would have been the value of DEC's lead engineers dreaming big about the artificially intelligent computers of the far future? No one at DEC could have built one of these machines. But in pursuit of the future, they would have recognized emerging trends. That foresight might have led them to develop the first laptop. With a constant push, they might have envisioned the fourth era of computing—and perhaps beyond.

Except for one problem: the company's senior leadership didn't see the trend. By 1998, most of DEC's divisions had been shuttered or sold. What remained of this once-great company was acquired by Compaq in January of that year.

It would be unfair to place the blame only on Olsen. Others at DEC did see changes afoot, but they were paralyzed by fear: trained in older technologies, they may have felt threatened by advances in personal computing that could devalue their skills. They didn't want to acknowledge the personal computing trend, which would cause so much disruption it could force the established computer maker to develop entirely new systems and models. Their reptilian brains took over, and they instinctively ran away from change rather than recognizing and embracing it.

GETTING IT RIGHT

Regardless of the industry or circumstances, one forecast has always been right throughout history: technology will advance, it will invariably intersect with other sources of change within society, and trends are the signposts showing us how changes will manifest in real life. Karl Benz's internal combustion engine eventually inspired the Ford Model T, which made Google's driverless car fleet possible. Da Vinci's contemporaries thought his flying machine was preposterous—indeed, the world had to wait another four hundred years before human flight became a reality.

We will never know with 100 percent certainty what, exactly, the future holds. There are too many variables to consider, such as the ten sources of modern change, natural disasters, and sudden accidents.

Earlier, I described three scenarios for the future of automated transport, and they may have sounded increasingly outlandish to you. But using three distinct labels before each scenario—probable, plausible, and possible—sharpened the focus of those ideas, clarifying what we know is true today and what we can assume might happen in the future. This method removed "how" from my line of thinking—at the moment, I was only concerned with what the future of transportation might look like. For now, I could focus my attention on research being done on the fringe. Futurists borrow these terms—probable, plausible, and possible—from statistics, and for many decades they've been used to help us generate concrete ideas about what's over the horizon.

Probable futures. If we assume that a current trend is likely to continue—for example, automated transport—then what is highly likely, given the technology that exists today and the emerging research being worked on in labs? Barring sweeping changes in funding for our highway systems, or how our law enforcement works, or how businesses distribute goods and packages around, it is very likely that we will still operate cars and trucks. In a decade, they will log in to a connected network, driving themselves in designated lanes on our highways. In two decades, they will drive autonomously around our neighborhoods, within cities and on country roads. Given what we know today, the automated transport trend has the highest probability of realization in this scenario.

Plausible futures. We have a current understanding of the trend. We also know the laws of nature, physics, and mathematics as well as the current systems, workflows, and processes that govern research, business, the government, and society—essentially, the concepts and rules operating within the ten sources of change. Therefore, we can look out on the fringe to determine which kinds of early experimentation are plausible, given how things work. Flying discs that use a skyway to take us short distances are an option. We can't exclude them from our thinking, since they are a plausible scenario for the future of automated transportation.

Possible futures. In our lifetime, we probably won't ever get beamed up like the Enterprise crew of *Star Trek*. But it's certainly thrilling to think about. We know that the rate of change in technology progresses exponentially: it took humans 2,000 years to get from horse-drawn chariots to self-driving Google cars, but only 20 years to advance from landlines to iPhones. Given where we are in the twenty-first century, how could anyone argue that 250 years from now, humans couldn't use quantum computing to teleport their minds into rented human bodies? To argue against such a scenario would require us to also argue that the currently accepted laws of the universe won't be tested, violated, or rewritten after future discoveries.

If your job involves managing risk, you may feel that there is no room for plausible or possible futures within your organization. Why pour money, time, and effort into investigating a trend's potential scenarios, when logic would dictate that the probable future is dependable? The story of Nintendo's remarkable longevity—and how, between 1889 and 2016, it used trends to create plausible and possible scenarios, and marshaled the gaming industry into the future—answers why it's important to allow for risk.

Focusing only on the probable future will serve you well in the near term, as it did DEC. For decades, staying just slightly ahead of the curve allowed researchers in the company to temporarily set the direction and pace for the computing business. DEC's first commercially available computer, the PDP-1, was cheaper than IBM's machines and relatively small, and it didn't require air conditioning. DEC's researchers built the first graphics display intended for the masses. They showed how computers could be used for more than computations—Spacewar!, the first computer game, launched on a PDP-1. Digital's later model, the PDP-7, was used by Ken Thompson and Dennis Ritchie at Bell Labs to create Unix, which included the first hierarchical file system and a command-line interpreter. In the early 1980s, DEC's VT-52 launched an all-in-one computer console with a screen and keyboard. It included the first WYSIWYG (what you see is what you get) editor.

These achievements were possible because DEC was focused on a probable future.[27]

However, when confronted with a plausible future—that everyday people would someday want to use computers in their own homes—the leadership at DEC couldn't make the leap. It was a perilous mistake, one that eventually caused this pioneer in computing to cease operations entirely.

Trends are only useful when we look at them through multiple lenses as we gaze across all six time zones. We must think of trends as signposts that can illuminate the conditions we will likely encounter at some point in the future, even if that future is a century away. Or, as we're about to see, as close as 1.3 light-seconds.

ALGORITHMS DON'T PREDICT MOONSHOTS

We know that our reptilian brains aren't to be trusted. Left to our own devices, most of us wouldn't dare venture into plausible or possible future territory. But we also know that without action, we are likely to be left behind. So that begs the question: Why not just entrust an algorithm to handle the prediction work for us instead? Why bother with a futurist's methodology? (Or, for that matter, even a futurist herself?)

Simply put, an algorithm is a set of rules that define a sequence of operations that have to be followed in a particular order. Combined with machine learning, artificial intelligence, and extremely powerful computers, algorithms can sort through massive, sprawling data sets to answer a number of complicated questions. They can also help predict changes, such as future public health crises. You encounter algorithms every day: Google's PageRank algorithm evaluates the quality and number of links on a web page to figure out how important it is relative to the words you search and your own search history, and that determines the order in which your search results appear. Sites like Netflix and Amazon use recommendation algorithms to suggest related books, movies, and other items you're likely to click on. The National Security Agency (NSA) uses powerful algorithms to analyze your personal data.

So here's a question for you, one that will illustrate why computers alone cannot forecast the future: Could an algorithm have predicted that Neil Armstrong and Buzz Aldrin would successfully land on the moon in 1969?

On a cold and clear day eight years earlier, John F. Kennedy had taken the oath of office. Kennedy was the youngest candidate to ever be elected to the presidency, and his Inaugural Address focused not so much on the past as on the future. "The torch has been passed to a new generation of Americans," he declared.[28] He and his young wife represented a fresh breath of idealism and excitement, even as events on the world stage pointed to a new kind of war. Tensions between the United States, the Soviet Union, and its communist allies had been escalating. Soviet leader Nikita Khrushchev taunted America's military, urging it to compete with his country in a missile "shooting match."[29] American pilot Francis Gary Powers was shot down over the Soviet Union while on a reconnaissance mission in his U-2 spy plane.[30] A special committee urged the US government to build fallout shelters throughout America. Fidel Castro had become the leader of Cuba, inspiring similar communist insurgencies throughout Latin America.

Just months into office, Kennedy suffered humiliation after his CIA-backed invasion into Cuba—the Bay of Pigs—failed to overthrow Castro. Meantime, halfway around the world, Yuri Gagarin became the first human to orbit the Earth in space during a 180-minute mission.[31]

Breaking from tradition, Kennedy didn't wait another year to address Congress. Instead, he assembled lawmakers on May 21 for a joint session. His address was intended as much for the ears of the Kremlin as it was for the approval of Congress. With the launch of the Soviet Sputnik satellite and a technological gap that seemed to be putting the United States ever further behind the Soviet Union, Kennedy wanted to catapult America beyond Earth's orbit and deep into space.[32]

At the end of a nine-point plan that included proposals for the establishment of the Office of Emergency Planning, a new Manpower Development and Training Program to retrain several hundred thousand workers who had been displaced through industrialization, and additional radio and television broadcasts to Latin America and Southeast Asia, Kennedy laid out an ambitious goal for an agency that had been created recently: NASA. "I believe that this nation should commit itself to achieving the goal, before this decade is out, of landing a man on the moon and returning him safely to the earth," Kennedy said. He called for the rapid development of a lunar spacecraft, alternate liquid and solid fuel boosters, new kinds of propulsion engines, and the Rover nuclear rocket, which promised unmanned explorations beyond the moon to other areas of the solar system. Kennedy also wanted space satellites for worldwide communications and better weather observation.[33]

The United States was well into the Cold War. Communist-inspired insurgencies were perfecting guerrilla tactics in the jungles and fields of Third World countries. Kennedy's plan to fight communism? Spending between $7 billion and $9 billion in taxpayer dollars not on tanks or nuclear weapons, but instead on a space race to the moon.[34] It was an absolutely insane proposition. At that point, both the Soviet Union and the United States had achieved suborbital flight. There were no rockets powerful enough to push a spacecraft past the boundary between Earth's atmosphere and outer space. Nor were there route plans, fabrics to safeguard astronauts outside their ship, communication systems that could relay information back to Earth, or the many thousands of other details required to get a human to space and home in one piece.

"Let it be clear," Kennedy said. "I am asking the Congress and the country to accept a firm commitment to a new course of action—a course which will last for many years and carry very heavy costs." Kennedy acknowledged that nine years was an extremely aggressive time frame, but reminded the country that the Soviet Union had a significant head start. "If we were to go only half way, or reduce our sights in the face of difficulty, it would be better not to go at all," he said. "While we cannot guarantee that we shall one day be first, we can guarantee that any failure to make this effort will make us last." Legislators, cabinet members, diplomats, and members of the public who were packed into the galleries interrupted Kennedy eighteen times with applause.[35]

Depending on who in the Kennedy administration and at NASA you asked, landing an astronaut on the moon's surface was a plausible future, something that theoretically could be done with the right circumstances in place. Others would have said it was a possible future—a literal flight of fancy. More would have said that our probable future looked like this: unrecoverable debt, dead astronauts, and national disgrace.

For Kennedy, though, it was his *preferred future*. We were in a space race to prove our technical and military superiority over the Soviet Union. During his emphatic address before Congress, the president didn't know with complete certainty that we could land on the moon—much less make it back to Earth safely. However, there seemed to be enough tangible evidence that setting the moon landing as a future goal would enable NASA to reverse-engineer the necessary processes, systems, and technologies to make it possible. Planning for the moonshot shifted Kennedy's goal from *possible* to *probable*, turning his idea into reality when Neil Armstrong and Buzz Aldrin stepped onto the lunar surface in 1969.

And yet all of Kennedy's charisma and our national excitement could not have persuaded an algorithm that Kennedy's moonshot was a good scenario for the near future. That's because these abstract, qualitative data points could not have been successfully evaluated by a computer.

It's possible to build an algorithm to forecast certain elements of the future. If the algorithm was completely bug-free, it would complete the sequence of operations in the order in which it was programmed to perform them. The code would reference a computational model, which in simple terms looks something like this: If certain events happen with an expected probability, then how does one event change the other probabilities, either positively or negatively? For Kennedy's lunar mission, we would have created a chart like the one shown in Table 1, which we could further visualize by constructing Table 2.

Table 1: Kennedy Lunar Mission: Events and Probabilities, Part 1

Event (E_i)	Probability (P_i)
Rapid development of a lunar spacecraft	P_1
Development of alternate liquid and solid fuel boosters	P_2
Development of new kinds of propulsion engines	P_3
Development of the Rover nuclear rocket	P_4
Feasibility of passing budget proposal	P_5
Availability of sufficiently trained astronauts	P_6
And so on …	$P_{...}$

Table 2: Kennedy Lunar Mission: Events and Probabilities, Part 2

If this event were to occur, then...	The probability would be...						
	P_1	P_2	P_3	P_4	P_5	P_6	$P_{...}$
E_1 Rapid development of a lunar spacecraft		increases	increases	—	increases	—	......
E_2 Development of alternate liquid and solid fuel boosters	increases		—	—	increases	—	......
E_3 Development of new kinds of propulsion engines	increases	increases		—	increases	—	......
E_4 Development of the Rover nuclear rocket	increases	increases	increases		increases	—	......
E_5 Feasibility of passing budget proposal	—	—	—	—		—	......
E_6 Availability of sufficiently trained astronauts	increases	increases	—	—	increases		......
And so on ...							

This is a simplified version with just a handful of computations. A computer would no doubt crunch the numbers much faster than a person, because it could factor multiple variables quickly. Quantitative data points can be addressed by a computer. But abstract, qualitative concepts, including enthusiasm, charisma, and our tolerance for risk, just could not have been computed.

THE GENIE PROBLEM

Here's the problem: The future isn't made up of predetermined, structured data alone. It changes as a result of people, and what we are learning, breaking, achieving, feeling, saying, thinking, and building in the present. Algorithms can't account for the introduction of new qualitative variables, such as hardheaded CEOs, temperamental developers, or the eruption of mob justice within online communities. Even the best algorithms can't, at the moment, auto-correct for unexpected real-time changes—like a stock market crash due to an unexpected technical glitch, which could deplete Facebook's reserves, which might lead to that company's $2 billion virtual reality project, Oculus, being put on hold indefinitely, which could lead to a different standard or version of virtual reality taking off instead.

Algorithms do exactly what they're programmed to do, which sometimes creates a challenge for programmers. They call it the "genie problem." Right now, machines will deliver you exactly what you wish for—and we're not capable yet of wishing for the right thing. We can certainly use algorithms to supplement our thinking, but knowing what's ahead still requires people who can listen, analyze, and make connections.

Government agencies are trying to put algorithms to use today in an effort to see how people will behave in the future. Predictive modeling promises accuracy and speed. The Intelligence Advanced Research Projects Activity, IARPA for short, is the intelligence community's research agency, working alongside DARPA, NSA, and other offices. IARPA is deeply interested in automated forecasting. Current and recent research initiatives include Project Mercury, which hopes to forecast political crises and terrorist activity. The SCITE program (for Scientific advances to Continuous Insider Threat Evaluation) passively monitors data (intranet search patterns, financial records) to forecast whether another government contractor, like Edward Snowden, will leak sensitive documents.[36]

Even with the considerable computing resources we have in the present day, it is still not possible to accurately predict how someone will think, act, or behave in every single situation. Moore's Law holds because it predicts that the number of transistors in a circuit will double within a given amount of time. Transistors don't have feelings, emotions, or ideas.

Would an algorithm have told Kennedy to shoot for the moon? Maybe. Some of the technological progress could have been forecast. But an algorithm would never have calculated the human ingenuity—the creative thinking born out of countless failures and bold experimentation—that eventually got us to space.

Algorithms alone cannot forecast the future. The process still requires people, who must continually monitor trends and relate them back to decisions organizations make in the present.

Smart leaders at Nintendo watched trends for the past 125 years, and that allowed them not only to forecast change on the horizon but to set a direction for an entire gaming industry. Meanwhile, the leaders of DEC doomed their once-revered company, not only by failing to watch for trends but by ignoring them altogether once it became clear how personal computers would evolve.

Now that we have established what a trend is and why trends matter to every organization, we can begin the first set of the instructions in earnest. For that, we'll need to take a trip to the fringe.

CHAPTER FOUR

Finding the Fringe

Seek Out the Unusual Suspects

THE FIRST STEP of forecasting the future requires a trip to the fringes of science, technology, design, and society, to where unusual experimentation is taking place. For it's at the fringe that all trends are born.

One such experiment involves Mango and Romeo, two monkeys who liked to solve problems and had a great love of orange juice. A few years ago, they were asked to perform a simple-sounding task: while looking at a screen, they were to guide a digital arm to a target. Get it right, and they'd be rewarded with a drink of juice.

But there was a twist. Mango and Romeo didn't have joysticks or keyboards. In fact, they weren't able to move their arms at all. To complicate matters, each monkey was only allowed to control either the vertical or the horizontal movements of the digital arm—the x-axis or y-axis of the screen—meaning that they would need to collaborate and synchronize their motions to successfully manipulate the digital arm toward the target. One final encumbrance: they wouldn't be in the same room together.

So if they didn't have a controller and weren't in the same room together, you might be wondering how, exactly, they got the juice. Mango's and Romeo's brains were connected to each other through the internet. (If you're suddenly imaging a sort of digital Vulcan mind meld, you'd be right.[1]) The monkeys had each been implanted with tiny electrodes in their primary somatosensory and motor cortices, which are the portions of the brain that control movement. Over time they learned a form of digital telepathy, working out how to send each other their thoughts in order to control the screen. By simply thinking about moving the digital arm in a particular way, and understanding that they needed to work together to move the arm toward the target, the monkeys saw a pattern of cause and effect. Synchronizing their movements, they successfully moved the arm and earned juice.

This groundbreaking study was the result of more than twenty-five years of work by Miguel Nicolelis, director of the Center for Neuroengineering at Duke University.[2] Nicolelis and his colleague John Chapin, a professor of physiology and pharmacology at Downstate Medical Center at the State University of New York (SUNY), first conceived of brain-machine interfaces in the late 1990s.[3] Just to put this in perspective, note that they were already trying to hook up brains to computers during the same time that *PC World* magazine named the Gateway G Series the best home computer and Nokia's 9000i Communicator "a cell phone, a fax machine and a handheld computer . . . a dream."[4]

The inspiration for their idea—connecting brains to other brains, as well as to computers and robots—didn't come from a horror movie. It wasn't ripped from the pages of a superhero comic book, though there are some unmistakable similarities. Instead, the researchers were trying to crack the future of mobility and help people suffering from paralysis to walk again. There were a number of prosthetics on the market, but none returned ambulatory independence. They theorized that in the future, maybe humans could control prosthetics using only their minds. If a patient remembered what it was like to move her legs, she might still be able to send that signal to a robotic prosthetic.

They started with a rat's brain, wiring it into an artificial neural system to make a robotic feeder dispense water through force of will. Next, Nicolelis wired a monkey's brain to see if it could send brain signals over a standard internet connection to control a robotic arm in another city. To many, his research sounded preposterous rather than pragmatic, something out of a wild Hollywood sci-fi flick.

Then, after years of work, the entire world watched as sci-fi intersected with reality. A twenty-nine-year-old named Juliano Pinto, with complete paralysis of his lower body, got dressed in a mind-controlled exoskeleton built by Nicolelis's team, walked out onto a soccer field, and kicked the first ball of the 2014 World Cup.[5]

Nicolelis had successfully built a real-life Iron Man suit.

What was in the farther future? How could Nicolelis push this research further? A human-machine interface might someday help people like Juliano walk again. But what about stroke victims? What if you had lost not only the ability to speak, but the very cognitive understanding of what language is? If the memory of moving your lips to form words had been erased, a brain-machine interface wouldn't work. What if you were wired in to the brains of two healthy physical therapists speaking normally? Could their brain activity be used to retrain your brain?

Nicolelis got to work building a way of networking animal brains, which he called a "Brainet," this time connecting a group of mammals to harness and direct their neural activity. In 2015, his team published their paper "Building an Organic Computing Device with Multiple Interconnected Brains," explaining the results of an experiment to see if networking rats together would allow them to solve a basic forecasting problem that individual rats struggled to complete on their own.[6] In every trial, the Brainet successfully solved the problem, and performance improved the more the rats worked together.

After his first rat study was published, Nicolelis said he couldn't predict what kinds of emergent properties would appear when animals began interacting as part of a Brainet. "In theory, you could imagine that a combination of brains could provide solutions that individual brains cannot achieve by themselves." Where is his research going? "We're just scientists," he quipped. "We're paid to go out to the edge and discover what is out there."[7]

If it isn't already obvious, the implications are breathtaking: the basis of Nicolelis's research implies that someday, humans might be wired together for collective intelligence. A Brainet of a sculptor, an architect, an ecologist, an engineer, and a dancer could combine their experience and knowledge to design a new kind of building that is aesthetically pleasing, beneficial for the environment, and able to nourish and inspire the people who live and work inside it. A Brainet linking a cardiologist, a vascular expert, and a roboticist with cardiac and thoracic surgeons might collaborate on a difficult emergency operation.

The "edge" for Nicolelis is what I call "the fringe." It's that place where scientists, artists, technologists, philosophers, mathematicians, psychologists, ethicists, and social science thinkers are testing seemingly bizarre hypotheses, undertaking wildly creative research, and trying to discover new kinds of solutions to the problems confronting humanity. Finding fringe thinkers is the first part of the forecasting process.

Trends, as we've seen, are signposts to the future, and we know that organizations must track them if they are to create their preferred futures. You have been introduced to the features and characteristics that trends share, and how the future of technology is invariably shaped by external sources of change. Nintendo understood this and has enjoyed more than 125 years of success. Instead of arguing that personal computers would never be used by everyday people, DEC executives could have ventured out to the fringe, where they would have seen the future of computing taking shape. A personal computer may have seemed like an impossible idea, but history proves that, over time, wild new concepts developed at the fringe—like self-driving cars and pocket-sized phone-computers— are iterated upon, adapted, and adopted as they move from the periphery to the mainstream.

But where is the fringe, exactly? How do you find it? And what should you do once you get there?

When looking for the future, many people begin with traditional market research, which is inherently a look into the past—not to what's ahead. By the time the average person in a focus group has enough knowledge to discuss an emerging trend, and newspapers and websites have published their reports, the fringe idea has already moved into the mainstream. If you're looking to reinforce a *probable* scenario that you've previously created, these sources will provide most of the information you need. While this is the accepted research practice by businesses and other organizations, it cannot surface what's happening now, at this moment, on the fringe.

For nearly every industry and interest area, there are pockets of re-searchers, citizen experimenters, and hyper-creative entrepreneurs hatching new ideas. Sony's future hackers, for example, were gather-ing on yet-unknown sites like 4chan and Reddit. Some of those on the fringe trade information on the dark web, hidden from public view. Sometimes, they're working in plain sight, in maker spaces, commu-nity laboratories, and academic departments. They're on the alpha lists to test startups, and then they hack those startups' new tools, giving them new and better uses. They listen to music, watch movies, and play games, but not like you do. They're using underground networks and devices that are still in development, and they're sharing content with each other outside of email, blogs, and Facebook.

The main problem, when an organization wants to map the future of x, is that it too often defines x far too narrowly, using the old market research paradigm. To identify emerging trends, you must gather infor-mation and observations from the fringe. But you must also broaden your definition of x. Remember, that Sony hack began not with a single action by a malcontented user, but as a result of what hackers viewed as a big corporation conspiring to take control over their enjoyment of music. Like many other people, they shared in a growing distrust of cor-porations and big banks that had been bailed out by the government. The economy had grown weak—lots of people were out of work, but they had PlayStations at home and ample free time to bemoan the com-pany on message boards.

If you're looking for the future of something, the first step is to con-sider the intersecting vectors of change. You need to seek out people who think differently. In short, you need to cast a wider net.

UNUSUAL SUSPECTS

To understand what's plausible and possible beyond the visible hori-zon—to broaden your definition of x—you must seek out and get to know the "unusual suspects," the people who aren't yet winning awards for their work or being featured in "40-Under-40" business lists. More often, they're stirring up controversy for their radical new ideas. Or they're silently working away, far away from the public spotlight. They are, however, vitally important, and their ideas are all-too-often ignored or discounted.

Some of the greatest advances in human history often come from outliers on the fringe—people working on a harebrained scheme that, at the time, seemed ridiculous, or even dangerous, to others. In 1610, Galileo Galilei published *The Starry Messenger*, detailing his discoveries that the moon wasn't flat, but was rather a sphere covered in craters and mountains; that Venus had phases like the moon; and that Jupiter had moons that revolved around it. Then came his paper refuting the official church doctrine that objects floated in water because of their flat shape, and another showing that the sun had spots on it and was not, as the church had decreed, perfect. By 1633 he was being tried for heresy because of his research showing that the Earth revolved around the sun. Once he was convicted, he spent the rest of his life under house arrest and was ordered not to have any visitors. It would take another two hundred years for the church to acknowledge that Galileo was right.[8]

In 1960, Jane Goodall went on a courageous quest to Africa to understand chimpanzees. Completely isolated from civilization, Goodall set up her tent in the Gombe Stream Reserve on the eastern shore of Lake Tanganyika in what is now Tanzania (Tanganyika and Zanzibar combined in 1964). It was an isolating, forbidding environment, where she would be the only human among Africa's wild animals. Goodall was there to study chimpanzees, but she wasn't an academic or a classically trained scientist. She didn't even have an undergraduate degree. In many ways, she was the most unusual of suspects. Her unconventional research methods—living with the chimps, assigning them human names rather than numbers, describing their personalities—was at first roundly dismissed by academics, who derided her homespun observation techniques and her obsession with primates. That was until she made important discoveries that challenged the anthropologists' assumptions: chimps weren't vegetarians, she said—they ate meat; they also made tools, not unlike humans, and they used tools in order to survive.[9] Her discoveries, made five decades ago now, were some of the most important scientific observations made in modern history: she shrank the intelligence and culture gap between humans and primates.

While his contemporaries favored lectures, discourse, and mathematical descriptions, Galileo instead drew elaborate diagrams as he worked through his heliocentric theory. Jane Goodall wanted to think like the chimps she studied, so she moved into their culture—acting, moving, and vocalizing like them to gain perspective.

Those at the fringe daydream productively. They are adept at using metaphors, and so they are able to focus on the hypothetical relationships between things, rather than the things themselves. This is why Nicolelis was able to conceive of his "Brainet"—a word he invented that itself is symbolic: if one computer can copy its information onto another machine, and if computers can learn from each other, what does that mean for the computers inside our heads?

Fringe thinkers define the future of x broadly, which allows them to wonder what's possible, rather than what's plausible and probable given the current state of the world. That's one reason why fringe thinkers make good companions for pragmatists interested in the future. Unencumbered by the need to prove immediate success, to meet a bottom line, or to show a positive return on investment, fringe thinkers can push the boundaries of their imaginations without having to worry about process—that is, how to turn that dream into reality. Their ideas or methods may seem unconventional, but that's only because not enough time has elapsed for their work to ricochet from the edge to other researchers, to early adopters, to businesses, to established academic circles, and finally to mainstream society.

Here's an example highlighting the fundamental differences between how the average person and fringe thinkers approach new ideas. On August 1, 1941, Isaac Asimov was en route to a meeting with his editor, where he was supposed to talk about new story ideas, but he had no plots or characters in mind. So he deployed a brainstorming technique he often used. He had a collection of Gilbert and Sullivan plays with him and opened the book to *Iolanthe*. The first thing he saw was an illustration of the fairy queen kneeling before Private Willis of the Grenadier Guards. That made him think about riding the New York City subway, military society, feudalism, Edward Gibbon's *The Decline and Fall of the Roman Empire*, World War II, the Battle of Britain, Nazi Germany's invasion of the Soviet Union, outer space, and life beyond Earth. By the time he arrived at the meeting with his editor, Asimov had a basic outline for what would become his best-known science-fiction series, which was originally published in magazine installments and later as a trilogy of novels called *Foundation*. Within a few hours, he had created a story about the fall of future galactic empires and a return of feudalism. One of the characters, Hari Seldon, used a new branch of science he called "psychohistory"—a combination of crowd-sourced psychology and math—to forecast the collapse of the empire. A small faction, called the Foundation, had to grapple with Seldon's predictions and figure out what to do next.[10]

Foundation went on to win the Hugo Award for the Best All-Time Series, trumping *The Lord of the Rings*. (Many, including Asimov himself, believed the award had been created specifically to honor Tolkien for his work.) Economist Paul Krugman credits *Foundation* with his career path: "I grew up wanting to be Hari Seldon, using my understanding of the mathematics of human behavior to save civilization."[11] Former House Speaker Newt Gingrich has also cited Seldon as an inspiration.[12] Asimov was a masterful fringe thinker, and we can borrow his technique of focusing on what and why rather than how: relying on signals in the present, context from the past, and free association.

It is important to pay attention to the unusual suspects at the fringe. Often, their work appears as a surprise once it reaches the mainstream, when it could have been tracked all along.

•

You may not immediately recognize the name of one of the most polarizing unusual suspects of the twentieth century, a soft-spoken, reserved British researcher from Hampton Lucy, a village in the Stratford-up-on-Avon district. His name is Ian Wilmut, and as a child he became fascinated with farming and agriculture. In his final year of undergraduate studies, Wilmut received a graduate scholarship to the University of Cambridge and a unique opportunity to study animal reproductive physiology. As a student, he was passionate about his work. His doctoral thesis concerned methods of preserving boar semen by deep freezing it; he had successfully implanted a cryopreserved embryo into a surrogate cow, which was carried to term. He nicknamed the calf Frostie.[13]

By 1973, Wilmut had been appointed a senior researcher at the Animal Breeding Research Organization (ABRO), a government-funded research facility in Roslin, a small community near Edinburgh, Scotland. Due in part to changes in government administration, ABRO required Wilmut to change his focus from investigating the underlying causes of embryo death in animals to studying the emerging field of genetic engineering. ABRO tasked him with a difficult goal: creating a genetically engineered sheep in order to produce mass quantities of human proteins that could be harvested for therapeutic uses.[14]

Wilmut worked on this problem for a decade. In 1989, Wilmut and a graduate student successfully used the embryonic cell nuclear transfer technique, in which the nucleus from an embryonic stem cell was injected into an enucleated egg. The experiment resulted in four lambs.

Fast-forward six years, to the winter of 1995. Wilmut and a small team began experiments transferring embryonic cells that they'd created from a cell culture into a host mother. The following summer, four Poll Dorset sheep were born: Cyril, Cecil, Cedric, and Tuppence. The scientists pushed the research further, using fetal fibroblasts, again from a cell culture. Two more sheep were born: Taffy and Tweed. Then they used isolated adult cells from a six-year-old ewe to construct a few hundred embryos containing adult cell nuclei. They implanted thirteen surrogate mothers with those embryos, but only one became pregnant. On

July 5, 1996, the Finn Dorset lamb was born, and her name was Dolly. The team had successfully cloned a living adult animal.[15]

Wilmut and his team published their research in the journal *Nature*, and to say it took the entire world by surprise would be gross understatement. The title of their letter made their discovery abundantly clear: "Viable Offspring Derived from Fetal and Adult Mammalian Cells."[16]

The news of Dolly's birth came as an absolute shock and rattled the scientific community. Wilmut's phone was soon ringing off the hook. He told the Press Association of Britain, "What this will mostly be used for is to produce more health care products. It will enable us to study genetic diseases for which there is presently no cure and track down the mechanisms that are involved."[17] He wanted to talk about his plans to clone animals with human diseases, such as cystic fibrosis, in order to research and test new therapies. He was also hoping to study ways of altering the proteins of certain pig organs, such as the liver, so that they might be viable for needy human patients waiting on long transplant lists.

Cloning wasn't a new concept. Some other researchers had been dabbling in cloning, and a few had successfully cloned amphibians. Others had some success creating genetically identical animals by dividing embryos early in their development. Dr. Daniel Callahan, a founder of the Hastings Center, a bioethics research institute, told the *New York Times* that there had been a tremendous amount of discussion on the future of cloning in the 1970s; however, most scientists had dismissed the topic, arguing that cloning was merely sci-fi fantasy. "They said that this is exactly the sort of thing that brings science into bad repute and [ethicists] should stop talking about it."[18] Wilmut's work was especially troubling to some because the previous experiments hadn't resulted in the creation of an exact genetic copy of an existing adult mammal, in essence replicating its youthful state.

In part because of their utter disbelief, scientists went to the media for public discourse. "The genie is out of the bottle," Dr. Ronald Munson, a medical ethicist at the University of Missouri in St. Louis, told the *New York Times*. "This technology is not, in principle, policeable." He went on to question whether the technology would be used to clone the dead. "I had an idea for a story once," Dr. Munson further told the *Times*, sarcastically describing how in his story a scientist cloned Jesus Christ using a drop of blood from the cross.[19]

An emergency summit on bioethics was held at MIT a few months after Dr. Wilmut debuted Dolly.[20] Though there had been some early cloning experimentation out on the fringes of the academic community, many scientists still clung to that earlier mindset—that cloning either couldn't be done at all, or that it couldn't be done for the foreseeable future. Trials on bacteria? A mouse? Sure. No one had anticipated a successful trial so soon, much less on a large mammal. Instead of remorse for dismissing the trend early, "How did we miss that?" turned into "Now what?!" and panic. Professor George Annas, chair of the Health Law Department at the Boston University School of Public Health, was incensed. "The reaction should be horror," he said, admonishing the biology and genetic experts gathered. "Parents do not have the right to collect cells from a child to reproduce that child. The basic public outcry against human cloning is correct."

It was not just the scientific community that was appalled. News of Dolly provoked worldwide terror. The Church of Scotland, located about seven miles up the A702 from the Roslin Institute, called a General Assembly and issued an official decree asking for an enforceable United Nations ban on reproductive human cloning. Quoting Jeremiah 1:4–5 in the Old Testament, the church argued that mankind could not take the place of God: "The LORD ... [said] ... 'Before I formed you in the womb I knew you, before you were born I set you apart.'"[21]

US president Bill Clinton held a press conference in which he announced a ban on federal funds that would allow scientists to clone human beings. "Any discovery that touches upon human creation is not simply a matter of scientific inquiry," he told reporters gathered at the White House. "It is a matter of morality and spirituality as well."[22]

When people bring their ideas from the fringe toward the mainstream—especially if those ideas cause a radical shift in what we know about science and technology—they can expect some form of condemnation.

Journalists write the first draft of history, and so Dolly was everywhere—a full-blown media frenzy. As with all first drafts, a lot of the important details had yet to be fully investigated by those reporting the news. A CNN/Time poll released on March 1, 1997, showed that the majority of Americans—who just a few weeks earlier had probably never once thought about cloning at all—had suddenly formed an opinion on this new technology and believed that it was morally unacceptable to clone either animals or humans. Fifty-six percent said they would never eat meat from genetically modified animals. About the same number said they wouldn't even consider eating modified fruits or vegetables. Twenty-nine percent said they were so troubled by the news reports about Dolly that they would participate in a demonstration against cloning humans.[23]

And yet, with enough time having passed for genetic engineering to move from Dr. Wilmut's fringe research to the mainstream, we barely talk about Dolly anymore. In the years since Dolly's birth, more sheep have been cloned from adult cells—along with mice, dogs, pigs, camels, donkeys, goats, cattle, rabbits, horses, cats, and a Pyrenean ibex—an extinct species that was briefly brought back to life for seven minutes.

Virology specialists at the University of Cambridge developed a chicken that can't pass the avian flu along to other birds.[24] Researchers at the Northwest A&F University in Xianyang, China, modified a cow so that it resists low levels of the *Mycobacterium bovis* infection, a bovine form of tuberculosis common throughout Asia and the United Kingdom.[25] Scientists in China and South Korea created a "double-muscled" pig that produces leaner meat, and more of it per animal.[26]

By most accounts, 80 percent of all the packaged foods in the United States contain genetically modified ingredients.[27] If you've been grocery shopping in the United States at all between 2000 and the present day, you have consumed a genetically modified product—crackers, chips, beets, cotton swabs, vitamins, hamburgers, edamame, eggs. After Dolly, we wound up with beneficial drugs, not the demons that many predicted.

You can blame the reaction, at least in part, on our reptilian brain's natural aversion to the fringe. When you don't anticipate technological advancement—when you're not actively thinking about the future— fight or flight dictates your next move. Your reptilian brain doesn't want you to wait around for a few weeks engaging others in rational discussion. The less you know about something, the bigger the shock you feel. And that sensation is especially magnified when the development comes from those who have great credibility and high stature within your own industry.

THE FRINGE REPEATS ITSELF

It's been twenty years since Dolly, and yet inextricably we find ourselves in nearly the same situation once again. This time around, the technology concerns genetic editing rather than outright cloning. Rather than making exact copies of mammals, today's researchers are copying and then editing the genes of adult populations of organisms in order to influence their offspring. Many in the scientific community, caught completely by surprise, are freaking out. Elected officials are scrambling to create policy. The media is stirring suspicion and unease among laypeople.

In the early 2000s, scientists on the fringe and doing serious research began testing a naturally occurring, ancient genetic defense mechanism found in a wide range of bacteria. The early research actually started even before Dolly's time. Anyone paying attention to the fringe and who knew how to connect the dots could have forecast what was coming next.

In 2012, researchers at the University of California at Berkley formalized what they called CRISPR/Cas9. CRISPR is an acronym for

"clustered regularly interspaced short palindromic repeats," and it refers
to the mechanism that finds where in the genome the desired edit will
take place. Scientists have discovered how to use these DNA sequences
as a gene-editing tool—for example, to edit the bad parts of genes that
cause life-threatening genetic mutations or spread disease. Cas9 is the
name for the natural protein that catalyzes the reaction.[28]

Today there are numerous scientists working with CRISPR all over
the world, and they're publishing research at a remarkable pace, an average of twenty papers a week.[29] That's in part because in the lab, CRISPR
has been able to prevent HIV infection in human cells. Scientists have
also discovered a way to eradicate malaria by simply editing out the ability of mosquitos to carry and spread the infection. Researchers believe
that CRISPR may be the key to curing most of our genetic diseases,
eliminating the need for environmentally harmful pesticides and more.
In June 2016, the journal *Science* published a paper about how CRISPR
can also be used to edit RNA, which is what our cells use to process
genes into proteins—and, importantly, how the technique might someday target and destroy cancer cells. It holds out the hope of improving
future generations of life on Earth.[30]

In 2015, rumors surfaced in the dark corners of the internet that a
team of Chinese researchers based in Guangzhou were planning to edit
the genes of a human embryo. Not many scientists believed the rumors,
and many warned that such sci-fi talk could discredit the serious work
being done.[31]

Then came the paper. The Chinese researchers published the results
of their experiments editing the genomes of human embryos in the
online journal *Protein & Cell*.[32] The team wrote that they had obtained
"non-viable embryos" from a local fertility clinic that could not have
resulted in a live birth. They were attempting to modify the gene responsible for a fatal blood disorder using CRISPR.

Astonishingly, this announcement—that scientists were using this
technology in a new way—to genetically pre-program humans, rather
than to treat diseases that were developed after birth—caught the

scientific community by surprise. The other scientists had been focused so narrowly on their own research—truly important work, like inhibiting hepatitis C in human cells—that they hadn't developed scenarios to describe the technique's farther-future implications.

High-profile scientists published an open letter in the Journal *Nature*, warning that this kind of experimentation was too early—that the scientific and ethical consequences of genetically modifying humans had not been fully discussed.[33] Outside of academia, CRISPR's potential is so controversial that headlines proclaim "Genetic Engineering for Our Babies Is Real" (*New York Magazine*),[34] "The Latest in GMO Panic: Human Engineering" (Grist),[35] and "Real-Life Mutants" (AskMen).[36]

Our collective subconscious may have been making its own analogy to understand the impact of a new technology that is literally life-altering. If cloning is the copy, then CRISPR is the "cut" of copy-cut-paste. The Chinese have raced forward in their efforts to edit the final draft of humankind, and in our current geopolitical climate, that has a lot of us feeling uneasy. What if they're working toward building a hyper-intelligent super-race in order to crack quantum computing before everyone else? What if they're editing a future army of double-muscled soldiers capable of strength, mental acuity, and steadfast nerves unmatched by anyone now on earth?

How did those in the highest ranks of the scientific community, the science journalists, and those in government charged with tracking these sorts of discoveries miss it *again*?

The answer is simple: they weren't following the forecasting methodology and monitoring the fringe.

Most of us will never fully grok exactly how CRISPR works, and that's fine. Most of us aren't professional scientists. But we know that our reptilian brains get in the way of smart decisions when it comes to emerging technologies. Our feelings—whether they drive us to panic and make us act too quickly, or trick us into thinking something is a one-off or novelty—are more dangerous than the ideas we're confronted with, because feelings aren't subject to rational evaluation. So we must be willing to monitor the fringe, to engage in a dialogue about stuff that seems like fantasy, and to actively track the trends across industries that are just over the horizon. If we don't engage in an informed conversation about technology, we'll start forming the wrong ideas. We'll assume technology can do something it can't. Worse, without taking the time to work out potential scenarios, we'll ignore what technology might be capable of in the future. We'll succumb to Nietzsche's eternal hourglass of existence, turning upside down again and again as we relegate ourselves to a continual cycle of ignorance, surprise, and fear with each new innovation.

WHY YOU SHOULD CARE
ABOUT FRINGE BIOHACKERS

The story of fringe thinker Zoltan Istvan will seem like it has nothing to do with you or your profession. It does, however. And it will make you squirm.

Istvan is a "transhumanist": he believes that technology can advance the evolution of our human intellect and our psychological and physical capabilities beyond our current biological limitations. In the fall of 2015, he embarked on a cross-country road trip, making a stop in a small mountain community in California. Like many transhumanists, he believes that technology can stave off death. "I think what we want is the choice to be able to live indefinitely," he said. "That might be 10,000 years; that might be only 170 years." Istvan, who at the time of his road trip was also running as a 2016 presidential candidate, likes to write about wildly speculative body modifications, such as robotic hearts, and suspending the aging of our organs. He claims to have invented a sport called "volcano ash surfing," which is exactly what it sounds like.[37]

Istvan had driven to California to visit Jeffrey Tibbetts, the founder of a local biohacking lab and a prominent figure in the small, fringe community of tinkerers who are repurposing emerging technologies and performing their own DIY biological research. Indoors, the lab looks as you might expect: there are petri dishes, soldering tools, scales, pipettes, and microscopes. Outside, the facility could be easily confused with a mechanic's garage.[38]

Tibbetts isn't working on the infinite extension of life, but rather, on small improvements to how we live in the present. During his visit to California, Istvan got a glass-encased radio-frequency identification (RFID) chip with near field communication (NFC) capabilities injected between his thumb and forefinger, just beneath his skin. Under the right circumstances, Istvan can now wave his hand over a car door to start the engine. He can unlock a mobile phone without having to remember his PIN or pattern. He can trigger the electronic locks on the door of a home or office.[39]

This may seem like a frivolous or even dangerous modification to you—What kind of lunatic would voluntarily inject a computer chip into his body, just so he doesn't have to carry around a key or remember a password? Maybe someone who's trying to be more efficient. The Silicon Valley venture capital firm Kleiner Perkins Caufield & Byers found that the average person now checks his mobile phone 150 times a day.[40] With an embedded chip, he'd be down to just one device, his phone, and he could program his chip to vibrate in different patterns, like a haptic form of Morse code. With training and time, he could receive text messages via pulsation—rather than 150 times a day, he'd only check his phone a few times. Meanwhile, every two years, on average, we trade in our mobile phones, which typically are in fine working condition, in order to get the latest model. What does this consumer behavior say about injectable RFID tags? Will we set up tents and sleep at the local mall every two years in order to get re-chipped with a faster model?

Maybe we shouldn't be so quick to dismiss Istvan. Maybe he's onto something—maybe even the beginning of a new, more personalized kind of medical care.

Consider the components already available in an RFID implant: a chip, an antenna, an inductor coil, and a capacitor. The microchip sends information that can be read within a distance of a few feet. It is possible for an RFID implant to continuously record a person's heartbeat, body temperature, and blood pressure, and to wirelessly transmit that data to an external device, like an iPhone. If such a chip can detect and track the cardiac enzymes and protein levels released into the bloodstream during a heart attack, it could also trigger your mobile phone to call or text 911 with a prerecorded message and your precise location. The emergency response team could monitor your vital signs as they drove their ambulance to you.

To Istvan—and to others in this fringe transhumanist community— injectable chips are a clear metaphor for our plausible future. They are still being tested, and while we cannot say with exact certainty how they will be used thirty years into the future, we can definitely build plausible and possible use cases for them given what we know in the present.

Why should you—you, who might be a small business owner, or a schoolteacher, or an investment banker—pay attention to what Istvan and a bunch of biohackers are doing out in the California mountains?

To answer that question, you'll need to ask yourself a series of other questions—and that's the basis of fringe thinking, our first step of the instructions. Just like Isaac Asimov did on his way to the meeting with his editor, allow yourself to freely associate. Add context from your own experience, draw from what you see happening today, and include ideas and concepts that may not have anything to do with your field. Find your industry from the list below. (Better yet, try a truly Asimovian approach: go through all of the fields that are completely unrelated to what you do, answer the questions, and allow your mind to wander.)

Doctors, Surgical Centers, Medical Schools

What is the basic human need these biohackers are addressing that isn't being addressed already in your field, even if you don't see a practical value in addressing it?

How do these biohackers inform the future of ophthalmic, prosthetic, cardiovascular, neural, and other specialties? For example, are they doing something with contact lenses that could be tweaked for glaucoma?

Many of their ideas and early experiments aren't practical at scale. Which ones should you pay attention to?

Scientific Researchers

What are biohackers doing now that informs your own research?

Especially for those in structural biology, robotics, and neurology, how are biohackers melding biology and technology in new ways you haven't yet considered?

Are there unusual or unorthodox research methods being used in the biohacking community that might inform your work?

Investors

Where are the potential seed investment opportunities that you might be able to take advantage of?

Where are users' pain points and everyday frustrations when it comes to medical technology—how do biohackers solve those pain points?

Where are the possible opportunities for a first round of venture capital financing?

Biohackers require parts and materials. Should you start investing in antennas and sensors?

What are biohackers doing today that might impact other areas of your portfolio tomorrow?

Government Agencies

Assuming that at least some of the technology that biohackers are using will reach the mainstream in the near future, what do you need to learn in order to make the best possible decisions regarding policy and regulations?

Will you need to form a new office or division to regulate biohacking?

Will a new division require a new kind of interagency partnership between the Food and Drug Administration, the Drug Enforcement Administration, and some yet-to-be-created agency that's dedicated to citizen data?

How can you ensure that any regulations, policies, or procedures you create will be updated regularly enough to keep pace with biohacking technology as it evolves?

Elected Officials and Staff Members

What do you need to learn and understand before proposing new legislation that might restrict, catalyze, or otherwise impact biohacking in the long term?

Which groups will be lobbying you in the future? What will they want, and what will you need to promise in return?

Universities and Other Public and Private Schools

What will be your student ethics policy on biohacking?

How will you create a harassment policy regarding students hacking into each other without explicit consent?

How will you determine what biohacks may be performance-enhancing in the classroom and on the field?

Equipment Manufacturers

Where are there potential opportunities to manufacture more parts and materials?

Where will parts and materials be needed? Can you offer a safer version of them?

Will there need to be multiple sizes of equipment in order to accommodate various body sizes, including men, women, children, and their pets?

Pharmaceutical Companies

Where are the potential investment opportunities that you might consider?

Where are the possible acquisition opportunities?

Does any of the biohacking community's research inform any planned paper submissions or patent filings?

What are biohackers doing today that might impact your existing products tomorrow?

Advertising and Marketing Companies

What is the biohacking story you will need to tell in the near future?

How will you run crisis management scenarios, especially on social media?

Are biohacking products gendered, and if so, are they gender-balanced?

Foundation and Nonprofit Boards

Will your foundation or nonprofit invest in biohacking? If so, what will be your ethics statement?

How will you evaluate biohacking proposals to determine which providers to back?

How will you develop a set of key performance indicators to measure the effectiveness of biohacking as it relates to your specific organization's mission?

Data Storage Providers

How will the cloud need to be reconfigured to safeguard biohacking data?

What new encryption will be necessary?

What levels of access will be required across what kinds of devices?

Law Enforcement Community

Would biohacking—chipping, for instance—allow you to reduce prison populations while monitoring qualified prisoners who could be returned to society?

Would chipping a prisoner allow law enforcement to chemically punish him or her? Could nanobots be deployed to control the behavior of violent offenders permanently?

How will you change your training so that officers and those in the field can recognize potentially dangerous biohacks?

Intellectual Property Lawyers

What future needs will there be for patents and trademarks when it comes to biohacking?

Can biological processes and mechanisms be protected?

Who owns the rights to biological data? Will consumers have a say in who gets to use their data? What happens when a company goes bust? Can it sell biodata to third parties without your direct knowledge?

Constitutional Lawyers

Does any part of biohacking constitute speech?

Do we have a constitutional right to embed devices into our bodies?

Do prisoners have a constitutional right to refuse biohacking, should it be forced upon them?

Retailers

Will there be a demand for biohacking tools, kits, and products?

Who are the likely early adopters, and will they want biohacking materials combined with your existing products? For example, athletic gloves that communicate with the RFID chip in someone's hand to display the wearer's heartbeat, lactic acid level, and perspiration rate?

Real Estate Agents and Commercial Maker Spaces

What will be the future demand for biohacking labs?

Will coworking spaces need advanced lab equipment?

Will you need to invest in more security systems to make sure that lab experiments and equipment are protected?

Will you need to require special background checks for buyers or maker-space members?

Insurance Industry

How will the underwriting algorithms you're currently using need to be rewritten to account for biohacking?

Will advancements in biohacking, human-machine interfaces, and genetic editing necessarily change insurance rates? If so, how and when?

If someone engages in biohacking, will it be considered a precondition?

If someone engages in biohacking and is injured, will her policy cover the bills? If not, does your language state explicitly why not?

Hopefully, your mind has wandered into places it had not yet explored as you connected biohackers to your own field, adjacent industries, and the future.

Remember, technology does not evolve in a silo—it is influenced by external sources of change. If you're in any of the industries or communities listed above, you can no longer claim to be surprised when biohacking emerges from the fringe.

CREATING THE LIST: MAP THE FRINGE

I've just rattled off seventeen industries and communities that will be impacted by biohacking and will also help to shape its future. Hopefully you saw yourself on that list, but I hope you also started to see a connection between yourself, a new technology, and others in adjacent or seemingly unrelated fields. When asking "What's the future of x?" for anything, it's imperative to both zoom in to your industry and then zoom back out, to think about the broader landscape.

Business school professors often talk about "value networks," how the set of relationships between organizations and individuals benefit the entire ecosystem. Networks can be visualized showing nodes (the members) and connectors (the relationships).

I've applied that model to help me visualize what's happening on the fringe. It's a way to help identify all of the organizations, individuals, and relationships impacting the future of x, and I call it a fringe sketch. It's something I draw, beginning with the x in the center—below, an example appears exploring the future of genetic manipulation—and then I continue to add nodes and connectors. A development related to x is plotted near the center, and something I believe is likely, but only as a result of other developments that must take place first, is plotted further away.

The fringe sketch is a visual representation of the unusual suspects, their relationships, and what they are likely doing in relation to that x. At this point, the sketch will not reveal exactly what the trend is, or even a definitive set of future scenarios. Instead, creating the fringe sketch is the first in a set of six steps to help you forecast what's beyond the horizon.

The fringe sketch is an outline of what and why, not how. Which is to say that now is not the time for process thinking, ruminating over procedures, or questioning whether something can actually be done. At this point in the forecasting process, our job is to expand our field of vision to include all of the unusual suspects and their work. Before starting a fringe sketch, it's important to observe a few rules:

1. Include theoretical or even poor information.

2. Assume that a present-day obstacle might be overcome in the future.

3. Assume that if something can be hacked (or adapted for a slightly different use), it will.

Then, in order to bring those nodes and connections to the surface, try to answer what I call the "Guiding Questions" as thoroughly as possible as they relate to your future of x:

1. Who has been working directly and indirectly in this space?

2. Who has been funding or otherwise encouraging experimentation in this space?

3. Who might be directly impacted by this development?

4. Who might be incentivized to work against this kind of change, either because they stand to gain something or because they might lose something?

5. Who might see this idea as a starting point for something bigger and better?

Let's revisit Dolly and CRISPR/Cas9. In the 1980s, the biological sciences community—at least those whose research was concerned with human DNA—was primarily focused on mapping. By 1990, the Human Genome Project had launched, and it was an international effort to sequence and map all of the genes of our species. Researchers were, for the first time, intent on reading nature's complete genetic blueprint for building a human being.

There was some controversy surrounding the project. Some argued that a complete map would enable us to engage in eugenics, whereby a government—or any interested party—might work to create a superior class of people. But scientists diffused those arguments, and even the notion that such a scenario would be possible. For one thing, where would you grow all those fetuses? There would never be a practical way to do it, as there would never be enough available human wombs, they argued. Moreover, while some scientists had posited that gene editing was possible, no one had done it successfully. The few who had thought about it doubted whether it could ever be done at all, much less safely or successfully.

By focusing on the usual suspects—germ cells, embryos, and eugenics—those scientists defined their x too narrowly. Process and procedure are the bedfellows of the paradox of the present. Meanwhile, others who were taken by surprise—government agencies, investors, pharmaceutical companies, bioethicists, and elected officials—didn't define genetic engineering as an x at all. By the year 2010, these groups should have been asking the Guiding Questions in order to foresee what was coming next. Here's one way a futurist might have approached the x:

1. Who has been working directly and indirectly in this space? Graduate student theses; published research in adjacent fields, such as microbes, structural biology, and virology; conferences, even decades ago, discussing the future of the human genome; patent applications filed on similar or adjacent topics; science fiction exploring the same issues.

2. Who has been funding or otherwise encouraging experimentation in this space? Corporate science fairs and talent searches; government awards and grants; foundation awards and grants; startup incubators.

3. Who might be directly impacted by this development? University researchers; pharmaceutical companies; patent and intellectual property lawyers; insurance agencies; global health organizations; agricultural companies; governments; fertility centers; intergovernmental partnerships; multinational associations or research projects.

4. Who might be incentivized to work against this kind of change, either because they stand to gain something or because they might lose something? Other researchers; criminals; pharmaceutical companies; activist organizations; patent and intellectual property lawyers; insurance agencies; religious leaders; hackers; intergovernmental partnerships; multinational associations.

5. Who might see this as a starting point for something bigger and better? Investors; intellectual property and patent lawyers; pharmaceutical companies; lab equipment manufacturers; medical and managed care consortiums; insurance companies; military units; governments; researchers in adjacent fields.

In answering those questions, you can gain a general sense of nodes. Without visualizing them in a map, however, there is no way to see connections and relationships. You would therefore make a fringe sketch looking something like the one shown on the following page about the future of genetic manipulation for the year 2010.

As you can see, I've drawn nodes that answer the five guiding questions listed above, and I've plotted them on three concentric circles representing now, soon, and farther out. I purposely haven't written down a time frame or exact years, because at this point the exact timing doesn't matter. Mapping the fringe reveals the ecosystem in order to define a broader x. I can't leap ahead to the definitive future of genetic engineering without first understanding and considering all these other likely influencers. This sketch doesn't present a full narrative of what's to come. It reveals a set of organizations and relationships to investigate at the fringe.

Taking this broader view, where nodes and relationships are both considered in tandem, is critical. It's why those on the fringe have a clearer vision of the future than most. The fringe sketch disallows the paradox of the present. Fringe thinkers aren't biased toward the usual research or ways of doing things. They often have a radically different

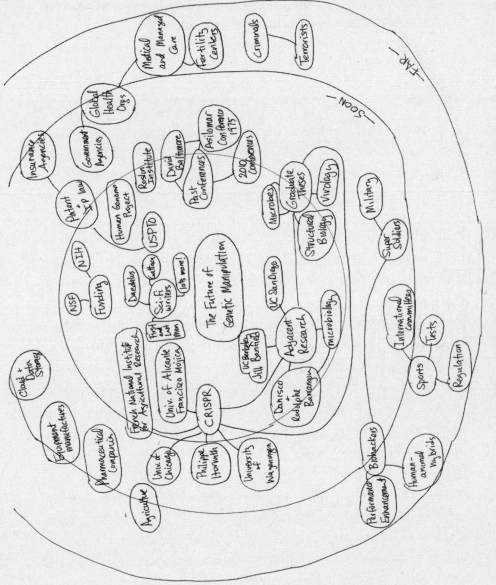

Fringe sketch for the future of genetic manipulation.

perspective on what's possible, and as a result, they are able to formulate new ideas. For example, Miguel Nicolelis was able to imagine his Brainet because the value network included the indirect connections between people, their bodies, computers, and robots.

It is helpful, after completing a fringe sketch, to try to separate your assumptions from your actual knowledge. Where did some of your cherished beliefs influence your thinking? For example, you might truly believe that even one hundred years into the future, there is no possible criminal use case for genetic manipulation, because the technique is too complicated or too expensive for anyone outside of a research facility to carry out. Or that there could never be a black market for gene editing, so that you wouldn't be able to get someone to add or remove particular parts of your genome even if it was illegal—and therefore you didn't include it.

If you were to review your fringe sketch with an objective eye, could you say it was comprehensive enough? What are the assumptions you've made versus the knowledge you have? I've coded my fringe sketch on the next page to reflect my own assumptions (no highlight) vs. my knowledge (highlight).

This fringe sketch is fairly straightforward. The same approach can be used to map the fringe for a product—for example, what is the future of credit cards? Or an entire industry, such as what is the future of book publishing? Sony might have used it to map the fringe of its own community and the future of gaming. DEC could have used it to map the future of personal computing.

To be fair, it's much easier to create a fringe map for the past, like the fringe of genetic manipulation as it existed in 2010. That map changed slightly in June 2012, when three sets of researchers rushed to publish that they had discovered how to edit life. Even today, as those three pioneers are now engaged in massive patent lawsuits, an updated fringe map is useful in thinking through future implications. The stakes are high: whoever wins the patent will be able to license it, and royalties will mean billions of dollars. Any products made will be worth billions more.

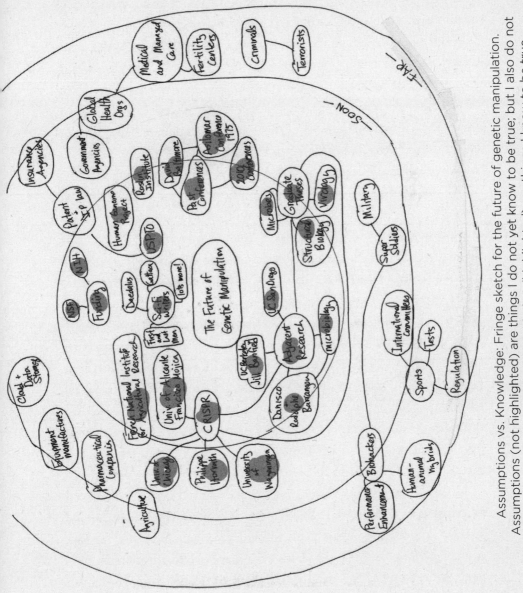

Assumptions vs. Knowledge: Fringe sketch for the future of genetic manipulation. Assumptions (not highlighted) are things I do not yet know to be true; but I also do not know them *not* to be true. Knowledge (highlighted) are things I know to be true.

YOU ARE THE FRINGE:
YOUR BODY HAS ALREADY BEEN HACKED

The MIT, Harvard, and University of California scientists each played a role in advancing the CRISPR/Cas9 gene-editing mechanism, and they did it in order to eradicate life-threatening diseases. Dr. Ian Wilmut cloned Dolly in pursuit of discovering new ways to grow tissues and organs for sick patients. Bell Labs researcher George Stibitz wanted a faster way to perform complicated math problems. Jane Goodall hoped to observe chimps in a new way. Galileo tried to understand our place in the universe. We revere these fringe thinkers now, but historically those working out on the edge have been chastised rather than celebrated.

We've been hacking our minds and bodies throughout our history as *Homo sapiens*. Hacks always begin out on the fringes before they move toward the center and enter mainstream society.

In the early 1800s, surgery was considered a fringe experiment, a treatment only of last resort. That's because there was no effective anesthetic beyond alcohol and opiates, which were no match against a scalpel and saw. Massachusetts General Hospital, arguably the biggest and best hospital in the country at that time, only recorded 333 surgeries between 1821 and 1846, or about one per month. While skilled surgeons could perform amputations—their primary procedure—with great speed and accuracy, most people would not submit to surgery unless their condition was truly life-threatening. Some physicians on the fringe began experimenting to see if there were effective ways to anesthetize their patients, to put them to sleep so they wouldn't feel the violent pain of surgery. Georgia physician Crawford Williamson Long thought that perhaps ether, a colorless, highly flammable liquid, could be vaporized into gas and breathed in by a patient before surgery. He tested his theory on a willing patient in 1842, but didn't publish the results of his experiment right away. Meanwhile, a Boston dentist on the fringe arrived at the same idea and used it on a patient at Massachusetts General. That led to obstetrician Sir James Young Simpson testing a different kind of colorless gas called chloroform, which seemed effective—but also proved deadly on occasion. Chloroform was hard to dose; slightly too much, and a patient's lungs would suffer from paralysis.[41]

It was difficult for these early physicians to reproduce the same results during public demonstrations, and so the medical community chastised them. For patients, the risks outweighed the benefits. With time, however, ether and chloroform both moved from the fringe toward the mainstream: first to the US military, where doctors used both methods during the Mexican-American War and then the Civil War. Nurse anesthetist became a profession in demand. By 1897, American pharmacologists began seriously studying the sympathetic nervous system and anesthesia, which eventually led to the science and medical specialty of anesthesiology.[42] Today, anesthesiologists are required to complete an undergraduate program, four years of medical school, and an additional four years of an anesthesiology residency program. Most go on to get additional certifications and training. So it may not surprise you to learn that currently, the best-paying job in America is in anesthesiology: doctors earn $113 an hour, on average, or a mean annual salary of $235,070.[43] Not bad for a controversial experiment that began out on the fringe.

In the sixteenth century, Italian physician Gaspare Tagliacozzi earned a reputation as an odd fellow who had developed a procedure to reconstruct the slashed-off noses of wounded duel fighters.[44] (Nose fixing was a busy, lucrative business back then.) The early anesthesiology work by surgeons Crawford Williamson Long and Sir James Young Simpson spurred others to experiment with what anatomist Pierre Desault called "plastic surgery," from the Greek *plastikos*, which meant "fit for molding." During World War I, doctors were required to treat horrific facial and head injuries: gaping skull wounds, shattered jaws, shrapnel-ridden noses. Surgeons on the fringe used those earlier techniques to create restorative procedures. Soon after that, the first cosmetic rhinoplasty was performed, followed by the first facelift in 1931. By the 1950s, Hollywood stars were having procedures done in secret: Dean Martin and Marilyn Monroe both had surgeries to reshape their noses. By the

1970s, men and women who could afford it were absconding to surgical centers for brow lifts, jaw sculpting, and fat reduction procedures, though no one would have dared speak of having any work done. There was a tacit agreement: those electing plastic surgery would go away for a few weeks, and their friends would remark that they simply looked "rested" upon their return.[45]

In 2014, Americans underwent 10.6 million surgical and nonsurgical cosmetic procedures, including eyelid surgery, tummy tuck, liposuction, chemical peels, and Botox and hyaluronic acid injections.[46] Patients are not only talking openly about procedures, they're offering real demonstrations on live television. E! Network's *Botched*, Bravo's *Real Housewives* franchise, Lifetime Network's *Atlantic Plastic*, ABC's *Extreme Makeover*, Fox's *The Swan*, and MTV's *I Want a Famous Face* have turned plastic surgery into a spectator sport. Not only has plastic surgery been destigmatized, it has become a status symbol. "Who did your such-and-such procedure?" is the new "What car do you drive?"

Can you imagine if you'd been able to foresee plastic surgery going from the fringe to the mainstream? A first mover could have invested in companies that make the necessary serums, surgical tools, and implants. Software engineers could have built the computer systems to show patients the likely results of their reconstructive work in advance of surgery. An entrepreneurial medical school could have built a world-class plastics program.

I'll offer just one more surprising biohack that started out on the fringe. There's a one-in-four chance that you are part of this biohacking community without even realizing it.

In the early 1950s, doctors working at Sea View Hospital on Staten Island were treating tubercular patients with a drug called iproniazid, which proved a better therapy than the previous drugs used, but did not control the intense tissue death in the lungs. They did, however, notice that patients treated with iproniazid suddenly transformed from sullen and despondent to happy and energized. Even in the midst of a challenging illness, these patients were asking to exercise, to be served enormous breakfasts, and to be allowed to dance up and down the hallways. Meanwhile, a few hundred miles down the East Coast, doctors had taken notice of some patients who suddenly complained of feeling lethargic, hopeless, and depressed after being prescribed a drug called Raudixin to control blood pressure. Some patients on the drug attempted suicide, after showing no other signs of emotional trouble.[47]

Within the decade, scientists knew enough about the brain to suggest that iproniazid and Raudixin were likely changing the brain's levels of serotonin, which would explain why they so dramatically affected the moods of the patients taking them. That early finding became the basis for a fundamental theory that is now core to modern psychiatry: that depression is caused by a "chemical imbalance" in the brain, where there is a direct correlation between raising or lowering serotonin levels and a patient's mood. The problem is that there is still no concrete evidence to back up this theory, which has become our modern practice of manipulating neurotransmitters for the past fifty years. Marcia Angell, a former editor of *The New England Journal of Medicine*, wrote that "the main problem with the theory is that after decades of trying to prove it, researchers have still come up empty-handed."[48]

This means that if you've ever taken a selective serotonin reuptake inhibitor (SSRI) such as Celexa, Prozac, Lexapro, Paxil, or Zoloft, you've willingly ingested an experimental neuroenhancer to modify your mood and well-being. Not only do we not know how, exactly, these drugs work, we don't even know what dose to administer. That's why the standard practice is to start with a base dose, and adjust it higher or lower over a period of months. Tinkering with dosage is an experiment, and you are the subject on which the medicine is tested.

There are a host of antidepressants that target different neurotransmitters—SSRIs as well as serotonin–norepinephrine reuptake inhibitors (SNRIs), norepinephrine–dopamine reuptake inhibitors (NDRIs), tetracyclics, and serotonin antagonist and reuptake inhibitors (SARIs). And yet researchers, including those working within Eli Lilly (Prozac),

Forest Laboratories (Celexa), Pfizer (Zoloft), and GlaxoSmithKline (Wellbutrin and Paxil), have yet to uncover the exact causes of depression. Although they know that neurotransmitters like dopamine, norepinephrine, and serotonin pass signals between nerve cells in the brain, and that antidepressants affect the transmission of those signals, they are still working off a forty-year-old theory.

You may take issue with my use of "experimental" above. SSRIs are truly a gift for those suffering under the heavy weight of depression. In her 1994 book *Prozac Nation*, Elizabeth Wurtzel wrote about how Prozac completely changed her life. Before it, she was living in "a computer program of total negativity . . . an absence of affect, absence of feeling, absence of response, absence of interest." After only a few weeks on the green and white pill, she had a literal awakening: "One morning I woke up and really did want to live. . . . It was as if the miasma of depression had lifted off me, in the same way that the fog in San Francisco rises as the day wears on. Was it the Prozac? No doubt."[49] What remains in doubt is how depression works and why SSRIs and other drugs make us feel better.

My point is that we don't think of antidepressants as experimental body modification. That's because enough time has elapsed for antidepressants to eclipse the fringe, move into the mainstream, and become common throughout society.

Antidepressants. Plastic surgery. Anesthetics. You would never refer to these as experimental body modifications from the fringe. It would be glib to even suggest that. It may even seem glib to lump all three into a single group. However, it's important to maintain our perspective. In the beginning, these were all novel, fringe body hacks—ways to enhance our daily living through new kinds of medical therapeutics and technologies. What society once discounted as a frivolous experiment emerged as three vitally important medical specialties, not to mention highly profitable global businesses. So who's to say that twenty years from now, we won't openly practice what psychiatrist Peter D. Kramer called "cosmetic psychopharmacology"?[50] Just as we self-diagnose the common cold and self-medicate with over-the-counter syrups, herbs, and pills, why wouldn't we someday self-medicate with low doses of Adderall and Ritalin, which have already become popular among Millennials, who use them to enhance their studying and work performance? Or with social drugs, like Stratera and Provigil, which boost alertness? Why wouldn't our future selves opt in to the idea of wearing technological neuroenhancer headbands to augment our general state of being no matter what situation we were in? We might dose ourselves up to bliss on our wedding day, or dose ourselves to focus so that we can concentrate fully on a complicated policy negotiation. For that matter, the same tools could be used to create a living hell on earth. A prisoner might spend a single twenty-four-hour period in solitary confinement, but feel as though he'd wasted away fifty years of his life inside a desolate cell.

FRINGE TO MAINSTREAM: THE SEVEN STAGES OF ACCEPTANCE

Throughout history, our reactions to scientific innovations such as antidepressants, plastic surgery, and anesthetics have followed a strikingly consistent pattern of acceptance as they moved from the fringe into the mainstream:

1. I've never heard of it. Why would I try it / invest in it / legalize it? Why should I care?

2. I've heard of it, but I think it's preposterous / dangerous / frivolous / unethical / will never work. It's a horrible investment. It will never scale.

3. I understand what it is, but I don't think it's useful / beneficial / helpful for me, my customers, my constituents, my investors, or my audience.

4. I think it's potentially useful / beneficial / helpful. I'd like to start gathering data, to see what traction there is in the marketplace.

5. I've started to accept it as useful / beneficial / helpful, but I still think of it as a novelty rather than a necessity in society. I'd like to make a small initial investment. I'd like to see some research on how early adopters are using it.

6. I now use it all the time; it's part of my daily routine! I'm participating in the Series A. I'm looking for ways to partner.

7. It's indispensable. How did I ever manage without it? I'm looking forward to the initial public offering (IPO). I'm thinking about making a competitive product. Damn—why didn't I think of that sooner? How did I miss it?

When you first learned about Zoltan Istvan and his drive to California to get chipped by Jeffrey Tibbetts, you probably found yourself somewhere between steps one and two. If you're like most people, you've probably never heard of the transhumanist movement, biohackers, and the DIY procedures they're performing to modify their bodies with technology. Perhaps you knew about biohacking, but you thought it was still a dangerous prospect. Maybe you still do. Or maybe you think it's a frivolous waste of time and energy. You would be in the same mindset as anesthesia's early critics, elderly surgeons whom nineteenth-century Scottish surgeon James Miller observed "closed their ears, shut their eyes, and folded their hands. . . . They had quite made up their minds that pain was a necessary evil, and must be endured."[51]

Or, upon learning about Istvan's quest to live forever, you might have started questioning the ethics of prolonging life indefinitely. That's an important point, one that is orthogonal to understanding the mindset of the fringe. Usually, those who are generating very early-stage research in areas that are entirely new, or that are new combinations of other work, do not forecast the future ethical quandaries posed. Their purpose is to ideate, test, and build—not to develop scenarios for the long-term consequences of their research.

This isn't to say that fringe researchers are purposely setting society up for doom, or that they somehow lack all concern for ethical considerations. It's just that life-altering breakthroughs usually start with questions regarding whether something *can* be done without simultaneously asking whether it *should* be done.

I am not saying, either, that all fringe thinkers deserve your attention. For every Isaac Asimov there are a hundred screwball hobbyists playing scientist after work. So you must seek out the Asimovs and the Gaspare Tagliacozzis, the Crawford Williamson Longs, the Sir James Young Simpsons, and yes, even the Zoltan Istvans, and check your present-day bias at the door. Just because you think that biohacking is strange doesn't mean that future generations will share your opinion. Anecdotally, we know that unless it violates a fundamental law of human nature, what is taboo today probably won't be tomorrow.

.

It's also worth noting that fringe thinkers don't always work in total isolation. They might have assistants, a team of researchers, or even collaborators in other fields. Or they draw inspiration from the other writers, theorists, artists, and scientists who came before them. In his book *What Technology Wants*, Kevin Kelly details a long list of inventions that were each discovered or built around the same time by multiple fringe thinkers: there were six inventors of the rotor cipher machine (an electromechanical machine used to encrypt messages during World War II), four of vaccination, four of photography, and three of the hypodermic needle. If there is one fringe thinker making headway in a particular area, there may be others.[52]

The first step of forecasting was to seek out the unusual suspects, future-thinkers like Nicolelis, Istvan, Tibbets, Wilmut, and Goodall. Their research alone didn't indicate a trend. Therefore, we cast a wide net by observing a few rules: we must use theoretical or even poor information when necessary; we should assume that present-day obstacles can be overcome in the future; and if something can be hacked, it will be hacked. And we asked some simple questions: Who will be impacted? Who will gain or lose? Who will see this as a starting point to something bigger and better? The answers reveal a fringe sketch with nodes and connections.

That begs the question: How do you make sense out of the fringe, now that you've found it? The sketch is merely a way to surface all the information we ought to consider. Now, we must look for patterns in that data, which will reveal possible trends.

CHAPTER FIVE

Signals Matter

Uncovering Hidden Patterns

The world is full of obvious things which
nobody by any chance ever observes.

—Sherlock Holmes,
The Hound of the Baskervilles

THE FRINGE, AS we've just seen, is that group of unusual suspects engaged in work that's directly or adjacently related to your own interests in looking for the future of x. You visualized what was happening by creating a fringe sketch to show the nodes (individuals or organizations) and connectors (relationships) impacting x.

Think of the fringe sketch as a set of clues. In order to solve the mystery of the future, you need to investigate the present by collecting data, intelligence, and information, adding details to the fringe sketch. This is the second step of forecasting. The answer is always there, waiting for you to make observations and connections. "You see, but you do not observe. The distinction is clear," Sherlock Holmes said.[1] "It is of the highest importance in the art of detection to be able to recognize, out of a number of facts, which are incidental and which are vital. Otherwise your energy and attention must be dissipated instead of being concentrated."[2]

In observing the fringe, how can you separate your assumptions from your knowledge to recognize the vital facts? How can you determine which facts are implicitly and explicitly important, and which ones are merely incidental? What can you make of the information before you? What does it tell you about what's to come?

To solve the mystery of the future, you must engage what Holmes, and nineteenth-century Irish physicist John Tyndall before him, called the "scientific use of the imagination." It's actually a skill that you are already adept at doing, because all humans are skilled experts in this technique. It's simple pattern recognition.

Let's try to solve a short mystery. Google has been launching all sorts of seemingly unrelated projects, from driverless cars to phones. Figuring out why Google is working on these disparate projects will reveal a key trend that will impact nearly every industry sector. Indeed, you are directly involved in what's happening.

Here are the facts as we know them:

Around noon on November 12, 2015, a police officer in Northern California noticed something unusual. There was a gumball-machine-shaped car ambling slowly along a busy, three-lane road. Unlike the other cars that would occasionally signal and brake to turn into one of the liquor stores or the Five Guys Hamburgers restaurant along the street, this car was driving along steadily at 24 miles per hour—about 10 under the speed limit. It wasn't swerving or violating other traffic laws. When the police officer finally pulled over the car, he was startled and completely unprepared for what he saw.

There was, as you probably suspected, no driver. Sergeant Saul Jaeger had unknowingly stopped a Google autonomous vehicle. The car didn't pull over to the side of the road itself; that was done by the passenger, a Google engineer. And if you're wondering whether Sergeant Jaeger issued a ticket, the answer is no. The Mountain View Police Department explained why on its blog: "In this case it was lawful for the car to be traveling on the street, as El Camino Real is rated at 35 mph." Sergeant Jaeger let the vehicle and its engineer go, but he said the car should allow others to pass if the slow speed of the Google car started causing a traffic jam.[3]

Google's self-driving car project has now logged more than 1.5 million miles along roads in California and Texas.[4] Its top speed is 25 mph, not only for safety reasons, but also to help local communities acclimate to cars that drive on their own. Rather than "zooming scarily through neighborhood streets," Google says that the unique design of the cars and their relatively low speeds are intended to make them feel "friendly and approachable."[5]

Google's response to the incident included a photo of the officer speaking with the passenger of the car. "Driving too slowly? Bet humans don't get pulled over for that too often," the cheeky post said. "After 1.2 million miles of autonomous driving (that's the human equivalent of 90 years of driving experience), we're proud to say we've never been ticketed!"[6]

So the mystery is solved, right? It was a self-driving Google car moving at a speed below the posted limit. Well, not exactly. From my point of view, the mystery is just starting to unfold. It's certainly interesting (if not irritating) that a driverless car is better at getting out of tickets than I am. What happened at noon on November 12 is an incidental fact. A distraction. The car is only one of many clues we must consider, starting with what is arguably a more important question: Why would an internet company build a car that can drive itself?

In forecasting, the second step tells us that we need to do some more digging.

Why is Google—a nineteen-year-old company that for much of its history has specialized only in products to help us use the web better—hiring teams of researchers to develop self-driving cars? What's the use in building such cars if they can't be properly road-tested? Which implies that Google must also be engaging lobbyists to convince local and state governments to allow the cars to drive in public, as well as risk-management specialists to deal with the daunting liability issues ahead. As an internet services company, Google doesn't have an auto manufacturing plant, so it is partnering with unusual collaborators. For example, the self-driving car requires radar and a whole series of sensors. Its onboard computer "sees" the road using a laser range finder to generate a detailed 3D map of the surrounding environment, which is then compared to high-resolution maps stored in its system. That produces various data models allowing the car to drive itself without hitting pedestrians, objects in the street, or other cars.

In 2011, when Google's secret self-driving car project was made public, cofounders Larry Page and Sergey Brin said that smart vehicles would make transportation safer and more efficient and would help the environment. On the highway, autonomous vehicles could tailgate intentionally, making better use of the 90 percent of extra space on our highways not currently being used, and would therefore increase the speed that everyone traveled. Stanford University professor Sebastian Thrun, who was leading the project, and Google engineer Chris Urmson had created a video detailing a concept they called Caddy Beta.[7] Vehicles could become a shared resource. In the future, one tap on an Android phone and a car would show up, ready to drive you wherever you needed to go.

As you're wondering why an internet company would build a self-driving car, let's take a look at some of Google's investments. It might not surprise you to learn that Google holds a stake in Uber, a car-sharing service. That's an adjacent startup, one that might play a role in the future of Google's fleet of self-driving cars. But there are other unusual suspects under the Google umbrella, such as Editas Medicine, a genomic editing startup with expertise in CRISPR/Cas9. And an investment in Kobalt Music, an independent music rights and publishing company.

The car project isn't Google's only fringe research. During the past few years, Google acquired a number of robotics companies, including Schaft, Industrial Perceptions, Redwood Robotics, Bot & Dolly, Meka Robotics, and Holomini. In 2013, Google made its eighth and arguably most notable acquisition in the robotics field, that of Boston Dynamics, one of the world's most advanced companies.[8] You've no doubt seen one of the BigDog videos, which went viral shortly after Boston Dynamics launched its YouTube channel. BigDog is that dystopian robot with four legs that are articulated like an animal's. It looks like a headless, steam punk–inspired bull as it climbs through the desert, wades through snow, and strolls along the beach. Boston Dynamics is also the company that famously created humanoid robots capable of walking on their own. But hardware is just one of their specialties. Their research portfolio includes computer intelligence and simulation systems, too. For years, the majority of the company's funding came from US military sources, including the army, the navy, the Marine Corps, and DARPA. Both Schaft and Boston Dynamics have repeatedly won DARPA's Robotics Challenge, which is viewed as a barometer for the future of the industry.

Self-driving cars. Wide-ranging investments. Robotics. We're just getting started.

What about Google's space elevator project? Imagine a cable attached to a satellite in synchronous orbit, tens of thousands of miles above Earth. Like a gigantic funicular, transport pods affixed to the cable would ascend up to a dock for transfers to the International Space Station or beyond. Speaking of space, Google is working on another project called Loon, which involves a series of balloons that float in the stratosphere, above the airplanes and weather (but below the space elevator, should it go into production). They've been overhead since 2013, rising or descending into a layer of wind in order to beam cellular spectrum back down to Earth. Telecom companies in Indonesia, Brazil, New Zealand, and Australia have partnered to harness Loon for LTE-capable smartphones in areas where service had been nonexistent.[9]

There are also 150 other projects that Google engineers have experimented with, launched, tweaked, and decommissioned.[10] Those included GOOG-411, which was a free alternative to dialing 411. Then there was Google Health, which allowed you to upload and store all of your health and wellness information in the cloud. And remember Google Glass? The wraparound headset that displayed information from your smartphone right over your eye? It was a wearable computer that allowed you to speak your commands and see the results, all in real time. As quickly as it debuted, Glass quietly faded away from public view. Are all of these projects really dead—failed projects that are gone forever? Tech reporters, especially, like to poke fun at projects like these.

But if you treat them as a series of yet-to-be connected dots from the fringe—as possible clues to the future—what are the obvious facts staring at you?

What *is* Google doing? Why does it matter to you, even if you don't work in a high-tech job or an internet-related field?

Have you figured it out yet?

To solve this puzzle, you need to first know a bit more about pattern recognition. Just as Sherlock was known to say, we need a process of observation and deduction. This next step will help you identify patterns when you're collecting signals from the fringe. In order to understand what Google is doing—what is the bigger trend?—we need to apply a system of analysis and uncover the patterns hidden in plain sight.

RECOGNIZING PATTERNS

Association and pattern recognition are necessary for forecasting an elemental mode of thought, often one we are not conscious of. Your senses consume raw data and take action based on the "category" of the pattern you recognize.

Our brains are hardwired to recognize patterns, and for good reason. In his book *Subliminal: How Your Unconscious Mind Rules Your Behavior*, Leonard Mlodinow noted that 95 percent of all human thought is unconscious.[11] We are overwhelmed with data—our senses transmit to our brains about 11 million bits of information per second—and we can't manually parse it all. "If your conscious mind were left to process all that incoming information your brain would freeze like an overtaxed computer," Mlodinow wrote.

You can almost sense the neurons firing in a toddler as she first learns how to grasp a bottle and combine sounds to form words. A musician becomes proficient once she can hear scales, arpeggios, and various sequences of notes. A star quarterback memorizes plays and the reactions opposing teams have to them. Over time, we begin to innately and subconsciously translate those patterns into actionable steps, whether it's speaking in full sentences, playing a hard lick, or throwing the perfect pass. If you've ever had a gut feeling that something's on the horizon, but you can't tell what, that's an instinct worth paying attention to. It is your unconscious mind making automatic connections between nodes.

With some practice, your mind will become attuned to recognizing the patterns that forecast our future. Honing your pattern recognition skills enables you to extract meaning from how the relationships, individuals, and organizations at the fringe are connected to the ten sources of change.

I'm going to describe a set of famous computer glasses. Take a moment to see if you can guess what they look like based on my description: they wrap around your head, need to be charged regularly, cover your entire field of vision, and require a smartphone to work. We'll come back to these glasses in just a moment.

Historians believe that eyeglasses were invented sometime between 1268 and 1289 in Italy, and that they were likely worn by scholars and monks.[12] If you traveled back in time to thirteenth-century Florence and showed side-by-side photos of the computer glasses and a set of reading glasses to an Italian monk, he wouldn't have formed the necessary associations required to connect one pair to the other. In contrast, as someone who has lived your entire life in the twentieth and twenty-first centuries, where glasses have been worn by everyday people, you've seen many frames worn over the eyes that you look through—you recognize their purpose without exerting any energy whatsoever. That's because your brain instantly categorizes the data using your previous experiences. It happens in less than a fraction of a blink.

For hundreds of thousands of years, we have been refining this cognitive and neural function, which is like a system of shortcuts for our brains. Things that we've learned or encountered in the past act as signals, helping to transmit sensory data into actions, reactions, and thoughts. Our realities are greatly influenced by those signals, which influence the ways in which we experience the world. For many of you, the following figure shows how your brain processed my description of the computer glasses.

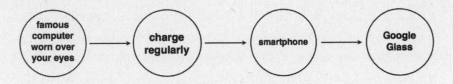

But the wearable computer glasses I described above weren't actually Google Glass, though to be fair, you are biased because I just mentioned them. Unless you've had direct experience with Glass, there was a relevant clue that you probably overlooked. It's a small but important distinction: I said that the "famous computer glasses cover your entire field of vision." Glass only has a single half-inch display affixed above the right eye. It augments your field of vision, but it does not cover it. Indeed, I was describing the Samsung Gear VR headset. It's a virtual reality system into which you insert a smartphone into a set of goggles. If you're unfamiliar with it, picture a scuba mask with a single, shiny black lens. Since I've used both Glass and Gear VR extensively, my brain instead recognized a different pattern, processing the information like this:

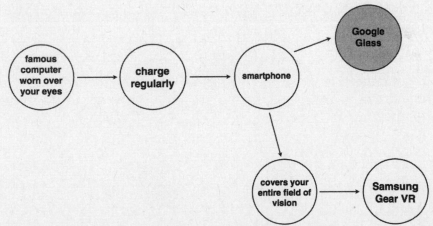

Our brains are continuously in search of patterns. That's why you see patterns in random noise, like an ink stain, tea leaves, or the clouds. It's also how your brain interprets Georges Seurat's dots and Claude Monet's wide brush strokes as clear snapshots of French life in the late

1800s. We've evolved to automatically filter out all unnecessary information—dots, blurs of color—so that we are consciously aware of only the most important data points. We therefore see a Sunday afternoon in a park rather than millions of tiny, colored points. We see a haystack and some farmhouses dotting the countryside rather than a haze of blues, purples, oranges, pinks, and reds.

Expert radiologists are capable of scanning an X-ray and determining within seconds whether or not there is an abnormality. Talented jazz musicians are able to improvise because they can hear a chord progression before it's ever played, their fingers moving reflexively to a few bars of music that haven't yet been written. With enough experience, factory workers are able to sort and spot bruised apples as they come down a packaging line at a tremendously fast rate. That is because they are automatically making connections between nodes within their own area of expertise. The more you learn to look for patterns, the more attuned your conscious mind will be to finding them.

Occasionally, your brain will trick you into recognizing a pattern and seeing something that isn't actually there. Take the Kanizsa triangle illusion.

The Kanizsa triangle illusion

Psychologists Max Wertheimer, Wolfgang Köhler, and Kurt Koffka collaborated on what they called the "Gestalt" theory of perception, and the Kanizsa triangle experiment was among their favorite examples.[13] It might seem as though a triangle exists in the illustration, but why do you see it? There are no lines drawn to designate the sides of a triangle. There are no colors shading in the surface area of a triangle. The circles marking the edges tell your brain to take a shortcut, and to recognize a signal in the noise.

It's a good example to remember because it illustrates why it's important not to focus on just one thing—the Kanizsa's Pac-Man-like circles, Seurat's dots, the Google car itself—but to simultaneously observe the motion between objects. Zooming out to observe not just the fringe, but the other sources of change, reveals a pattern you would otherwise miss.

As it happens, pattern recognition is also a fundamental component of modern computing. Everything from the autocorrect in your word-processing program to the code in your antivirus software relies on seeing and acting on patterns. For example, Google search can now recognize patterns in videos and photos, even if it doesn't "see" them the way that you and I do. In one sense, Google's pattern recognition is akin to that Italian monk staring at the Samsung VR headset and a pair of reading glasses. But there is one important exception.

If you type "cute cats" into a Google search, the system is able to infer that you want images of cute house cats playing, yawning, sleeping. Google can look through millions of digital images and filter out all the other possible cats on the web that you probably don't want, such as old drawings of the Garfield comic strip. Or baby tiger cubs—after all, tigers are the biggest members of the cat family. It also won't show you photos of a young Brian Setzer and his popular 1980s band the Stray Cats. (By 1980s standards, his big makeup-rimmed eyes and bleached blonde pompadour hairstyle had Valley Girls calling him "like, you know, so cute.")

The reason you see kittens and not rockabilly musicians is because Google has also learned to distinguish between patterns. But Google is relatively young, and it's still learning. In order for Google's systems to recognize the patterns—the colors, shapes, dimensions—from our everyday lives, it must practice going forward and backward. Google's image-recognition neural network progressively extracts higher levels of features of an image with each pass until it is able to decide what the image is showing. The first pass might have to do with identifying corners. A second might look for colors. Then features and shapes, and so on until the system responds with "Siamese cat." Engineers are training the system to work in reverse, too, in order to better understand how the networks function. So they can take a digital photo that might look to humans like static and ask the network to use patterns to generate an image. On its own, it has "seen" ants, starfish, anemonefish, parachutes, and measuring cups.

In order to work out what Google is doing—why it would make a car, Google Glass, and so on, we need to Kanizsize the facts we've collected at the fringe. We need to zoom both in and out. We need to look for both the Pac-Man pieces and the picture that emerges as we consider all the developments in aggregate.

And, of course, we need to collect more clues.

GOOGLE'S PATTERNS

One clue worth considering is a press release Google sent out on April 1, 2004, to journalists and tech bloggers.[14] It announced a new service called Gmail. The search giant promised storage of 1 gigabyte (GB)— an implausible *500 times* what Microsoft's Hotmail then offered—and anyone could use it, for free. "Search Is Number Two Online Activity— Email Is Number One; 'Heck, Yeah,' Say Google Founders," the press release started. The date of the release wasn't lost on the tech community, which at first assumed the announcement was some kind of elaborate hoax. Neither businesses nor universities paid much attention. They were enterprise Microsoft users, with deeply entrenched technology workflows and long-term contracts.

But Gmail was real, and its storage capacity was actually the least of its interesting new features. With all that storage, you could keep your email forever. Google was offering special features to scan old messages for keywords, to help you search through your inbox (and to serve up targeted ads at the bottom of each message). Plus, it automatically extracted names, email addresses, and other personal details to a contact list. The only way to get a Gmail account was by invitation from a current user, which was intended to allow the service to roll out slowly and methodically. But within days, people were clamoring for an invite. Gmail had become tech's golden ticket, and some early adopters were bidding as much as $150 on eBay to get one.[15]

In 2006, Google launched Calendar, which promised to seamlessly integrate with all the data Gmail was storing on your behalf. A few months later, it released the web-based applications Docs and Spreadsheets, and it also launched something called Google Apps Premier, which enabled businesses to port much of their office activity over to the cloud using their own company name and logo.[16]

Around this time, large businesses and privacy advocates were beginning to question Microsoft's more traditional software, which had been valued, in part, for its proprietary code and its vigilance in patching security holes. Google came out of the startup shadows and declared war on Microsoft Office, offering an alternative to expensive, static software. "The whole industry looked at us like we were crazy," said Rajen Sheth, who had worked on those early products as a member of Google's Enterprise team.[17]

Gmail. Calendar. A suite of cloud-based office software. It's all very interesting, but our Kanizsa triangle is not yet in focus.

As mentioned above, another one of Google's product launches that year was GOOG-411, which enabled people to dial a phone number and speak a search query. It was intended as a free alternative to calling the operator or 4-1-1, both of which were costly services provided by local and long-distance carriers. Users could call 1-800-GOOG-411 and get not only a phone number, but the answer to virtually any question they could think to ask. You could dial and say, "Sushi, Philadelphia, Pennsylvania," and a voice would automatically respond by reading you a list of options. Saying "Details" would prompt the service to read the address and phone number, and you could say "Text message" to have the information sent to your phone. GOOG-411 would even patch you through for free.

I used GOOG-411 that October, en route to a conference being held at the Palace Hotel in San Francisco. Driving from the airport, I was in the mood for dim sum, so I dialed up 1-800-GOOG-411. It recommended Yank Sing, a sprawling restaurant in the Financial District.

The theme of the conference I was attending had to do with the web's fringe, and one of the speakers was Mark Zuckerberg, whose relatively new social network, Facebook, was about to launch pages for businesses. Marissa Mayer, who was then Google's vice president of Search Products & User Experience, was there, too. She opened her talk with an awkward joke, a self-deprecating list of hypothetical health-related Facebook competitors that Google might someday launch: Rashbook, Boilbook, and Wartbook. She spent the rest of her time talking about yet another new Google project called Google Health, which would allow users to store their personal medical and wellness information online.

Later in the day, a reporter stopped Mayer to ask some questions about video and the new Google Health project, but her conversation steered back to GOOG-411: "The reason we really [created GOOG-411] is because we need to build a great speech-to-text model that we can use for all kinds of different things, including video search." This is a detail worth pausing to think about. Google was venturing into voice recognition, which could have wide application across numerous products and services.

Mayer continued: "If you want us to build a really robust speech model, we need a lot of phonemes, which is a syllable as spoken by a particular voice with a particular intonation. So we need a lot of people talking, saying things so that we can ultimately train off of that. So 1-800-GOOG-411 is about that: Getting a bunch of different speech samples so that when you call up or we're trying to get the voice out of video, we can do it with high accuracy."[18] Mayer went on to say that her engineers had started some very early research into machine learning so that Google could automatically recognize faces and objects in videos.

Let's apply the Kanizsa triangle here. The Pac-Man figures are the pattern-recognition processes to recognize the phonemes. The triangle isn't GOOG-411. Zooming out, we can see the relationship between us, the users, and Google's suite of internet offerings. Google wants to allow us to speak to our phones and computers, to have a conversation with them.

But why? Let's consider what was happening at the fringe, since at the time there were concurrent, tangential movements outside Google.

Mobile equipment providers were creating smarter, more effective GPS hardware and software.

Coders were starting to develop more sophisticated search algorithms for text. Some had even figured out how to make an algorithm that understands our intentions.

Researchers were experimenting with new programs that could translate speech into different languages.

Developers had started to hack online calendars, since the standard applications didn't offer all the functionality they could.

Meanwhile, engineers within Google had been making significant progress in semantic language, machine learning, and artificial intelligence. This would enable the Google system to infer context and intent. Typing "What day is it" would return the day, date, year, and location right at the top of the screen, even if you hadn't defined what "it" meant. Meantime, Google was preparing for the launch of its Android mobile operating system and Google Voice, a free telephone service that would transcribe voice mails into email.

By 2010, we were in the middle of a mobile phone revolution. One-third of Americans owned some kind of smartphone, and not just for business.[19] BlackBerry was out, while the iPhone and Android were capturing more and more market share. Apple reported 14.1 million iPhones sold in the fourth quarter, up 91 percent from the previous year. "We are blown away to report over $20 billion in revenue and over $4 billion in after-tax earnings—both all-time records for Apple," said Apple CEO Steve Jobs.[20] While that might have been a record for Apple, Google's Android mobile operating system had quietly become the worldwide market leader, and by a significant margin.

Of Google's many projects between 2004 and 2010, I was captivated most by GOOG-411. Not because it was particularly useful to me on a daily basis, but because of something Marissa Mayer had told that reporter back at the Palace Hotel.

Google was training its systems how to recognize voices. In the near future, would we speak our searches? Why, I wondered? How would that prove a better experience than typing—even using the keypad on a mobile phone? In the back of my mind, I kept thinking that Google must also be trying to work out how to identify us by voice alone—our unique inflections, tones, and pitches. The difference in amplitude displayed when I, as someone who grew up in the Midwest, say "Mississippi" versus someone from Jackson or Biloxi. But why?

And then, just as swiftly as GOOG-411 had come online, it was retired at the end of 2010.[21]

Is our mystery solved? Google was an internet search company providing cloud-based spreadsheets, calendars, email, and contact lists. It had successfully ventured into the mobile space. Maybe GOOG-411 was intended as a new profit center that didn't pan out? Since so many people were now using Google's mobile internet search, maybe it never turned a profit? Perhaps that's why they killed the product. All this time, was Google just trying to capture market share away from Microsoft with a suite of productivity tools?

Stop and think: Where are the Pac-Men and where is the triangle?

I'll reveal what I saw. I was sitting in an uncomfortable chair at that same conference at the Palace Hotel three years later when it happened. Google's chairman, Eric Schmidt, was on stage, answering questions about the future of the internet, and I started a fringe sketch of Google's internal projects and external relationships, as well as what I knew was happening outside the company, in my notebook:

- GOOG-411 wasn't just an information service; it was a massive, unprecedented database collecting and learning from our voice queries.

- Gmail and Google Calendar were windows into our daily lives. Data from both could be more useful to users if they were ported through and accessible from other applications and networks.

- Google had acquired software and was testing new tools to help it learn to identify faces and the people with whom we associated closely.

- Blogger, a blogging platform that Google had acquired earlier, was a great vehicle for advertisements, but it was an exceptional window into understanding sentiment.

- Semantic search was starting to make the web more conversational.

- Early experiments had produced a handful of clunky but functioning virtual assistant mobile phone apps that could schedule meetings, make dinner reservations, and send reminders—all without your direct involvement.

Where is the vital information, and what is only incidental? Recognizing patterns in those clues, I gained an early glimpse into what's unfolding today. Google wasn't trying to squeeze Microsoft out of the market. Rather, the search giant was creating a ubiquitous exo-brain, one that could anticipate my every need, even before I did. Google had to be working on some kind of digital life assistant, something like Computer from *Star Trek*, or J.A.R.V.I.S. from the Iron Man comic book series.

Indeed, we were introduced to this new reality on July 9, 2012, when Google announced something called "Google Now."[22] It was a massive integration for mobile phones. All of your data across Google's vast programs and tools would be merged with data from outside platforms and services. Soon, Google would check your calendar, the weather, and traffic, see if it's snowing, and offer to remote start your car twenty minutes earlier than you'd planned on leaving for work. It would power the mundane tasks of everyday life.

That's what I saw when I zoomed in and out, and it indicated an emerging trend in voice-based digital assistants. I knew that Apple, Yahoo, and Microsoft had been acquiring applications that could perform similar functions. I envisioned a near future in which we would have conversations with our devices, which would be listening for triggers—patterns in the ambient noise—and respond to our every need, perhaps even before we knew to ask. Soon, an operating system wouldn't just run our devices, it would help operate the tasks of daily living.

But how did I see the trend? I followed the second step of the instructions and brought hidden patterns to the surface.

THE CIPHER MODEL

"Okay, Google. What is a cipher?" I say aloud.

A soothing woman's voice emanates from the Android phone on my desk. She understands my question and answers accordingly. "A secret or disguised way of writing." She pauses briefly, then continues: "a code."

"Can you give an example of one?" I ask.

She offers a few, along with a deeper explanation. I'll summarize it for you here.

A cipher is a method of disguising information within text to send a message in a secret code. In computing, ciphers are algorithms—a series of defined steps—that encrypt or decrypt an email, a document, or a sensitive file. In order for a cipher to work, it must use a reliable pattern.

Julius Caesar was said to have created a cipher to communicate with his army. His generals would shift each letter in his message a certain number of letters to the right, so a message reading "RETURN TO ROME" would have been sent as "UHWXUA WR URPH."[23] In World War II, the Germans used the Enigma, a sophisticated machine that required a series of interlocking rotors to decrypt messages. A handful of literary conspiracy theorists believe that a cipher created by Francis Bacon in the 1600s proves that he—and not William Shakespeare—was the true author of all those plays and sonnets.[24] (It's a theory that has been debunked numerous times.)

A cipher is a helpful analogy for understanding how to decrypt and find the hidden patterns that emerge in the fringe. After many years researching how technology evolves, I have refined a model with six pattern identifiers that help to reveal trends. Those identifiers are the basis for what I call CIPHER: Contradictions, Inflections, Practices, Hacks, Extremes, Rarities.

Contradictions. When two or more things succeed or fail simultaneously, though usually they would track in opposite directions; or when things track in the same direction, though typically the reverse would be true. Additionally, a node—an organization or individual—becomes connected to another node, when typically that connection has been shunned or prohibited in the past. For example, the number of injuries and fatalities due to distracted driving continue to increase. Yet the number of technology features in our cars, such as touchscreens that access the internet, speaker systems that connect to our phones, Wi-Fi—the reason we're distracted—are also on the rise. We're making it easier to distract ourselves, when logic would dictate that the opposite should be true.

Inflections. When something happens to catalyze a great acceleration in emerging research. This might include a sudden round of fundraising; the acquisition of a new company, product, or team; the passage or defeat of legislation; an unanticipated natural disaster, a market crash, or an act of terrorism.

Practices. When a new technology threatens the established orthodoxy. This orthodoxy might be a long-standing design exemplar (all phones have buttons), a mindset (people value their privacy), or a certain way of doing things (watching TV only on a television).

Hacks. When consumers or companies are creating off-label uses for something such that it becomes more useful; or when someone finds an experience related to technology or digital media so frustrating that she builds something smarter, more intuitive, and easier to use. Although Twitter was invented to make it easier for people to connect with each other, in the beginning users had no easy way to tag topics or follow conversations as they did within chat and message boards. Early adopter Chris Messina proposed using the number sign, or hashtag, as a workaround.[25] His hack not only completely transformed how we aggregate and share content across social media—it also became a key part of the 2009–2010 Iranian election protests and many other large sociopolitical movements.

Extremes. When people are truly pushing boundaries in an attempt to break new ground. In many cases, they are pursuing research no one else has ever attempted. Or they are theorizing new ways to build, explore, see, manipulate, or replicate something that already exists. Remember Zoltan Istvan from the previous chapter? He's just one of many thousands of biohackers who are using themselves as test subjects in order to reach extreme frontiers in human-machine interfaces.

Rarities. When something—for example, a social movement, an object, a community, a business practice, or a policy—is so unusual and unique that it seems like a meaningless outlier, but it actually solves a fundamental human need or transforms some element of society. It could also be something that seems out of place but is succeeding, even if it is not the cause of disruption or transformation itself. The hacker collective Anonymous is a decentralized community that began on the imageboard 4chan back in 2003. No one took the social movement seriously—there were no leaders, it was impossible to trace who was involved, and so those who even knew about Anonymous wrote the community off as a meaningless group of pranksters. And yet Anonymous evolved into a new kind of social activism, taking down child pornography sites, launching cyberattacks on numerous governments (Angola, Russia, the United States), threatening China's political leaders, hacking into 2016 presidential candidate Donald Trump's personal data (Social Security and mobile phone numbers),[26] and more.

We can reverse-engineer Google's various projects between 2004 and 2010 and the audacious research being conducted at the fringe to see how the CIPHER pattern indicators were triggered.

There was a staggering *contradiction (C)*: By 2007, universities, Fortune 500 companies, and nonprofits alike were flocking to a company that used open-source code and didn't have any actual software to download. They were giving Google—a search engine company—access to office documents, emails, and calendars—as well as the search histories and preferences for each individual user. The products were so revolutionary and cost-effective, it was easy to imagine, as myriad tech-industry watchers did, an emerging trend in cloud-based office systems, with Google at the forefront.

Launching a suite of office productivity tools was also in contradiction to Google's core product, which was search. However, if Google was working toward a more comprehensive system—incorporating internet searches into all those other tools—that could be a real benefit to the user, and it would become a competitive advantage. Maybe "Googling" would soon apply to both the web and to my professional life: I'd enter the name of a coworker, and all of our interactions, as well as our shared calendar items and documents, would show up in one place.

Machine learning and computing power was reaching an *inflection (I)*. Between 1995 and 2005, engineers had been focused on natural language processing, search, and information storage and retrieval. Google had been at the forefront, using simpler tools, like logistic regression and support vector machines, to help build the Gmail spam classifier. In 2005, all of that changed when the computer science community embraced neural networks, which were first theorized in the 1960s. A sudden movement in neural network research was making computer vision possible, and that development had catalyzed research for new uses like machine translation. Google was at the forefront yet again, publishing a paper about how it had managed to distribute neural networks. It was evident that computers were getting smarter faster. That included our mobile devices, which are really just tiny, handheld computers. And it would lead to hyper-personalized computing, and then another inflection just over the horizon. It was no longer a matter of "if" someday far off in the future, but "when" in the coming years.

Standard *practices (P)* were being challenged. Talking computers, like HAL from Stanley Kubrick's *2001: A Space Odyssey*, have been a popular sci-fi theme for decades. But in practical terms no one had created a voice interface that worked well. And certainly not one that was conversational and context-aware, where pronouns could be substituted for names and the system would return accurate answers.

Early in 2009, the Siri voice assistant app went into testing. Originally, it was a third-party iOS application that offered a decent voice interface. Those who used the app loved it—they could simply speak to send messages, make a dinner reservation on OpenTable, search through Google maps, and more. For those questioning the power of natural language processing, there were some clever "Easter Eggs" hidden in the system. Ask it "What happened to HAL?" and a somber Siri would respond, "I don't want to talk about it." Ask it to help you find a local gym, and it would joke, "Yeah, your grip feels weak."[27]

Talking to a mobile device solved the persistent challenge of typing on a tiny keyboard. But this research previewed a new era of conversational computing. Combined with artificial intelligence, our devices could someday know all of our tastes and preferences, our needs and desires, and the most likely pathways to optimize our everyday lives.

Way off on the fringe were a handful of clunky but functioning virtual assistant applications. They were the result of *hacks (H)*: developers, frustrated with the projects they had been working on, broke free to build what they thought could be better versions. An Israeli student had entered the Y Combinator tech accelerator program, which is famous for having launched hundreds of startups, including the peer-to-peer apartment rental service Airbnb, Reddit, and Dropbox, a file-sharing company. One of the founders asked him to build something that would solve a problem the young student faced every day, so he built a digital secretary. His project, Greplin, was a search engine for your entire digital life, looking through your instant-message chat transcripts, emails, Facebook, Dropbox accounts, and other data with just one simple query. Elsewhere, an early Siri developer had been prototyping a smart notepad application, while a former Microsoft designer was working on an easier way to transfer the meeting details from an email into an online calendar. They eventually teamed up to figure out how to build a virtual mobile assistant. It's worth noting that in Silicon Valley, allegiances can be fickle. Developers might sign nondisclosure agreements, promising not to divulge company secrets. But as they move around from Google to Facebook to Apple, they bring their institutional knowledge and imaginations with them.

To me, Google appeared to be pushing an *extreme (E)* in an attempt to revolutionize our personal relationships with computers. Mobile phones didn't have to be an extension of our offices. With deep integrations into so many other areas—learning who we were communicating with and when, tracking our locations and travel patterns, observing when we used our phones—Google could theoretically soon know us better than we know ourselves. (At least when it comes to our digital lives.)

Finally, I thought it seemed odd that Google would offer a voice-based service to compete with 411. A project like that was rare in Silicon Valley, and at the time it was a rare tangent within the search giant. While it was certainly handy to call GOOG-411 while driving, it wasn't a practical long-term investment in company resources. A high call volume would at some point strain finances, assuming that Google had to cover the charges to patch people through using a third-party telecom service like AT&T or Sprint. Unless GOOG-411 started charging to be listed in search results, or it played advertising pre-roll at the beginning of calls, it was difficult to see how the service would become profitable.

To me, it was a signpost: GOOG-411 couldn't be just an information service. It was a real-time effort to data-mine our voices.

The CIPHER model proved to be an invaluable tool in helping me to see the relationships between the people, organizations, and projects on the fringe. These pattern indicators were a reliable signal in the noise. Assuming that Google was merely trying to compete with Microsoft would have been defining an extremely narrow x. For one thing, Google wasn't a software company. It was a search engine. Surely, a search engine company would have thought about and defined the future of cloud-based office systems quite differently from the reigning market leader in office software. How could it not?

There are certainly other categories that could be added, and not every trend will be revealed through all six CIPHER indicators. (In the Google example, only five were present.) However, in my research, I've consistently found using the six CIPHER model indicators to be a reliable way to spot emerging trends.

Now we have a better understanding of what Google was doing, and, more importantly, what the trend is. Google was building an exo-brain accessible via a mobile phone. Mergers and talent acquisitions would indicate that Apple and Microsoft were onto something similar, and to me, that indicated a possible emerging-trend candidate in ubiquitous virtual assistants. This trend—ubiquitous virtual assistants—meant that our machines would soon learn about us, anticipate our needs, and complete tasks in the background, without our direct request or supervision. The ubiquitous virtual assistant trend would be pervasive, spanning mobile phones at first before moving to other ambient interfaces and operating systems. Perhaps in the future, we might subscribe to a single assistant capable of interoperating with all of the people, devices, and objects in our lives. (However, I think that's highly unlikely, given entrepreneurs' predisposition against standardization in tech.)

CIPHER revealed a trend in the fringe: ubiquitous virtual assistants. It is one that we should begin to track and to investigate further.

Still, we ought to ask *why*. We still don't know what Google's space elevators, self-driving cars, and stratosphere balloons have to do with voice search. That answer would no doubt further inform the trend.

BANDWIDTH AND THE TOOTHBRUSH TEST

Legend has it that in 1996, Larry Page woke up in the middle of the night with a vision. He was a twenty-two-year-old graduate student at Stanford, and in that vision he saw a way to index all of the content on the web. What he wrote down became the basis for PageRank, which was an algorithm that powered a new search engine he called BackRub. A year later, Page and a fellow student, Sergey Brin, would rename the service "Google," a play on the word "googol," which refers to the large number represented by a 1 followed by 100 zeros. It is a number almost beyond comprehension, and yet it was an early sign of Page's ambition. Together, the pair intended to organize an infinite amount of information on the web. But Page had bigger plans.[28]

By the end of 2010, Google had 24,400 employees[29] and had amassed $35 billion in cash equivalents and marketable securities.[30] Page was about to take charge of Google's day-to-day of operations as chief executive officer, a role that had been occupied by Eric Schmidt, who assumed the executive chairmanship. Sergey Brin continued working on new products and strategy.

Page had been complaining that Google wasn't working on anything big. He wanted to tackle what he called "n-squared problems," long-term projects that would fundamentally change how we live. Page believed that Google was facing an existential question: What was after search? Google owned search, and soon it would own most of the world's mobile operating-system market, which was quickly adopting Android. What was next?

Google didn't need to get *more* people online. It needed to connect *everyone*—the entire world—to the internet. Tackling the world's biggest problems would require the very best minds, dedicated research, and new kinds of tools—but all of that costs money. The company would need to create new services, find new customers, and ultimately, convince everyone to spend more time with Google.

To that end, Google Fiber was launched to connect homes in Austin, Kansas City, and Provo (Utah) with internet service that's one hundred times faster than broadband. Google never intended to become an Internet Service Provider. Rather, this is about forcing the established providers in each market—Comcast, AT&T, Time Warner Cable, CenturyLink, Verizon, Charter—to lower their prices and increase their bandwidth. In developing countries, a similar strategy is in play. Google is helping to build out fiber backbones for entire cities, such as Kampala, Uganda. Where the ground or the local government proves tricky, there is Project Loon. Laying a massive backbone would be an expensive proposition for a rural community, hence those giant floating balloons.

Thanks in part to Google, by the year 2020, 90 percent of the world's population will be covered by mobile broadband. This will have a transformative effect on the way we live, learn, relate to each other, do business, and govern. It is our generation's steam engine.

Wiring communities won't have any impact if they don't have access to affordable computers. PCs and laptops can be cost-prohibitive and power hungry. But Android smartphones are devices within reach. Scaling the volume of cheaper devices, and getting them into the hands of billions of people, would change the worldwide digital landscape.

But not if they're only sending email or making phone calls. In 2015, Google released a "conversation mode" update to its mobile translation app.[31] All that was required to operate it was—wait for it—your voice. When it launched, I immediately tried it with a Spanish-speaking friend. I opened the app, selected the two languages needed (English and Spanish), hit the microphone icon, and spoke. We talked about technology, restaurants, and Madrid for more than fifteen minutes, each of us using our native languages, neither of us ever missing a beat. Next, we tried to push conversation mode to an extreme, to see if it would break. I switched over to Japanese, and my friend began speaking with an Argentinian accent. Aside from some momentary confusion resulting from some obscure Argentinian slang, Translate fulfilled its promise.

Instantaneous translation is a neat trick, but is it really necessary? Why does this matter?

With Google, search is now passive and ubiquitous. Rather than simply pointing us to relevant web pages, Google has become an omniscient digital oracle, one that we have access to via Google Now. Page was part of the driving force behind the launch of the project and the more recent upgrade to Google Now, On Tap. When prompted, Android now observes your behavior and queries more than seventy different partners, such as Airbnb, Spotify, Nest, Kayak, and Waze, and displays what you need to know on digital cards that appear on your mobile screen. They can be flicked away or opened for additional information. If you're looking for a new home, Google Now will know and can display Zillow cards with houses for sale as you drive by them. On your mobile phone, Google infers what you might need even before you do.

It's because of this functionality that Google Now has passed what Page refers to as the "toothbrush test."[32] If it is something you'd use once or twice a day and it makes your life better—like a toothbrush—it wins approval. Google Now is revolutionary in many ways, but it alone won't change how we live on this planet. How does it factor in to the bigger picture?

Think about all of the invisible infrastructure you take for granted today. You wake up in the morning and flip a switch to turn on your lights. A knob in your bathroom brings you clean, hot water within seconds. After you finish using the toilet, a lever creates enough force and pressure to flush your excretions through a massive underground sewer system. All of this infrastructure passes the toothbrush test, and you don't even notice.

As more people adopt the Android mobile platform, Google Now will become more ubiquitous. It, too, will become an invisible infrastructure someday. You won't think about it, but it will be an indispensable part of your daily routine. And it will require you to use the internet more.

CIPHER tells us that there's a reason Google wants everyone to be online, using our devices as much as possible.

In part, it's because the more people use internet sites, tools, and services, the more robust the network becomes. And, of course, because of money: 90 percent of Google's revenue comes from advertising, and 70 percent comes from search ads.[33] The more money amassed, the more likely some of those bigger ambitions can be realized. Google is a corporation with shareholders, so it needs to make money. But that isn't what's really happening here. Google needs enough revenue—orders of magnitude more than any normal Fortune 500 company earns in a year—to change the world.

Which brings us back to robots. Page envisions a society in which robots help care for our elderly, acting as their constant companions. With a fleet of well-trained robots, we may not need nursing homes in the future. Many of us could eventually outsource domestic tasks to robots—grocery shopping, house cleaning, laundry—which would follow a set of protocols while we're doing something more fun, like relaxing with family.

Robots would plug into an "Internet of Things." Along with other connected devices, like thermostats, garage doors, lights, refrigerators, and more, an army of subservient machines would communicate with each other, making decisions to power a seemingly invisible layer of everyday living. To make that future reality work, those objects, as well as our mobile devices, wearable computers, and all of the backend systems that they connect to, must speak the same language on the web.

What about that space elevator? It's an ongoing fantasy of Google's founders (and many others in Silicon Valley), who believe it would revolutionize how we might someday work and live beyond the Earth's atmosphere. A space elevator would allow research scientists to collect information, to transport things into space, and perhaps even to ferry humans back and forth.

This brings us back to the Google autonomous vehicle and that November day back in 2015. Page likes driverless cars because they would theoretically reduce the number of deaths and injuries due to everyday accidents. And because they are more efficient, they could begin to chip away at the pollution challenges posed by traditional vehicles.

But think about it. The less direct supervision our cars need from us, the more time we can spend streaming YouTube videos, answering Gmail messages, and reading sites that are part of Google's Display Network for advertising. Which means we're spending more time with Google.

Steve Jobs once reportedly told Larry Page that expanding so far beyond search and mobile into all of these other areas—cars, space elevators, robots, and other initiatives, like Calico, which is meant to expand the frontiers of human longevity—was a bad idea. Page thought that was ridiculous. But shareholders have expressed the same concerns, and so, in August 2015, Page announced a new operating structure in a blog post called "G Is for Google."[34] A new umbrella company called Alphabet had been formed, and Google would become one of its subsidiaries, along with Fiber, Calico (an age-related disease company), Nest (a smart home products company), and Google X, which would manage all of the "moonshot" projects (space elevators, driverless cars) that Page wanted to pursue. The move was literally a bet on alpha, giving Page and Brin leeway to separate their moneymaking businesses from these bigger, riskier projects.

If you're looking for technology trends on the horizon, it's not just a matter of seeing new research from the unusual suspects. You must also try to discover patterns that point to a trend, and show why that trend is emerging. This analysis will illuminate a possible trajectory for that trend, other people and organizations that might someday be involved, and a likely set of new, unusual suspects to begin tracking on the fringe.

After we cast a wide net, CIPHER narrows all of our brainstorming to help identify signals in the noise. Those signals indicate a possible trend candidate. But did we hear them correctly? Did we identify the right trend? Even Sherlock Holmes was known to make a mistake every now and again.[35] As we applied CIPHER, there were possibilities for missteps—How can we be sure we know what Google is doing?

That is the third step of the forecasting process: assess whether we've identified the right patterns, and whether we can trust what we saw.

CHAPTER SIX

The "Uber for X" Trend

Ask the Right Questions

FORECASTING THE FUTURE requires us to identify trends and track them as they move from the fringe to the mainstream. Once you've cast a wide enough net at the fringe for unusual suspects and applied CIPHER to identify trend candidates, you must stop and interrogate your work and what you think you know. It's a crucial step of forecasting that entrepreneurs, investors, and leaders often neglect, especially when it comes to technology. When a new technology becomes popular, they assume that it will jump across industries and scale the same way, earning the same revenue and proving just as indispensable to users in one field as in another.

It's precisely because so many people skipped the third step that "Uber for X" was the one ubiquitous phrase people throughout the business community uttered again and again starting in 2010 and through 2016. "X" was any established business sector (such as package delivery) that someone was promising to disrupt with new technology like Uber's.

"Uber for X" has been the headline of more than four hundred news articles.[1] Thousands of would-be entrepreneurs used the phrase to describe their companies in their pitch decks. On one site alone—AngelList, where startups can court angel investors and employees—526 companies included "Uber for" in their listings.[2] As a judge for various emerging technology startup competitions, I saw "Uber for" so many times that at some point, I developed perceptual blindness. The words became invisible to me as I focused attention on the rest of the pitch.

Nearly all the organizations I advised at that time wanted to know about the "Uber for" of their respective industries. A university wanted to develop an "Uber for tutoring"; a government agency was hoping to solve an impending transit issue with an "Uber for parking." I knew that "Uber for" had reached critical mass when one large media organization, in need of a sustainable profit center, pitched me their "Uber for news strategy."

"We're going to be the Uber for news," the news exec told me.

Confused, I asked what, exactly, he meant by that.

"Three years from now, we'll have an on-demand news platform for Millennials. They tap a button on their phones and they get the news delivered right to them, wherever they are," the editor said enthusiastically. "This is the future of news!"

"Is it an app?" I asked, trying to understand.

"Maybe. The point is that you get the news right away, when you want it, wherever you are," the exec said.

"So you mean an app," I pressed.

"Yes!" he said. "But more like Uber."

UBER FOR X

The mass "Uber for X" excitement is a good example of what happens when we don't stop to investigate a trend, asking difficult questions and challenging our cherished beliefs. We need to first understand what, exactly, Uber is and what led to entrepreneurs coining that catchphrase. Today, Uber is a wildly successful, six-year-old ride-sharing service that's now found in most major cities around the world. Anyone who has a valid license and access to a car, who owns a smartphone, and who can pass a criminal background check can become an Uber driver. Riders flag down a driver via a mobile app, which connects to the Uber dispatch and payment platform on the backend. A user's credit card is stored in the platform, so cash isn't part of the transaction. Drivers and riders are connected through Uber's platform, cutting out all of the other parts of the taxicab industry.

Those who use Uber rely on the service for its ease of use, seamless transactions, and customer service. Because of its astonishing growth, hundreds of "Uber for X" startups have popped up all over the world. In fact, "Uber for X" has become a kind of shorthand for convenience—a technological solution for any of life's frustrating, dull tasks, one that either makes them more convenient or automates them completely.

Before everyone was talking about their "Uber for X" startup, there was UberCab (Uber's original name), the company. It was founded in 2009 by Travis Kalanick and Garrett Camp as a sort of digital hitchhiking service. With the tap of a smartphone button, a driver in a black car would locate you on a map and take you wherever you needed to go.[3]

Kalanick, a UCLA dropout, had been working for years on the fringes of what became known as the "sharing economy." His first attempt was a multimedia search engine called Scour and a Napster competitor called Scour Exchange. The Recording Industry Association of America and the National Music Publishers Association—as they did with other peer-to-peer file-sharing networks—brought suit against Scour, which then filed for bankruptcy protection. Even so, Kalanick was back the following year with another peer-to-peer file-sharing company called Red Swoosh. Bandwidth had become more affordable and reliable, and Kalanick's team had figured out a more efficient way to allow users to send very large media files (including videos and music) over the internet. The company was acquired for $19 million by Akamai a few years later, and Kalanick got to work on his next idea. This time, he would build a smarter, more efficient system to share transportation.[4]

Today, Uber is a global company with hundreds of thousands of drivers. While there are competitors in the market, such as Lyft, they are dwarfed by Uber's sheer size, capital, and global user base.

But back in March 2010, before Uber made its first $5 in revenue, Kalanick posted a message on Twitter, complaining: "Trying to explain an opportunity this sick is tough."[5] Angel investors and venture capitalists weren't exactly lining up to write him checks. Kalanick approached Sequoia Capital, the storied Silicon Valley venture capital firm, but they passed. Investment from a venture firm like Sequoia wasn't just money—it was the stamp of legitimacy that catalyzed others to participate in a funding round, and it usually meant coverage in several of the tech-industry blogs.

Alfred Lin, a Sequoia partner, said that Sequoia "looked at the service and loved it" and thought that Kalanick was a "relentless, original thinker."[6] But the investors got stuck on the market and on the app itself, rather than the larger technology platform Uber was building. Another black car service? How could it possibly survive?

Well, it did more than just survive. Uber made history in December 2015 when media outlets reported that the company was looking to raise as much as $2.1 billion in its seventh financing round. That would value the company at $62.5 billion and make it the world's most valuable privately held startup.[7] For context, Facebook, when it went public, was valued at $50 billion[8] and soon made its founder Mark Zuckerberg the sixteenth wealthiest person in the world, just behind the Arnault family, which runs the massive LVMH luxury goods empire (Dom Perignon, Bulgari, Louis Vuitton, Fendi).[9] Let that sink in for a moment.

Privately held companies do not have to publicly disclose their revenue, margins, or any other financial data. Every time a company seeks investment, an independent party must appraise and estimate its worth in something called a "valuation." Uber, which was less than five years old at that December valuation, was said to be worth the same amount of money as Unilever, Vodafone Group, Softbank, PepsiCo, Google, and Comcast. Of course, Uber doesn't actually have $62.5 billion in tangible assets. But investors have already given the company more than $12 billion in cash that went into a real bank account.[10]

Uber isn't a unicorn. It isn't a decacorn, either (a company valued over $10 billion). It's a one-of-a-kind mythological siren, enchanting investors and entrepreneurs, beguiling competitors, and teasing journalists. In the span of just six years, Uber has expanded to sixty-seven countries and more than three hundred cities, from Baku, Azerbaijan, to Xiamen, China, to El Paso, Texas. Uber facilitates more than a million rides every day around the world.[11] On Christmas Eve 2015, Uber announced its billionth ride when a customer identified as Marvin went from London Field, Hackney, to Hoxton on London's East End. Marvin was given a gift of a year's worth of free Uber rides, and his driver got a free vacation to an Uber city of his choice.[12]

With all the excitement and buzz, scores of entrepreneurs wanted in and tried to build their own "Uber for X" companies. With its remarkable success, who wouldn't want to emulate Uber's global hegemony? Consider this very short list of startups:

Lugg: Uber for movers

Wag: Uber for dog walkers

Coders Clan: Uber for computer coding

Heal: Uber for doctors

Minibar: Uber for alcohol

Animan Robo: Uber for drones

Eaze: Uber for medical marijuana

LawTrades: Uber for lawyers

BloomThat: Uber for flowers

Plowz: Uber for snow plows

Shortcut: Uber for haircuts

Glamsquad: Uber for makeup

Transfix: Uber for trucking

Washio: Uber for laundry and dry cleaning

JetMe: Uber for private jets

IceCream.io: Uber for ice cream

Nimbl: Uber for cash deliveries

Tomo: Uber for long commutes

Zeel: Uber for massages

On the financial news site Quartz, humorist Jason O. Gilbert published a poem[13] about the "Uber for X" zeitgeist, inspired by descriptions of startups as an "Uber for something" by the tech press.

There's Uber for planes,
And Uber for jets,
An Uber for pills
And Uber for pets.

There's Uber for dogs,
And Uber for cats.
Need a hot stone massage?
There's an Uber for that.

An Uber for nails,
And an Uber for news.
And while your nails dry,
There's an Uber for booze.

There's an Uber for kids,
And an Uber for maids,
There's an Uber for hair
So you can Uber your braids.

There's Uber for bikes,
And an Uber for gifting,
There's an Uber for beauty,
If your face needs a lifting.

There's Uber for house painting,
And Uber for car towing,
There's Uber for clothes washing,
And Uber for lawn mowing.

If you don't have a green thumb,
There's Uber for flowers,
With all of these Ubers,
We could drone on for hours.

There's an Uber for groceries,
For all lazy cookers,
And if you feel lonely,
There's an Uber for hookers.

There's an Uber for pot,
For sticky green nugs,
And an Uber for cash,
To pay for your drugs.

Between Uber for weed,
And Uber for sex,
You name it,
There's likely an Uber for X.

So with startup reporters
Facing ever tight deadlines,
Perhaps what we need
Is an Uber for headlines.

Uber the company is an undeniable success. But does that necessarily imply that "Uber for X" is a real trend? "Uber for X" is certainly *trendy*, but is it worth tracking? People are busy and time is scarce. Everyone wants convenience. A technological solution for frustrating, dull tasks—an "Uber for laundry," for example—seems like it could capture a big audience.

Or is "Uber for X" merely a red herring, a shiny object in the business, while Uber the company is quietly building a new kind of technology platform that will usher in omnipresent on-demand services of the future? Which parts of the Uber story are worth paying attention to?

To answer these questions, we turn to step three of the process, which tells us that we need to stop and investigate what we think we see so far. Our own experiences and belief bias influence the way we parse any set of facts, and we are further swayed by the milieu of popular sentiment. Maybe "Uber for X" represents an upcoming boom in the sharing economy. Or maybe it's the opposite: with so many start-ups, maybe it means that the sharing economy is in a bubble, one that could soon burst.

Let's go back in time and try to see the world as Kalanick did. What trend patterns were emerging? How does the CIPHER model come into play?

UBER'S X-FACTOR

Let's forget what we know about the world today and instead pretend like it's January 2010, just a few months before Kalanick posted that Tweet complaining that investors couldn't see his vision. If we zoom in and out—if we "Kanizsize" the facts—we might be able to interpret the emerging technology landscape as Kalanick did.

In 2010, America was still rebounding from our Great Recession, which had been sparked by the subprime mortgage crisis. The Bureau of Labor Statistics forecast an ongoing decline in the growth of consumer spending. America's unemployment rate reached 10 percent, and experts offered a bleak outlook for most job seekers. "We will likely see elevated unemployment for at least the next five years," Heidi Shierholz, at the Economic Policy Institute, said at the time.[14] Former Department of Labor secretary Robert Reich urged Americans to prepare for "high unemployment for the next few years" and warned that "even when the jobs come back, they're not going to be very good jobs."[15]

We hadn't seen unemployment climb above 9 percent since the 1981 recession, in which three-quarters of job losses came from goods-producing sectors, like auto manufacturing. This time around, white-collar and public-sector workers were hit hardest. They were teachers, civil servants, sales department managers, journalists, and postal workers. We reached an inflection point, and almost overnight, there were far more people who needed jobs than positions posted by the relatively few companies able and willing to make new hires.

But unlike those who were laid off in 1981, the people who lost their jobs in 2009–2010 had lived through a decade-long dot-com boom. The tech bubble may have burst, but even that implosion couldn't dampen America's renewed sense of entrepreneurial spirit. There may not have been jobs available, but a lot of people still needed assistance getting things done. TaskRabbit emerged as an online marketplace for small jobs and tasks. There were no more buyers for bad second (and third, fourth, and fifth) investment properties, but there were rooms to let. Airbnb soon enabled anyone to make a few bucks off of their empty houses, condos, and rooms as a bed-and-breakfast purveyor. The unemployed no longer had disposable income to buy new power tools or designer handbags, but there were neighbors willing to lend their goods—for a fee. SnapGoods and NeighborGoods were platforms allowing communities to rent items to each other.

Zooming in and out, we can begin to see CIPHER pattern identifiers come into sharper focus.

We had reached an *inflection* point. Something happened to catalyze a great acceleration in emerging research: the job market tanked, and myriad developers got to work thinking about and tinkering with new kinds of sharing-economy platforms.

In 2010, a lot more people were buying smartphones than those economic indicators would lead us to believe. Even in a down economy with so many people out of work, Apple posted record iPhone sales and what had at that point been its highest earnings in company history. Sales of iPhones, at 14.1 million, were up 91 percent year-over-year.[16]

It seemed like a staggering *contradiction*, one that could favor Uber. That's because the Uber platform relied on mobile technology. Would-be riders had to mark their location within an app, which would connect them with a nearby driver, who received the notice on her own mobile phone. The rider's credit card information was stored in the app, as was the driver's account—Uber was completely cashless. Once a ride was completed, the total amount would be charged to the stored credit card, and a percentage would be posted to the driver's account.

Wi-Fi was also becoming more ubiquitous. It was freely available in coffee shops, office buildings, and shopping malls. Smartphone users were free to gobble up bandwidth without paying fees. This benefited Apple, Google, and anyone else hoping to gain users for mobile apps: the easier it was for people to hop onto a mobile service, the more valuable that service would become to other people, who would in turn join and make the service even more popular. Uber's astonishingly simple mobile app would create a "network effect" on both sides of its platform: for riders and drivers alike.

In the taxi market, there are three operators: the taxi driver, a dispatch company that facilitates transactions (as well as other logistics and infrastructure, like fleet maintenance and scheduling), and what's called the "medallion holder." Medallions are special permits required to own and operate a taxicab, and they're a requirement in most US cities. Without the official permit, a local government could impose hefty fines.

By the time the medallion idea originated in the 1930s, cabs had become wildly popular in New York City.[17] So had crime. There were increased calls for regulation to make cabs safer. But medallions weren't free. By 2010, the onetime cost of a single New York City medallion averaged $775,000 to $850,000.[18] It was less in other cities, including Boston and San Francisco, but not by much. That fee trickled down to drivers, who had to pay the medallion owners $100 or more per shift just for the privilege of working. It could take half the day to break even. Medallion owners had to pay down the debt on the permit, and they also had to pay the dispatch companies.

Back when the medallion system was introduced, there were 6.9 million people living in New York's five boroughs.[19] While no office was keeping annual city tourism numbers at that time, we can use the 1939–1940 World's Fair for some context. The fair brought an unprecedented number of people into New York City over the span of two full years—44 million.[20]

By the time Kalanick was pitching Uber to investors, the city's population had increased to 8.2 million.[21] Even without a major global event like the World's Fair, the city was managing an average of 50 million tourists every single year.[22] And let's not forget about the 117 million passengers served at New York City's three airports.[23] Some are tourists, but many are local residents who use cabs to get to and from their flights.

In 1937, guess how many taxi medallions were issued? 11,787.[24]

Now, guess how many medallions are in circulation today? Only 13,270.[25]

In 2017, there are many more people living in New York City—and millions more needing airport transportation—but there are only a few hundred more medallions in circulation than there were back in 1939.[26] This is why in crowded metropolises, like New York City, it's so hard to hail a cab, even in Manhattan, where taxis appear to be everywhere, a rippling blur of yellow with occasional accents of red flashing lights. If you've ever tried to hail one of those cabs during what's known as "shift change"—the dreaded 3 p.m. to 6 p.m. block of reduced service as drivers end and begin their shifts—you've no doubt experienced a level of frustration that's difficult to convey without the assistance of expletives. Same goes when it's raining in Washington, DC, and you're trying to get a cab outside of Union Station. Or when it's snowing in Chicago and you need a ride out of O'Hare.

It's another *contradiction*. One would think that a great increased demand would lead to a corresponding supply when it comes to public transit, but that just hasn't been the case.

Uber is also a workaround for a standard *practice*, threatening the established orthodoxy. It creates instant competition in a field dominated by a singular monopoly in just about every market. Kalanick wasn't just building another car service. His ride-sharing idea was, at its core, about building an advanced, pervasive peer-to-peer network. Instead of circumventing the intermediary to move files, he'd get around the medallions, dispatchers, and operators—as well as those irksome government regulators—to move people.

In 2010, the taxi owner-driver-dispatch trifecta hadn't evolved at all, even as technology had changed consumer expectations and behaviors. Hundreds of mobile apps had made paying for things easy and seamless, but cabs were stuck in the old cash-based system. Although drivers were required to take credit cards in most cities, the machines were often difficult to use or couldn't make the connection back to the dispatcher. Drivers wanted cash tips, not credit card receipts—and so they would discourage passengers from using the machines.

Uber was a very clever *hack* for paying with cash. Its payment gateway—the infrastructure that works securely between the passenger's phone and Uber—uses client-side encryption written in a mobile language. Which means that rather than the passenger having to enter her credit card information again and again, or having to load slow web pages onto her mobile device, the entire transaction happened lightning-quick in the background. Credit card information only needed to be entered one time, and the passenger was the only person to see it. This and other advanced technology made the Uber transaction invisible—once a ride was finished, the passenger was simply free to leave the car. A receipt would be emailed.

No one had ever before launched such a seamless mobile payment interface. This wasn't a simple update to the cash transaction—it was a creative solution to an experience that had long frustrated riders throughout the world. It was such a revelation, and the payment interface was so tremendously easy to use, that Uber-style payments started to change the consumer mindset. Why wasn't every transaction that easy?

Uber totally upended established payment practices. And the technology platform was so good that when the company introduced its so-called surge pricing, in which fares can be multiplied anywhere from 1.2 to 10 times the usual price during peak demand, Uber's business actually continued to grow. Think about the practical implications of surge pricing for a moment. If a regular taxicab changed its rates throughout the day, such that a short ride to the airport could range in price from $30 to $300, most people would look for another alternative. I certainly would, even if the rate was explained to me before the driver started her meter. For one thing, there are cheaper reliable ways to get to the airport. And knowing that the driver's credit card machine might not be working, there's a strong possibility that I wouldn't have enough cash on hand to pay her at the end.

With Uber, when surge pricing goes into effect, it's made abundantly clear on the app. That the cost per mile can be upward of $10 with a minimum fare of $30 should come as no surprise to users, even new ones. And yet, attendees at the 2016 Consumer Electronics Show in Las Vegas, where regulated taxis are already scarce, railed against Uber on social media. With an estimated 170,000 people in town for the convention,[27] Uber invoked surge pricing of five to six times the usual rate, and it alerted users when they opened the app. Throughout the week, there were hundreds of Tweets, Facebook posts, and Instagrams about how Uber was unfairly charging people attending the show. But many of those posts included screenshots of time-stamped, paid receipts, throughout the week—and even toward the end of the convention. Like this one from an angry techie, which read: "#Uber robbed all of us today at #CES" and included a receipt showing that he'd paid $47 on a fair that was normally $9.26.[28]

This means that the angry techie opted to use Uber in spite of the fact that it ran counter to his best interests at the time. We embrace Uber even when it's bad for us, because the technology—on-demand service, widely available drivers, seamless payments—is too good to pass up.

Finally, it isn't as though Uber has come this far without controversy. Kalanick's previous file-sharing startups had to declare bankruptcy in the wake of lawsuits and legislation. With Uber, he's hired scores of lawyers and lobbyists, and he's putting up a formidable fight across several fronts:

Taxicab companies. Medallion holders have partnered with local lawmakers around the country to push for new regulatory frameworks that would unravel much of Uber's business, from its mobile platform to the independent-contractor status of its drivers. When Yellow Cab of San Francisco filed for Chapter 11 bankruptcy protection in January 2016, its losses were due in part to tort liabilities and lawsuits—but they were also due to Uber's presence in the city.[29]

State governments. Insurance agency officials from eleven states, including California[30] and Nebraska,[31] have sued Uber over what it calls "coverage gaps," arguing that standard car insurance doesn't extend to cover commercial driving.

Drivers and unions. Some of Uber's drivers filed a class-action lawsuit, alleging that the startup misclassified drivers as independent contractors, when they should have been classified as part-time or full-time employees.[32] Drivers in the suit say they are entitled to reimbursement for expenses like gas and vehicle maintenance.

Riders. There are numerous individual complaints against Uber, which have been cataloged by the Taxicab, Limousine and Paratransit Association (TLPA), a membership group that represents more than 1,100 taxicab, black car, and other transportation company owners. The list includes dozens of alleged physical and sexual assaults by Uber drivers as well as many alleged harassment incidents.[33] Although Uber drivers are supposed to pass a screening and background check, the list outed several Uber drivers who had criminal histories.[34]

Yet even with the widely reported lawsuits involving Uber, the company is succeeding. It's another *contradiction* within such a heavily regulated industry as transportation. In Silicon Valley, where most startups launch first and work out the bumps later on, lawsuits are common. They're one of the costs of doing business.

Zooming in and out with CIPHER, we can see the pattern emerge. Uber had created a rich, complex pool of opportunities, solving for the customer experience problem and—though they might not recognize it as such—for the taxicab owners' outdated technology and the regulators' restrictive business model. "We didn't dream with [Kalanick] about what it could be, that it could transform transportation," said Lin, the Sequoia partner.[35]

Indeed, if we Kanizsize the facts, it becomes clear that Uber's promise wasn't a well-designed mobile app. Uber had a certain x-factor—a set of qualities that was special and significant. If an x-factor wasn't in play, then the copycat apps launched by the taxicab industry itself, such as Hailo, would have found big, captive audiences. To date, the industry has not been able to replicate Uber's success. It hasn't even come close.

Uber the company was more than just an app, which is why for years it succeeded in the wake of so many external pressures. Maybe if Kalanick's technology platform took hold, it might transform how we think about logistics—not just in the realm of taxis and black cars, but in how we move around people, packages, groceries, pets, and just about everything else.

COGNITIVE SHORTCUTS AND DISADS

In trying to understand important events looming on the horizon and forecast what's to come, most people stop looking when they identify (or hear about) a possible trend. That's especially true when the trend comes wrapped in a catchy, linguistic ribbon like "Uber for X."

Nobel Prize–winning psychologist Daniel Kahneman and his collaborator Amos Tversky call this the "availability heuristic."[36] Our brains make cognitive shortcuts, and we think that the possibility of something happening is higher simply because an example comes to mind easily. Four hundred headlines? Five hundred startups? A poem? It must be a trend!

The availability heuristic can be triggered by a catchy phrase—like "Uber for X"—since it's an analogy that's easy to understand and applicable in lots of situations. We base our judgment on what we can remember, rather than the available data. In this era of consumer-facing technological innovation, company names—Google, Facebook, Instagram, Slack, Twitter, Uber—enjoy dual use as verbs. We "Google the best island resorts for families" and then "Facebook our friends" to see if anyone has suggestions. From the plane, we "Tweet that we're going to be offline for the weekend" and then remember to "Slack that file to our colleagues at work." Relaxing on that gorgeous beach, sipping piña coladas, we can't help ourselves. Out comes the mobile phone so we can "Instagram the clear blue water" and the sun and all the rest of it.

It is especially problematic when a brand's name *is* the catchphrase and becomes shorthand for a complicated concept. That's because it makes us lazy. Eventually, we read, hear, and see a phrase like "Uber for X" so many times that our brains leap to conclusions that may not be accurate. The availability heuristic is responsible for goading us into believing that what's trendy is a tech trend worthy of attention.

"Uber for X" was approaching fever pitch among investors in late 2015, just as Kalanick sought that unprecedented funding round and sky-high valuation. It's worth taking a short break from our "Uber for X" story to learn the fate of another buzzy catchphrase—one that similarly got investors into a tizzy—just a few years ago. (You may argue that I've just spoiled our "Is Uber for X a real trend?" question—but there's a twist. So read on.)

The phrase was "flash sale for X," and our story opens just as "Uber for X" did. Lots of headlines. Inexplicable exuberance. Wild valuations. Except in this case, several "flash sale for X" companies, rather than just one with a few very distant competitors, took off quickly.

The startups—Gilt, HauteLook, Rue La La, One Kings Lane (OKL), Zulily—offered steeply discounted goods for a short period of time, usually twenty-four to forty-eight hours. Like Uber, these were internet and later mobile platforms that required people to sign up via email to become a member. Flash-sale sites were a blessing for designers, for whom the slumped economy had dampened consumer appetite for high-end goods. Leftover handbags and shoes from a slow season could find a new audience, and the brief sales could help the designers earn back lost revenue. Just like Uber, flash-sale operators fulfilled needs on both ends of the platform—customers, who wanted to buy luxury goods but could no longer afford them, and designers, who needed to offload their wares.

Gilt Groupe launched in 2007, and by 2009 its user base had soared to more than 1 million members. By 2012, venture capitalists (VCs) believed so fervently in the "flash sale for X" trend that they started making deals. Big, fat deals. Gilt Groupe was given a whopping $1 billion valuation.[37] That's unicorn territory.

One Kings Lane's post-money valuation came in at just below that, but not by much—$912 million.[38] The news had energized everyone in the company. I remember a visit I made to meet with OKL executives at their offices in Lower Manhattan, just across from the entrance to the Holland Tunnel. OKL had taken over a few floors in a gigantic, non-descript building. It was an enormous but beautiful mishmash of temporary walls and shelves stuffed with colorful pillows, picture frames, lamps, and rugs. OKL was now expanding from housewares and furnishings into jewelry and accessories, and they were launching a line of OKL-branded merchandise that would include candles and bedding. There was talk of growing OKL into a technology company in its own right, with a white-labeled platform that others could use.

Soon after my visit to OKL, Zulily, a flash-sale site for moms, went IPO. By the end of its first day of trading, enthusiasm for the "flash sale for X" trend had driven the stock's price up 71 percent, making the site's founder, Mark Vadon, a billionaire in just a few hours.[39]

Entrepreneurs, succumbing to the availability heuristic, jumped on the bandwagon, launching dozens of "flash sale for X" sites. VCs began circling, term sheets already prepared, pens uncapped, dotted lines ready for signature. There were "flash-sale" operators for outdoor enthusiasts (The Clymb), travelers (Jetsetter), home design (Joss & Main), fine wines (Lot18), men's fashions (JackThreads), babies (The

Mini Social), five-star hotels (SniqueAway), surfing (Driftwagon), and even fishermen (Tightlinz).

After steps one and two of the instructions, we only have a trend *candidate*, nothing more. As the bandwagon swerved and rolled full-speed ahead, with lead-footed investors excitedly driving the "flash sale for X" trends, I hopped off, forcing myself to take a contrarian view. I wasn't ready yet to buy into the trend. I wanted to make sure I couldn't weaken the premise.

Shredding a trend candidate apart and challenging assumptions and knowledge is the third step, and it required starting with one big question: What would have to be true in order for the "flash sale for X" trend to prove out as a manifestation of sustained change within society? We know that a trend represents sustained change within society—to me, flash-sale sites seemed like a temporary business gimmick, one that didn't have strong enough technological legs to stand on in the farther future. In order to answer that big question, I broke it down into smaller parts, trying to psychologically distance myself from the trendiness of flash sales and to separate my knowledge from my assumptions.

It turned out to be an easier question to answer than I'd imagined. Consumers are capricious, and the flash-sale platform was too easy to replicate. The successful operators were aggressive marketers, sending around one or more email messages a day, in addition to mobile push notifications and sponsored posts on social media. Originally collaborators, traditional retailers discovered that they could lure customers back by offering their own steep discounts or by partnering with designers for lower-priced goods. Suddenly, flash-sale operators had formidable competitors whose brand relationship with customers went back decades or more.

Eventually, sales growth waned, ushering in layoffs and a soft market for "flash sale for X" sites. The once mighty, magical unicorn Gilt lost its horn, agreeing to sell itself to Saks Fifth Avenue owner Hudson's Bay

Company for $250 million.[40] Zulily's share price tanked 46 percent, and the company agreed to sell itself to Liberty Interactive Corp's QVC for just $18.75 per share, a far cry from its per-share peak of $72.75.[41] By the end of 2015, OKL was shopping itself around, hoping to find a potential buyer. News reports cited unnamed sources that said the brand would have a difficult time fetching more than $150 million.[42] All those "flash sale for x" sites were merely a flash in the pan.

When a conclusion fits within our existing systems of belief and we don't challenge the facts, that's called "belief bias," and we all suffer from it at times. Gilt, OKL, and Zulily were exciting! Everyone was talking about them in social media: if they weren't bragging about some great steal, they were clamoring to become members. Add to that the excitement among investors, the rapid growth in memberships, and the positive response to marketing, and it was easy to believe that "flash sale for X" sites represented something more fundamental than a temporary response to a down economy. Many thought it was an entirely new way to do business, one that consumers would expect to see across all the different retail sectors. Challenging such zeal would require an intentional fight against some heavy-duty psychological peer pressure. It can be hard to disagree with everyone just for the sake of disagreeing—to look for and poke holes into established thought. Who wants to be the person slamming down on the brakes when everyone in the bandwagon is having a jolly good time barreling forward?

Moving past belief bias requires deliberate disagreement, even if you believe in what you're seeing. If you're a natural contrarian, this process will be easy. If you were on a high school or college debate team, you've already learned to do this.[43] For every resolution you argued, your team had to break the big concepts down into smaller parts and then see if you could prove each one wrong. These counterarguments were called "disads," or "disadvantages," and they broke apart every part of the opposing team's assertions, bit by bit, in order to show every single way in which the assumptions, evidence, and impact were wrong, untrue, or overblown. I know a lot about disads because I spent eight years as a competitive debater in high school and college. Scientists, investigative reporters, lawyers, police detectives, politicians, and engineers all have their own versions of "disads," though they are called something different.

Getting in the habit of poking holes in a hypothesis, even taking the contrarian view when you agree with the idea, will help make you a good forecaster of the future. Be warned, however, that it may mean that your friends and family members won't discuss politics with you. (That, however, may be a good thing, given political discourse today.)

So let's now go back to our story about "Uber for X," and complete step three of the instructions. Our objective is not to evaluate Uber the company, but rather to determine whether or not "Uber for X" is a trend. We must reexamine our belief bias and consider the trend as though we're debaters arguing the opposing side. The position we are refuting is this: *"Uber for X" is a trend, a new manifestation of sustained change within an industry, the public sector, our society, or the way that we behave toward one another.* What would it take for that statement to be true? And what can that statement tell us about the future of Uber itself?

In order to create our disads, we need to break that question into many smaller parts. There is no set formula for this and no standard line of questioning. Instead, the best way to start the process is to address the biggest, most obvious point straight away and then narrow the focus to more granular details. At the end of our interrogation, if we haven't been able to make any compelling disads, then we haven't disproven the position. "Uber for X" is a trend. On the other hand, if we've successfully poked too many holes, that tells us we've merely found a shiny object—a phenomenon that's only *trendy* for the moment.

What would it take for "Uber for X" to represent a new manifestation of a sustained change within the society? That's a very big question. In order to answer it, here is what we would need to know:

- Is "Uber for X" habit-forming? Does it pass the toothbrush test? We already know that people will continue to use Uber even when it runs counter to their best interests. But that fact about Uber the company doesn't necessarily represent other "Uber for X" brands. What about them? If Minibar, the "Uber for alcohol," initiated surge pricing every Saturday night or during football games, how long would people still use it?

- Do we see the "Uber for X" model changing the behavior of consumers in other industry sectors? Do consumers anticipate and expect an on-demand, transactionless experience in unusual arenas, such as religion, education, or medicine?

- Have "Uber for X" companies impacted any economic indicators, such as the stock market, manufacturing, the housing market, or jobs? Has the on-demand business model and the technology required to support it caused a ripple effect throughout other sectors? Or, if we haven't seen any tangible effect yet, is there a likelihood we might in the near future?

What is the basic human need being addressed by "Uber for X," and is it catalyzed by new technology? This is another big question. To answer it, we should think about how people interact with their mobile devices, since the "Uber for X" apps all require smartphones. We should also try to think through other aspects of daily living, both as individuals and collectively as a connected community.

- Does the "Uber for X" platform greatly reduce consumer friction points? Is the technology so seamless and easy to use that it alleviates frustrations connecting people to services or products?

- What percentage of mobile users continue to use an "Uber for X" app after a particularly steep surge price? Do people stick with a service even when it is financially disadvantageous? Overall, have people continued to use the service, and is that user base growing?

- Does the "Uber for X" on-demand model solve any human-centered challenges? Is it succeeding only because we are too busy or too lazy? If so, is there a possibility that in the future, we will prefer to be more busy and more active?

- Have "Uber for X" companies alleviated any public health issues? Do they address the needs of the members of our aging population, who will increasingly need assistance, but for whom mobile apps may be a challenge?

The "Uber for X" trend is timely, but what will cause it to persist? The "flash-sale" trend didn't stick because it was a temporary reprieve in a down economy and because initial collaborators too easily became eventual competitors.

- Does "Uber for X" create partnership opportunities in other industries, such that the two are stronger together than apart?

- Are these partnership opportunities with companies that are more likely to benefit financially from a long-term collaboration rather than competition?

- Is "Uber for X" a perennial service, or does it rely on the seasonable availability of people and products?

- Does the "Uber for X" trend require a down economy to work? What happens when jobs are plentiful and money is flowing again?

In what ways did the "Uber for X" trend materialize as a series of unconnectable dots that began out on the fringe and moved into the mainstream? Remember, this factor is a key insight into understanding the evolution of a technology trend. It helps to distinguish a trend from what's really just a hot new product, service, or app.

- Has "Uber for X" created widespread use of a new kind of technology, code, or product?

- Has "Uber for X" inspired second, third, and fourth iterations of a technology? Is the technology evolving, with accompanying breakthroughs—or is the field growing by virtue of copycat competitors?

- Does the "Uber for X" technology encompass more than a consumer-facing app? If we were to reverse-engineer the platform model, in what ways would we see it serving multiple audiences?

Just now, our goal was to take the contrarian view—to acknowledge the availability heuristic, jump off the bandwagon, and leave our belief bias at the curb. Everyone we normally pay attention to—the big-name Silicon Valley investors, business journalists, and tech bloggers—thinks that "Uber for X" is an important trend. Were we able to refute their position? *"Uber for X" is a trend, a new manifestation of sustained change within an industry, the public sector, our society, or the way that we behave toward one another.*

There are too many counterarguments that can be made, and we now have even more questions than before we started this disad exercise. The "Uber for X" trend is based on evidence that is self-perpetuating. For one thing, headlines beget more headlines, and funding rounds beget more funding rounds. We assume that there is a direct correlation between our enthusiasm for something today and that thing's success into the future.

We were blinded by our belief bias.

There are too many problems with the "Uber for X" position for it to survive as a trend. Those 526 companies calling themselves the "Uber for" makeup, laundry, private jets, ice cream, massages, and flowers will inevitably go the way of Gilt, Zulily, and One Kings Lane. Actually, that's not quite right: few (if any) will ever come close to achieving unicorn status. Most will go under, just as we begin hearing that siren call, tantalizing us with the next buzzy-sounding "Tech Thing for X" catchphrase.

And yet, while I don't expect the "Uber for haircuts" startup Shortcut to be around much longer, there's something about Uber the company. It has an *x*-factor we've sensed but haven't entirely identified. Uber the company is a juggernaut too massive to ignore. Perhaps we've been distracted by all the weird and wild "Uber for X" startups to notice.

Could it be that *Uber itself* is the trend?

UBER-POWERED POTATO FARMS

Let's revisit the facts. What do we know to be true about Uber today? The genius of Kalanick is that he recognized pain points—everyday frustrations and inconveniences—and figured out a way to address it using an enormous, peer-to-peer network. Uber didn't just solve one or two problems plaguing the taxicab industry: the scarcity of cabs, the high price of running a cab business, drivers who refuse to take credit cards, poor customer service. Uber completely reimagined every piece of the experience: circumventing the arcane medallion requirement, obviating the middleman dispatcher, creating a seamless mobile payment system, and allowing users to rate their drivers. For example, in 2016, Uber was already leveraging the GPS coordinates and accelerometer within a driver's phone. If a user complains that the driver is going too fast, or too slow, or hitting the brakes too hard, the app reports that data back through the system, where Uber staff review it and act to improve passenger safety. Uber is a twenty-first-century, omnidirectional technology and logistics platform that services multiple customer segments.

The calamitous impact that Uber has had on the taxicab industry, and will eventually have on other industries, is difficult to oversell. In

January 2016, the Obama administration proposed $4 billion to be spent over ten years for research related to a system of autonomous vehicles.[44] What would it take for Uber *the platform* to represent a new manifestation of a sustained change in society? Let's start with a specific instance and see how far we get:

- Uber is a ride-sharing service operating in cities around the world.

- Uber is a ride-sharing service that has beaten incumbents, causing the value of the industry's most prized asset (medallions) to collapse.

- Uber is an on-demand logistics service, which you can hire to drive you to the airport, pick up your kids from school, or take your elderly grandmother to her doctor appointments.

- Uber is a car you don't have to maintain, lease back, or sell. Uber replaces your monthly car payment.

- Uber is a supply chain management solution, delivering people, packages, and other goods to destinations around the world.

Now let us include some other information about Uber that we know to be true. In 2013, Uber closed a significant round of funding—$361.2 million—and the largest investor wasn't one of the usual venture-capital suspects. It was Google Ventures, which contributed $257.79 million and represented 86 percent of Google Ventures' annual $300 million fund.[45] Quite a sizable investment!

Why did Uber need so much money? It wanted to acquire deCarta, the company that originally powered General Motors' OnStar turn-by-turn navigation service. Uber was also after a strategic partnership with Carnegie Mellon University, whose world-renowned National Robotics Engineering Center (NREC) employs some of the smartest engineers and research scientists on the planet. Or rather, I should say "employed." Just four months after the partnership was announced, we learned that forty of the NREC's top scientists and researchers left Carnegie Mellon for Uber, including six principal investigators, thirty-four engineers, and even the NREC director himself. It was a devastating, behind-the-scenes raid, in which Uber poached from the best, offering the new hires more than double their former salaries without forcing them to relocate. The robotics researchers had a sole focus, one that might surprise you: driverless car technology.[46]

Uber had purchased a 53,000-square-foot former restaurant-supply center on the Allegheny River, not far from Carnegie Mellon's campus. But that wasn't all. Uber had also bought commercial advertising space around town, which included a billboard just outside Carnegie Mellon's computer science building that read: "We are looking for the best software engineers in Pittsburgh."[47] Graduate students were being aggressively recruited. Tianyu Gu was one of them: a doctoral student who was researching algorithms to help an autonomous car's computer plan its next moves while driving.[48] Uber's interest in Gu's work and the cutting-edge work being done by others at Carnegie Mellon was revealing. So what do we know so far?

- Uber is a fleet of driverless cars and buses that take us anywhere we need to go.

- Uber is a fully automated, global supply chain management solution, delivering people, packages, and other goods to destinations around the world.

- Uber is an interconnected system of service vehicles and equipment that automate tasks previously done by people.

- Uber is the invisible logistics layer powering our everyday lives.

In the previous chapter, we asked why Google was developing self-driving car technology. It wasn't because Google wants to own and manage a fleet of automobiles, or to complete with General Motors or Toyota. Rather, in order for Alphabet—Google's parent company—to accomplish its moonshots, it needs a bankroll an order of magnitude away from any company we've seen to date. Self-driving cars offer you the freedom to sit back, relax, and consume vast quantities of information and data. Just as it has in adjacent arenas—like how it introduced Google Fiber to force internet providers to increase their speeds—Google is making investments, forging partnerships, and creating competition that forces us to think about something—in this case, vehicle ownership—in a new way.

- Uber is slowly, inconspicuously becoming the toothbrush we can't live without.

Let's fast-forward to a plausible scenario for the year 2040. Uber is now three decades old. The tens of thousands of contract drivers who worked with Uber were obviated once self-driving cars became mainstream. Fully autonomous Ubercars drive us to work and pick up our kids from soccer practice. We order our groceries, our toiletries, and our medications, which arrive automagically—by Uberdrone or Uber's fleet of microtrucks—when we need them. For those who still need to send physical letters and documents, the U-USPS (Uber-US Postal Service) sends a robocourier to any destination imaginable. A tiny camera scans and identifies the correct recipient before releasing a delivery. Infrastructure developed by Uber and Google now power most US cities as well as cities around the world. Just as Google has become the invisible information layer that powers our everyday lives, Uber is now the invisible logistics layer, servicing just about every market.

Generation Alpha—those who were born between the years 2010 and 2025—are the most formally educated generation to date. They are also the most technologically advanced. By the time they entered the workforce, there were very few labor-intensive jobs. That's because machines have rendered manual labor positions unnecessary. In 2040, Uber and its agribusiness partners, DuPont-Dow and Monsanto, have made working farms more efficient than ever before in human history. Of course, each company is successful in its own right. But as collaborators, they have completely upended modern farming.

In the year 2040, at the beginning of the growing season, an Uber-tractor drives itself through a few dozen acres, planting genetically enhanced hyper-productive seeds. Ground sensors track the level of moisture in the soil and plants. Drones fly above the crops, scanning for pest infestations, viruses, and overgrowth.

At potato farms, the long harvest season is heralded by an Uberharvester, a complicated machine that digs potatoes out of the ground in wide swaths and gently separates them from dirt and plants. An Uberscoop transports the potatoes back to a washing facility, where machines automatically sort, wash, and chill potatoes before they're driven by an autonomous Ubertruck to a nearby potato-chip factory. There, the potatoes move through a series of machines that wash, peel, slice, fry, salt, and inspect them before they're portioned into bags, sealed, and boxed. Ubertrucks are waiting at the end of the production line, where they will transport the chips to local grocery stores, across the country, or wherever they are programmed to drive. (This assumes, of course, that farms are still outdoors and haven't relocated deep underground. A modified version of an indoor Uber-powered farm works, too.)

I count just one, highly skilled mechanical botanist on the farm, adroitly managing both the equipment and the crops. Remote support staff would probably include an Uber IT specialist, who can service the machines and their computers.

This is a plausible future for Uber, considering the facts and variables available at the time I'm writing this book. You might completely disagree with me. Sure, you may concede that some of what I've written could be *technically* feasible in the farther future. But I'm suggesting that agriculture writ large—American farming as we've always known it—will be completely disrupted by a company whose founder once said that he started Uber so that "me, my cofounder, and our hundred friends could roll around San Francisco like ballers." It's almost impossible to imagine a young, spirited Travis Kalanick, traipsing all over Silicon Valley, trying to persuade VCs to invest in his idea.

I'm saying that in our far future, the largest transportation and logistics companies, like DSV, C. H. Robinson, CEVA, DHL, and UPS, will see their global businesses shrink. A significant portion of the human-powered jobs in logistics will be obviated . . . by what started as a ride-sharing platform. We will look back in the year 2040 and realize that all this time, we were acclimating ourselves to automation as we unwittingly and methodically trained our future job replacements.

UBER *IS* THE X

"Uber for X" is certainly trendy, but after completing step three of the instructions we realize that Uber itself is the wheel from which many technology trend spokes protrude: automation, the sharing economy, invisible infrastructure. Uber represents more than just an app. It's more than an easy way to get back to your hotel after a late night at CES.

In fact, Uber represents a "transportation-as-a-service" trend, and it will eventually market and sell this service to its partners, just as Google, Microsoft, IBM, Oracle, SAP, and Adobe sell their "software-as-a-service" to companies and organizations all over the world. Uber will have consumer-facing products just like Google and Microsoft do for office documents and Intuit does for your taxes.

We know Uber represents a trend because it leverages our basic human needs and desires in a meaningful way and aligns our human nature with emerging technologies and breakthrough inventions. To boil that down to a cognitive shortcut would be impossible, but maybe that's a good thing. It reminds us to Kanizsize the facts rather than blindly accepting what we assume we're seeing.

Mapping the future is a process, and we can't stop once we think we've correctly identified a trend. After we've considered the modern sources of change, cast a wide enough net at the fringe to gather research, identified CIPHER pattern indicators, and connected the dots, we must complete step three and investigate what we think we know, since it's possible we've gotten distracted by shiny objects.

After poking holes in our own assessment of "Uber of X," we should feel confident now saying that it isn't a trend. Entrepreneurs hoping to emulate Uber's success may or may not weather this cycle of "Uber for X" buzz, but they most assuredly will fail if they distill Uber's complicated matrix of innovation down to a simple app and ride-sharing service.

However, I do acknowledge that there are events and variables that might catalyze further change. Kalanick could run away and join the circus. Uber's entire executive management team could simultaneously quit. Given what we know about Kalanick and his team, it's highly improbable that either event would happen. And yet, it isn't *impossible* for either event to happen, either. I believe that the year 2040 scenario I described is plausible, but that changes in technology may cause the rate of change in technology to accelerate.

The Uber that exists in the year 2040 will be the result of technological advances created in response to outside challenges—like not being available to pick up your kids after school or not having enough farmhands to harvest potatoes. But is the timing right? Where is Uber on that trajectory? How can we be sure it won't happen sooner?

CHAPTER SEVEN

Is It *Really* Awesome?

Know When the Timing Is Right

M Y PLAUSIBLE SCENARIO for Uber in 2040 would have the ride-sharing company building an expansive invisible infrastructure layer that provides transportation as a service. Fully automated vehicles—cars, forklifts, combines—take us where we need to go, make warehouses more efficient, and do the majority of the work on our farms.

My focus on 2040 was neither arbitrary nor the result of carefully working through any particular scenario first. Rather, I considered a number of factors, including the current state of the auto and ride-sharing markets, the accelerative nature of technology, the progress of certain proposed transportation regulations, and more in order to determine not just what the future might bring, but in what time frame. Notice that I also didn't say that Uber *definitely will* power our potato farms in the year 2040. This isn't me hedging my bets in case I'm wrong. (Though, to be fair, who likes being wrong?) Instead, I am acknowledging that certain events could influence both the trajectory of a trend and the speed with which certain milestones are achieved.

The year 2040 may seem like a very long way off, and in some ways, it is. If the car you use to get to work is falling apart and needs to be replaced, you shouldn't wait around for driverless Uber cars. On the other hand, if you're an early-stage investor, a government regulator, or an auto manufacturer, you need to judge where the trend is right now in order to take action. Even if the action you take is merely to actively monitor the trend as it moves forward.

This is the next step of our instructions. Trends are signposts to the future, and we now know what it takes to identify them correctly, but identifying a trend isn't the end game. We must also understand where a trend is along its development path. Recognizing a trend early enough affords tremendous competitive advantage. Think of how much further along Google is compared to its competitors—we now know that it enjoys an effective monopoly in search, of course, but also in space elevators, balloons that float in the stratosphere, self-driving cars, and the personal information layer. Google was early to recognize and act on trends. Google's former rival, Yahoo, had a ten-year head start and at one point far more capital, but it waited too long to act. Even if it had been granted unlimited resources in 2015, many would argue that was just too late for Yahoo to put up a respectable fight.

Yet jumping into a trend too early could have equally disastrous results. Think back to all the excitement about moving sidewalks after the 1900 Paris Exposition. What if you were an investor, and you'd sunk all your cash into this newfangled technology?

You need to not only follow the path of a trend, but evaluate how quickly it's evolving. That's tricky as well, since events will influence momentum. For example, the drive from Baltimore, Maryland, to Washington, DC, is about fifty miles. The average posted speed is fifty-five miles per hour, so the trip should take about an hour. But as every commuter knows, it could take as little as forty minutes for those with a heavy foot and no traffic, or as long as three hours (or more) when there is heavy traffic or an accident.

After visiting a friend in Baltimore, you begin that drive back down to DC. You enter your phone address into your car or phone GPS, which displays your estimated time of arrival. But keep in mind that travel time is subject to events, like a police officer pulling someone over or an improperly secured mattress suddenly flying off the back of a truck. Drivers slow down or slam on the brakes, causing a ripple effect, and your estimated travel time increases. If the traffic eases up, the road opens up, and your favorite song starts playing. You crank up the volume. It's a beautiful day, and you temporarily lose track of the speed limit—now your estimated travel time decreases. Along your journey home, you have accelerated, decelerated, and even stopped between events. That's why your GPS keeps changing its mind when it comes to your ETA. As you'll soon see, calculating the timing of a trend uses the same general principles. That's why tracking a trend's trajectory isn't as simple as anticipating when a new technology might reach critical mass in the marketplace. It isn't a linear process.

ESTIMATED TREND ARRIVAL

Determining whether something is a trend before you act on it is just as important as calculating where that trend is along its trajectory. But figuring out timing is a difficult task. Just as with your GPS, that initial estimated arrival time might stay constant, but the more challenging your route—the more stoplights, turns, and potholes—the more likely it is that the timing will fluctuate. The same is true of trends, where forward momentum changes in relation to a wide array of variables.

I've borrowed the math that a GPS uses to calculate a trend's estimated time of arrival, because it's a helpful representation of what's going on here:

$$\text{ETA} = (\text{distance} \div \text{speed}) \; +/- \; (\text{events along the route})$$

In my loose adaptation, "speed" and "distance" mark the advancement of a technology's development or the internal advancements of the primary driver of a trend. The evolution of a science or technology between two waypoints—moving from a simple hypothesis to the first round of testing, or from operational use to widespread production—might take more or less time depending on the stage of development. Distance ÷ speed is how we directly evaluate the movement of a technology trend.

But, as we know, independent variables can and do affect the speed with which a technology gains enough critical mass to influence business and how society operates. For that reason, we need to be on the lookout for adjacent events along the route. Some, such as the passage of new legislation, are more substantive than, say, a minor software glitch. Therefore, we know in advance that certain events will influence the momentum of a trend more significantly than others.

So for our purposes, I'll recast the equation like this:

Trend's timing = (internal tech developments, or I) +/− (external events, or E)

When I calculated plausible, far-future scenarios for Uber, as well as timing, I used that formula. What are all the advances Uber is making internally—and what external events might influence the company's growth and evolution? Here's what went into my calculation:

External events (E)—Adjacent developments and circumstances that will impact the trend's future, even if technology leaps forward. Often, these events are completely outside an organization's control.

For example, Uber's technology platform might be hampered by the US patent process. Another company might sue for infringement. Uber may face other lawsuits having to do with safety, or worker rights, or any number of other issues.

The government might establish a new federal agency to handle licensing and regulation for all autonomous vehicles (air, land, sea, and hybrids). That agency could create new policies and rules that would impact Uber's operations. For an autonomous fleet to be fully operational, the government will need to invest heavily in our highway infrastructure, and we will need new kinds of regulated indoor lanes as well. (Remember, autonomous vehicles would likely bring us directly into covered structures and buildings in order to drop us off.)

Components for driverless vehicles—sensors, microprocessors, and sonar, for example—will need to be widely available and affordable to make highway infrastructure upgrades and to allow companies to scale up their capacity for manufacturing driverless cars. Components such as these are designed and built in the United States, China, Korea, and Japan, so the strength of those economies are necessarily influencers, too.

There are additional social and cultural factors that come into play which have nothing to do with computer parts, highway infrastructure, and laws. For example, the failure or success of driving-related public health initiatives, such as those regarding texting while driving, will influence our attitudes about driverless cars. If the youngest Millennials and Generation Alphas increasingly rely on the present-day Uber car service to get around, they may not value driver's licenses in the future, which could increase social pressure for driverless cars.

Some of these external events, such as establishing and funding a new federal agency, or working through licensing and regulations, could hold up progress for several years. Both, however, are inevitable if the widespread adoption of autonomous vehicles is going to happen, at least in the United States. Meanwhile, other events—the availability of components, public attitudes toward autonomous vehicle accidents, and the like—also impact momentum, just not with as much weight.

Internal tech developments (I)—Technological advances specific to or directly impacted by a trend. These advances often happen within the organization, or as a result of a partnership between the organization and outside researchers.

When it comes to Uber, the list on internal tech developments is a long one. So I'll include just a few relevant examples:

- Development of semi-autonomous driving technology features to keep cars in lanes, slow vehicles down, assist with parking, and so on.

- Development of mobile monitoring technology, which transforms an Uber driver's mobile phone into a "black box" that collects data on speed, braking, routes, etc.

- Developing fluid "handoff" technology, in which the car's computer puts the driver back in control for designated situations.

- Development of cybersecurity measures to continually protect against hacking an autonomous vehicle's computer system.

- Development of highly detailed 3D maps for every drivable, flyable, or swimmable area . . .

And so on. Fully automated planting and harvesting equipment will require extremely complicated technology, so naturally there are thousands of R&D advancements and steps necessary in order to get us from Uber's current ride-sharing service to Uber-powered potato farms. Each one of those broad *I* waypoints include many smaller points underneath.

It's worth noting that internal and external events intersect and influence each other. Trade or other sanctions could force the price of semiconductors to increase, which might slow the pace of getting a test car into operational use. Or a significant development in automation—an autonomous car's computer system will soon be able to make a life-or-death decision—could catalyze new government regulations and therefore slow down testing. This is a real concern. Autonomous vehicles must be programmed to make a decision when avoiding an accident: if swerving to the right means hitting a single person, swerving to the left means hitting a dozen people, and stopping short means impacting the passengers, how will the car decide what to do? The car's programming will have to determine which group to injure or kill and which to spare.

When it comes to emerging technology, most of the internal waypoints—all the little software, systems, and platform waypoints—are invisible to us. That's because most of us want to see radical change before we'll accept that it's taking place.[1] The heads of corporations, organizations, and governments too often remain skeptical about technology until they've had direct experience with it. So we had bioethicists and government officials who were shocked when Dolly the sheep was cloned, and when CRISPR/Cas9 successfully edited out the gene carrying malaria from a mosquito's DNA. That's why Sony executives ignored the copious warnings for nearly a decade before that game-changing hack in 2014. It's why the stadium cheered when that young paraplegic man outfitted with a brain-controlled exoskeleton kicked a soccer ball at the World Cup—but why that same crowd wasn't also talking about the ramifications of direct brain-to-brain communication. They can't believe it until they see it.

External events—the obvious things, like lawsuits and rules—are easy to see, even if you're not working in the industry. That's because news organizations write stories about them, and commentators discuss the pros and cons on talk shows. One external event you can count on: I am certain there will eventually be a new federal agency to address autonomous vehicles—for our purposes, I'll call it the Federal Autonomous Vehicle Agency (FAVA)—and it will be charged with working alongside the twelve existing agencies concerned with transportation, from highways to aviation. When it's announced, FAVA will garner major news headlines. The establishment of a new government agency is an external event we can wrap our heads around. Society will understand how to think about it and which questions to ask, the majority of which will be drawn from our Kanizsa Pac-Men—the explicit details that we can see and that are familiar to us—rather than the triangle—which we can only see when zooming out to take in a shape that would otherwise be invisible. Who will run FAVA? Is the proposed director qualified? How much will our taxes be raised to pay for it? What kind of enforcement will the agency actually have? What do the commercial service providers have to say? Will this raise the cost of my own travel?

Internal waypoints are visible, but only when you are intentionally tracking them. Compared to the establishment of a new federal agency, waypoints are boring, or involve technical language. Unless you were watching Uber's product development, you probably missed an app update in early February 2016 that made it easier for the company to track driver performance, compare drivers, and view rider complaints. This was an important movement between waypoints, since it laid the technical groundwork for mobile monitoring, which will inform the R&D going into driverless cars. While this update was being applied, Uber also announced a new logo and new branding. Which do you think received a 3,000-word story in *Wired* magazine?[2]

If we can't see or even visualize a trend as it is emerging, we subjugate it to the distant future and assume that we can have no bearing on it today. This is why you see so many *predictions*, where experts in various subject areas guesstimate when a particular tech innovation will arrive. We assign a timeline that sounds far-off (twenty-five years from now, fifty years from now), and then we essentially allow ourselves to stop tracking it. This is especially true of trends that are still emerging from the fringe, such as a Brainet connecting a cardiologist, a vascular expert, and a roboticist with cardiac and thoracic surgeons for a complex operation.

In order to calculate where a trend is on its trajectory, we have to resolve our own belief biases and fight against our desire to confirm the existence of a future scenario before we believe in its plausibility. We have to calculate a trend's ETA—its *I* with *E*.

A GPS FOR TRENDS

Just like we can't drive a car between DC and Baltimore as the crow flies, a trend can't move forward in a singular, unwavering direction. There are too many internal waypoints and external events influencing how the trend evolves, as shown in Figure 1 on page 204.

Forecasters often use an S-curve to describe a trend's timing. A technology's movement between waypoints emerges slowly and incrementally from the distant fringe, becomes operational, and finally enters the mainstream. For example, if we were to look backward, given what we know now, we could track the advent and popularity of smartphones. While there are numerous variations, most forecasters tend to use the same basic structure, as shown in Figure 2 on page 205.

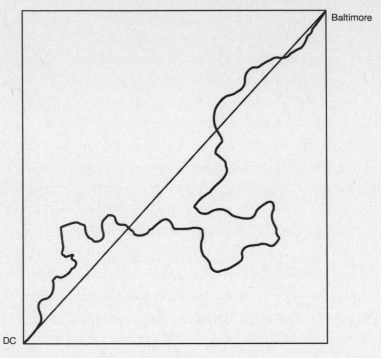

Figure 1

Back when I lived in Japan, smartphones were just experimental prototypes starting to emerge from the fringe. More time was devoted to tinkering and pushing the boundaries of what mobile phones could do, which meant focusing on rapid prototyping and new research. The internet expanded. New digital maps were made portable. Screens were suddenly in color, and cameras became smaller. New operators were promising free email. At the time, these were all new ideas and technologies from the fringe, and they began to surface as patterns within CIPHER and converge as a unifying trend: portable phones that could do more than simply place a call.

First movers got excited and bought early versions of the new devices, which caused manufacturers and third-party companies to increase the phones' functionality. The curve began to spike upward; with momentum building, a tipping point was reached, and the trend—smartphones—plateaued as it moved into mainstream use.

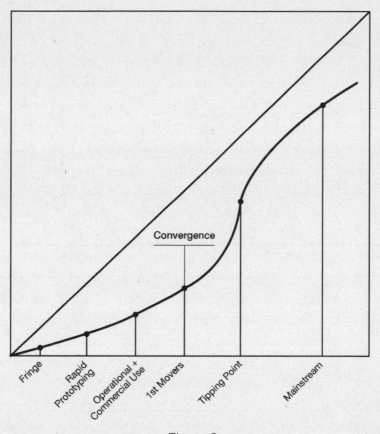

Figure 2

S-curves are helpful retrospective visualizations—but they aren't as effective in real time. An S-curve helps us understand the adoption of a new technology like the smartphone, but it doesn't allow us to visualize *events along the route*, since those events are independent variables, and they don't necessarily build upon each other in the same way that technology advances do.

Instead, we need to think in terms of roadblocks and express lanes. The more significant the event, the bigger the block, and the more time it will take to drive around it. Prototypes for smartphones have been around since the mid-1970s, and not just in Japan. Why did it take two more decades for smartphones to move out of the labs and into the global consumer marketplace? The technology worked, but the mobile internet had been a commercial flop—it was an external event that slowed down consumer awareness and adoption. The Wireless Application Protocol (WAP) that was supposed to have ushered in a new era of portable connectivity throughout Europe and the United States didn't take off, in large part because of clunky infrastructure and a lack of capital in the amounts needed to build up the networks.

Conversely, smartphones proliferated in Japan because NTT Do-CoMo, a spinoff of Nippon Telegraph and Telephone (NTT), had developed a different kind of network and standard, called "i-mode." In Japanese, *dokomo* means "everywhere," and the company made good on its promise: the service was available everywhere, it was fast, and within eighteen months, one-fifth of Japan's population converted to the service, becoming i-mode subscribers.[3] In Figure 3, you'll see various events—accelerations (shorter lines) and decelerations (longer lines), that had to do with external forces—on the top of the chart.

While many organizations monitor either the first or second parts of the ETA equation, they don't often look at the two together. That was certainly the case a few years ago with a flashy new startup and a charismatic founder so compelling that many big organizers shut off the GPS entirely and went for a joyride.

CHECKING IN

At the 2011 South by Southwest (SXSW) conference, thousands of people crammed into the Austin Convention Center on March 12, quickly flashing the badges hanging around their necks to security guards. Veterans knew to get there early if they wanted a seat. Soon, a twenty-two-year-old Princeton dropout would take center stage to recreate some of the magic they'd seen in his TED talk and at other tech-industry conferences.

The lights dimmed and Hugh Forrest, the venerated SXSW director, took the stage to introduce the festival's first keynote speaker. "Seth is

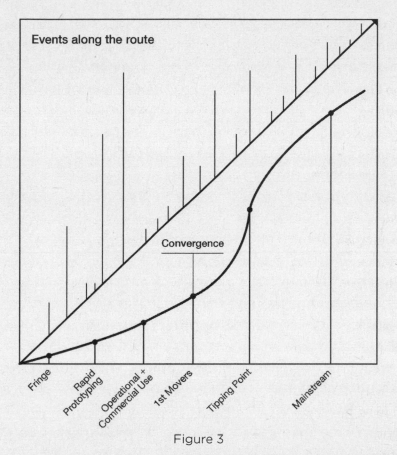

Figure 3

very, very young. He's very, very creative. And he is full of passion and energy for what he does," Forrest said over enthusiastic applause. "He raised his first million in venture funding before he was 20. Please join me in welcoming Seth Priebatsch, founder and CEO of SCVNGR!"

Suddenly there he was, wearing his trademark bright orange polo shirt, baggy jeans, and a pair of neon orange sunglasses atop his head. With everyone still clapping, the founder of SCVNGR (pronounced "scavenger") jogged out to greet Forrest, squinted at the audience, and began to speak.

"I'm Seth Priebatsch and I'm the chief ninja of SCVNGR!" he shouted. "I'm here to tell you about the game layer on top of the world and why it's awesome!"

What was a "game layer"? Why was it awesome? Was it a tech trend? Was it an event along the road leading to something else? At that time, no one really knew—but it didn't seem to matter. SCVNGR had launched amid a torrent of buzz, joining an already-competitive field of similar social networks that rewarded users for sharing their locations in the physical world. They could "check in" to a restaurant, classroom, or even a conference venue and earn virtual merit badges that displayed cheeky messages.

Initially, location-based networks like SCVNGR, and its competitors Foursquare and Gowalla, solved a critical problem for early adopters: the networks made it much easier to find other people at tech conferences, where the best parties happened in private rooms and bars. Simply open the map, locate yourself on it, and announce that you've arrived. These early networks were like a GPS for friends.

Checking in to the networks also meant bragging rights. You'd earn virtual merit badges, which were only awarded for certain activities (like checking in to an exclusive SXSW panel, or checking in to a bar at 3 a.m. with three friends of the opposite sex). That virtual merit badge could be seen and shared throughout the networks as well as on Twitter and Facebook. Location-based networks took advantage of a basic human emotion, one that became a hashtag meme as a result: #FOMO, the Fear Of Missing Out.

Soon after those first movers, the general public caught on and began using the networks. It appeared as though location-based networks were a tech trend rapidly ascending the S-curve toward the tipping point and about to enter widespread adoption throughout mainstream society.

Again and again, journalists and tech bloggers proclaimed "location-based networks" as a new trend, one that threatened to completely supplant pure social networks like Facebook and Twitter. TechCrunch wildly speculated that SCVNGR may have achieved a $100 million valuation just a few months after launch.[4] CNN devoted a long biographical feature story to Priebatsch's young life, calling him "the modern tech CEO."[5] Media reports cited early adopters who were eager to share where they'd visited, who they were with, and what they were doing. (To be candid, many early adopters were actually the bloggers and journalists using the services.)

Thousands of companies, nonprofits, universities, advertising agencies, and even government agencies hopped onto the location-based networks bandwagon, spending time and money to take advantage of what seemed like an exciting new trend. Many of them devoted significant time and money to creating location-based marketing strategies. Several early movers partnered with SCVNGR.

Location-based networks were certainly trendy. But what was their ETA? What were the external events and internal waypoints worth noting?

Sometimes, a technology hasn't fully formed at the point of convergence, as we've seen several times. Samsung and Sony both released a wearable watch-phone hybrid device years before the Pebble Watch became one of the most funded startups on Kickstarter. Two decades before it launched the Wii, Nintendo debuted the Power Glove,[6] a game controller powered by motion control. In both cases, the technology was still being developed and improved. Rather than heading toward the tipping point, occasionally a trend is instead dipping back along the S-curve toward a second convergence. That's exactly what was happening during that SXSW speech in 2011, as Figure 4 on page 210 depicts.

At the same time, there were a number of *events* which stood to impact the sustainability of a location-based networking trend. Just as Priebatsch had proclaimed, SCVNGR, Foursquare, and Gowalla had indeed built a game layer for our everyday activities, and for a time it really was awesome. A trip to the grocery store could turn into a competition between family members—additional check-ins yielded more points and the potential for more badges. On one of the networks, whoever checked in the most to a particular venue was crowned—quite literally, with a virtual gold crown avatar—as the mayor.

But was this a game we'd play indefinitely? Businesses glimpsed the future of location-based marketing using a customer's personal data.

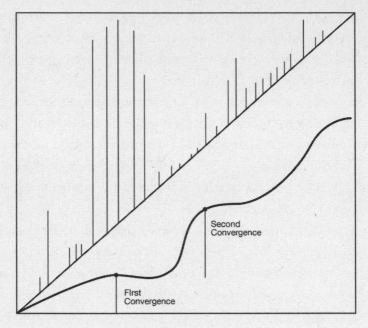

Figure 4

Political campaigns, television shows, and conferences learned that co-alescing an audience around a shared experience increased engagement and a sense of brand affinity. Consumers started worrying about the data that these apps were collecting. You may remember some of the ensuing backlash and fears about privacy. Countless news and morning talk shows aired segments about enterprising thieves prowling users' accounts to see who was out of town on vacation.

Beyond badges, there weren't other incentives sustaining these net-works. Universities and other organizations, which had been paying top dollar to build out custom integrations, ended their contracts.

There was no as-the-crow-flies path between Priebatsch's original idea at the fringe and a global, location-based-service app so valuable to us that we would need to use it every day. Stop and think for a moment: Does SCVNGR pass the toothbrush test for you?

There were elements of SCVNGR, Gowalla, and Foursquare that informed later technologies, but it should have been clear that the location-based services trend was still evolving. And yet, in a very short period of time, Foursquare had secured a $760 million valuation (that's three-quarters of a unicorn!) and had raised more than $162 million in financing.[7] SCVNGR came in lower, raising a total of $41 million on a $172 million valuation.[8] Financing came from Morgan Stanley, Greylock Partners, Google Ventures, Andreessen Horowitz, O'Reilly AlphaTech Ventures, Union Square Ventures, and others.

SCVNGR, Foursquare, and Gowalla were on to something early—location-based services. It was clear that limited utility would curb our appetite for stand-alone apps; however, those apps had created tremendous excitement among developers and researchers. So other developers started barreling ahead with the technology, even if for the time being users had lost interest.

With ever more smartphones entering the market, developers started using that same location-based technology as part of other experiments and prototypes. Soon, a few emerging startups were combining the personal information layer trend with location-based networks to create apps that automatically tracked friends or family members for you in real time, whether they were driving home from work or ambling around a farmers' market. Now there was a practical benefit—not just a virtual badge—for location sharing outside of conferences and events. Rather than sharing a location with everyone, a user could instead share her estimated time of arrival or where she was sitting in a big conference room with only a designated coworker or group of friends.

Step four of our forecasting methodology informs us that failing to keep watch on a trend, or assuming that it will travel along a straight path at a set speed, is a mistake that is often made by forecasters and the businesses who rely on trends research. The businesses, universities, and government agencies that acted too quickly on location-based networks discovered what happens when you get the timing wrong.

By the following year, Gowalla had evaporated.[9] Foursquare pivoted into a location-based recommendation service. At the beginning of 2016, Foursquare quietly went through what's called a "down round" of financing, where a startup raises a round of money at a lower valuation than its previous one. Its founder had stepped down to make way for a new CEO, and it was announced that the company would focus on data.[10]

As for SCVNGR? The company never publicly said that it folded, but it stopped updating its app and took its website offline a year and a half after Priebatsch, SCVNGR's "chief ninja," took the stage at SXSW.

Ironically, the word "ninja" comes from the Chinese and in sixteenth-century Japan meant "one who endures."[11] Unlike the samurai, who wore extremely colorful clothing and were all about public display, the Ninja were understated, reserved, and hidden. They were spies—cleverly and secretively gathering information to protect their communities against invading warlords. Originally, their sole purpose was to figure out timing. Attack too soon, and they would reveal their position to the enemy, or miss additional soldiers. Wait too long, and their village would be decimated. Perched along rooftops high above the ground, they watched, listened, and calculated the right time to strike.

CHAPTER EIGHT

If This, Then That

A Formula for Action

HOW TO SURFACE present-day data to understand and map the future has been our focus until this point. New technology is being imagined, created, and iterated at the fringe. We recognize patterns within the fringe to identify a trend, and then investigate what we've discovered to ensure that our assumptions are accurate. That trend is in continual motion, so we calculate its estimated time of arrival to understand the influences—both those within the company and the external ones—shaping its trajectory. At this point in our process, we should have enough information to understand what is happening. But we do not yet know yet what to do about the trend, how to make use of it, and how to prepare for the future.

Amazon's founder, Jeff Bezos, has said that when mapping the future, leaders must "be stubborn on vision but flexible on details."[1] You may have correctly forecast a new trend and set a course of action; now, you must explore the particulars of that course, looking for possible roadblocks. You might be inclined, as many often are, to stop now and skip ahead to making a strategic decision. If you proceed now, you may discover that while the trend is accurate and the timing is right, you've still made a mistake. It's the future-fallacy trap: when your inflexibility on details causes mistakes in your planning for the future.

Nearly a decade ago, as smartphones were emerging from the fringe, a big news corporation I worked with fell into the future-fallacy trap. The company's executives agreed that smartphones would play a major role in how people got their news, and we developed a big-picture mobile forecast for them. However, when the company's team got to work on executing the strategy, its members made inaccurate assumptions on one important detail, and they didn't course correct when they should have. That inflexibility led to download targets being missed, and ultimately, some very unhappy executives. Here's what happened:

My team advised the news organization's leadership that consumers would soon use smartphones as their primary devices for reading news. In 2007, Amazon's Kindle and the first-generation iPhone were preparing for launch. The company's managers were watching both closely, and together we cast a wide enough net at the fringe, asking how mobile screens would evolve, whether phones would get larger or smaller, how consumers would subscribe to content, and if consumer behavior would change—so that, for example, people would start watching TV and their mobile phones concurrently.

At that point, all of the news company's competitors thought that big websites—certainly not apps, and definitely not on phones—would be the future. It was, however, becoming clear that the news organization's audience, as well as the audiences of its competitors, would migrate to phones and tablets. Meantime, advertisers would shift away from print to mobile advertising. The company had become one of the largest and most profitable news organizations in the world precisely because of its traditional business model. This emerging smartphone trend, even though it was a few years away, threatened to upend the news business entirely.

That consumers might prefer shorter stories on their smartphones that consisted mostly of text was a rather shocking revelation at the time. Photo galleries and big, interactive features were popular on the web, and it was relatively easy to repurpose print content for digital stories. On the web, consumers had full-sized screens and the ability to scroll, click through elements, and immerse themselves in a story. But on a phone? Back then, the BlackBerry still dominated the smartphone market, and it didn't display news stories very well.

It became clear that the best way to move the trend into action was to build a new kind of mobile app unlike any that anyone had seen. The news organization's executives agreed with our forecast that smartphones would soon become the primary device for their readers, and they were stubborn on that vision of the future. With our forecast in hand, the strategy and details just needed to be worked out by the organization's team.

Their digital staff decided that they should build an iPhone app and hired a development firm to begin work. During initial testing, some junior staff members raised a question that concerned them: What mobile platform would the news organization's audience be using by the time the app was ready to launch? Historically, their entire mobile audience had used BlackBerrys, which had either been given to them through work or they'd purchased personally via two-year contracts. Sure, the future of news was mobile, the staffers agreed—but in the short term, *which* mobile?

The team could have pushed forward, carrying out the leadership's vision for mobile news while recalibrating the details. It could have built a version of the app for the BlackBerry, which would get used by its wider audience, and treated the iPhone app as a first-generation experiment that they could make more robust as more people bought Apple's phones. Instead, the team put all of its eggs into the iPhone basket.

The resulting app was a gorgeous representation of the news brand. There were articles and photos, and readers could easily share their favorite content with friends. It didn't require a subscription or sign-in, and the user interface was easy for anyone to use.

But after several months, the iPhone app was missing download and use targets by a wide margin. The question the junior staffers had mentioned early on in the development process turned out to be a valid concern. The team had created a groundbreaking digital experience for its customers, and at that time, its customers were all loyal BlackBerry users. The relatively new iPhone had captured the zeitgeist, but most people were already locked in to their two-year contracts with mobile carriers.

The future-fallacy trap happens in every organization, and quite often within those that are pushing the boundaries of innovation. When a decision is made to act on an important trend, details must be considered before putting a trend into action.

Developing a business strategy is complicated enough, but when it involves a new technology trend, something we know involves complicated concepts and sometimes an entirely new lexicon, it can be difficult to manage all of those disparate elements. Or even to identify them.

How can we transition from identifying all the elements of a technology trend to taking the right kind of action? There is a better approach, and it involves telling a good story, the fifth step of our forecasting process.

Data is a critically important part of any story, but it should be contextualized before any decisions are made. Data alone can lead us to creating strategies that might work—or that could be catastrophic. Data without details won't satiate our instinctive need for a narrative, and as a result we'll have a difficult time analyzing impact in advance.

DETAILS, NOT JUST DATA

People are instinctive storytellers. Our ancestors, according to evolutionary psychologists, preferred descriptive storytelling over facts. Thousands of years ago, if you had heard that "behind that rock over there is a four-legged animal," your curiosity might have enticed you to go have a look. However, if you were told instead that "my sister was mauled and shredded alive by a giant saber-toothed wombat, which is standing behind that rock over there," you'd hide and immediately look for some kind of protection.

In their 1944 study at Smith College, psychologists Fritz Heider and Marianne Simmel asked thirty-four college students to watch a short film showing two black triangles and a black circle moving in and out of a rectangle. When asked to describe what they saw, all but one student described a bully triangle chasing around a little "worried" circle and a "little triangle," which was just an "innocent young thing."[2] The video itself is mesmerizing[3]—it's impossible not to interpret the bigger triangle, which only moves in the direction of one of its points, as an angry, rage-filled intimidator. I've watched the video dozens of times myself, and when I talk about it, I reflexively describe a helpless triangle trying to get away from a bully.

Storytelling is hardwired into human existence, as we can see from narratives about dreadful futures published centuries apart. In 1550, Michel de Nostredame—you know him by the Latin name he adopted, Nostradamus—published his first set of his many predictions.[4] His popularity grew because he told terrifically entertaining, vague stories (mostly dreadful) mirroring the epic narrative of humanity. He wrote of uprisings and invasions, the rise of powerful dictators and the development of dangerous weapons:

> *Near the gates and within two cities*
> *There will be scourges the like of which was never seen,*
> *Famine within plague, people put out by steel,*
> *Crying to the great immortal God for relief.*[5]

Nostradamus enthusiasts argue that this passage from his *Prophecies* predicted the United States dropping two atomic bombs on Hiroshima and Nagasaki during World War II. You could also argue that this passage applies to the war between the Qing dynasty and the Ming dynasty, which decimated 25 million Chinese between 1616 and 1662. There were epic floods, rebellions, economic chaos, and multiple famines, and a once powerful Chinese emperor committed suicide.

Nostradamus wasn't a prophet—he was a gifted storyteller. And while I wouldn't take his forecasting advice on Uber, there's a lesson to be learned in how he described the future.

A latter-day Nostradamus was Herman Kahn, a physicist at the RAND Corporation who was asked in the 1950s to help military planners answer questions no one wanted to think about, such as, "What happens if the Soviets strike New York City with a thermonuclear weapon? How could New York City be evacuated safely and on short notice?" Data and facts alone weren't going to provide the context or thought leadership needed.

Using US Air Force intelligence—warfare technology trends, along with many other data points—Kahn put his team to work creating narratives. They were fictional stories rooted in the "if this, then that" formula intended to be read as though they were reports prepared by people from the future. But Kahn had a problem. He didn't want the military to either discount his work as science fiction or take it too seriously, and think that the narrative illustrations were meant to be interpreted as facts, because none of the stories were definitive outcomes. He needed a new word to describe what his team was writing.

Kahn explained the predicament to his friend Leo Rosten, a writer and humorist who happened to be working in Hollywood, and Rosten suggested that Kahn steal a term from the movies—"scenario"—which at the time referred to what we now call a "screenplay." "We deliberately chose the word [scenario] to deglamorize the concept," Kahn later said. "In writing the scenarios for various situations we kept saying 'Remember, it's only a scenario,' the kind of thing that is produced by Hollywood writers." Kahn defined scenarios as "attempts to describe in some detail a hypothetical sequence of events that could lead plausibly to the situation envisaged."[6]

The point of Kahn's scenarios was to fill in that necessary descriptive detail, the imagery and narration needed to give those who were charged with creating strategy more than just data points to consider. Scenarios proved to be an incredibly powerful tool.

Kahn went on to give a series of public lectures about his work, which were collected, rewritten, and published as a hefty, 651-page book called *On Thermonuclear War*. He used the same scenario technique in the book in order to "think the unthinkable."[7]

Nothing like it had been published before, and it enraged everyone, even if for very different reasons. Kahn had thought the unthinkable—we were to accept thermonuclear war as a foregone conclusion, and to live as though radiation fallout was no more unusual than smog—and published it. Some protested the book, arguing that Kahn had effectively published a how-to guide to destroy the United States. Others read it and demanded that doctrine be changed to something less drastic. But everyone agreed on one thing: Kahn's vivid scenarios couldn't be ignored. Those within government were forced to consider broader impacts—not just the geopolitical outcomes—of President Dwight D. Eisenhower's "New Look" theory, which put nuclear strategies first in the nation's national security policy.

Scenarios are still used today, for the same reasons that Kahn introduced them to RAND, Nostradamus employed them in his writings, and our primeval ancestors carved them onto clay pots: because they help us understand the meaning of facts. "If this, then that" thinking allows us to interpret how trends, and in our case, emerging technologies, will impact an organization, an industry, and even our entire society.

The logical next step after determining where a trend is on its trajectory is to follow with an "if this, then that" statement. Step five of our forecasting method is to use Kahn's technique of storytelling and put the facts into a narrative context to develop possible scenarios for the future. Our goal isn't to predict something that will definitely happen. Instead, we must envision all of the possible outcomes and use them to help us make an informed decision about strategy to employ in the present.

GOOD STORIES REQUIRE FORMULAS

"Formulaic" can be a nasty word, especially when it's used by reviewers to deride a film for its lack of originality. *Variety* called *42*, the movie about Jackie Robinson, "a relentlessly formulaic biopic."[8] The *Charlotte Observer* chided the "formulaic storyline" in Hugh Jackman's *Eddie the Eagle*,[9] a movie the *Seattle Times* also called "formulaic and overstuffed."[10] *The New Yorker* couldn't stand the "formulaic romantic comedy" *27 Dresses* starring Katherine Heigl.[11] And yet every one of the top-grossing films of 2015 followed formulas with which we are all familiar: a new Jedi went on a quest, met up with some bad guys, bested her foe, and learned something important along the way. An astronaut went to a strange land—Mars—overcame great danger, and returned home changed by the experience. A poor, forgotten girl forced to clean up after her stepsisters finds new power, temporarily loses it, and gains it all back (along with Prince Charming) at the end.[12]

The details that underline the case you want to make may be complex, but if you want attention paid to your story, it must be easy to follow. Our human biology limits us to noticing, interpreting, and understanding the vast amount of data that surrounds us. Formulas help us to parse those details into a structure—a story—that enables us to comprehend all that data with less effort. Social anthropologist Sir James George Frazer, Shakespearean scholar A. C. Bradley, psychiatrists Carl Jung and Sigmund Freud, mythologist Joseph Campbell, writer Christopher Booker, psychologist Bruno Bettelheim, and a host of other thinkers all believed that there are really only seven basic plots for storytelling: they represented the comedy, the tragedy, the rags-to-riches story, the quest, the voyage, the return, and stories of humans versus humans, monsters, nature, or society. Throughout our history, every story we've ever told—which includes scenarios about the future—fits into one of those categories.

Taxonomy aside, it turns out that our human attention spans have a unique rhythm that further necessitates the need for an if/then formula. Professor of psychology James Cutting and his team of researchers at Cornell University investigated how well humans were able to pay attention to the top-grossing movies made between 1935 and 2005. They discovered that the composition of certain scenes and the length of shots followed a mathematical pattern that mirrored human attention spans. When they translated attention measurements into wave forms using a mathematical function called the Fourier transform, they saw an interesting pattern, one representing human attention rhythms: the waves increased in magnitude as their frequencies decreased. We're paying attention when that pattern is present, and the storylines of the films that were most successful followed this pattern identically. In fact, the *Star Wars* franchise follows the pattern without deviation.[13]

In order to extract signals and meaning out of the trends so that we can take informed action on the future, a formula is necessary. The goal is to write a scenario that includes enough detail and description to help build the right strategy. In our case, a scenario should follow an if/then pattern:

IF [Facts, Perspectives, Framing] . . . THEN [Outcomes]

Let's start with a very familiar trend as an example: automation in banking. Various technologies—from automated systems to optical character recognition to biometric security systems like face and iris scanners—will soon significantly decrease the need for human employees by up to 30 percent. Much of the transactional work employees now perform can be done more efficiently and reliably by machines. So what does that mean?

Data and research would show the *fact* of financial technology forcing traditional banking to a tipping point to be the case. For example, in his 2015 annual letter to shareholders, JPMorgan Chase CEO Jamie Dimon said, "There are hundreds of startups with a lot of brains and money working on various alternatives to traditional banking."[14] Around 30 percent of bank jobs could be eliminated between 2015 and 2025 as a result of automation, making it attractive to invest in new platforms, apps, websites, computers, and technical equipment. The investment in emerging financial technologies jumped from $1.8 billion in 2010 to $19 billion in 2015, 70 percent of which focused on the what's known as the "last mile" of the user experience (interfacing with mobile screens, ATMs, and websites) in the consumer space.[15]

External events completely outside an organization's control—the adjacent developments and circumstances—also impact a trend's future, especially as a technology leaps forward. In banking, it is currency itself that is changing. Bitcoin, a digital currency that promises complete anonymity, uses a crowd-regulated public ledger system called a "block chain," a transaction database that removes the need for intermediaries such as bank tellers or customer service people.

In addition, biometric security devices are being developed for use in circumstances when it makes sense to track the location of people. In banking, these devices will be used to secure transactions that previously required a bank employee, who would have checked a customer's identification and signature.

What about the internal tech developments—the technological advances specific to or directly impacted by a trend, which happen within an organization or as a result of a partnership between an organization and outside researchers? Optical character recognition (OCR) was invented in the 1970s to help the blind. A computer scanned in and read aloud text, even if it was handwritten. In the 2000s, OCR was further improved and made available as an online service. One of the most popular applications of OCR includes automated data entry from business documents, such as checks. Many banks now allow customers to deposit a check by snapping a photo of it with a mobile phone camera. Advancements in OCR, combined with stronger encryption, will make it easier for consumers to process payments this way—without ever having to talk to a bank employee.

•

Once we have the facts and understand the related developments of external and internal technology, we then need to consider *perspectives* from all the possible players—the "characters" for our story—involved within the network: *Who are they? Why do they matter?*

We can return to a modified version of the fringe sketch from Chapter 4 to work out all the possible nodes (the characters) and connectors (the relationships they have to each other), thinking through the following seven questions:

1. *What are the possible converging trends associated with this technology trend? Who's involved?* Automation in banking involves a number of other players: venture capitalists and investment banks funding financial technology startups; technologists working in fields of recognition (OCR, biometric); those working on blockchain applications; people mining bitcoins.

2. *What is the impact to various people and organizations if this trend succeeds or fails?* With a potential 30 percent reduction in the banking workforce, there will be many skilled workers out of a job; associations will see their memberships drop (the American Association of Bank Directors, the Consumer Bankers Association, the American Bankers Association). Specialized IT firms will be required to monitor, maintain, and service the computers needed to run financial technology platforms, apps, and services.

3. *How does this trend impact one particular industry, company, or government and all of its parts? Who are the players?* As just one example, automation in banking will reduce the need to write physical checks, so dozens of adjacent organizations will be affected, too, like those companies that manufacture the specialty paper required for bank checks, the printing companies contracted by banks to personalize and produce the checks, and the delivery services (US Postal Service, FedEx) contracted to deliver the checks.

4. *Which people and organizations are the drivers of change?* These will include company leaders who need to reduce operating costs and deliver better profits; organizations curating the entrant pool for startup contests and accelerators; early-stage angel investors and venture capitalists; business school students who are interested in technology; and companies working in encryption and security for banks.

5. *Which groups of people—customers, constituents, civilians—does the trend address?* The automation of banks positively affects younger consumers, who are accustomed to making payments digitally; newer businesses, which don't have the time or staff to visit bank branches for various services and transactions; and offshore call centers, which will be increasingly used to process customer service requests. It negatively affects many other groups, including older bank customers, who visit their local branches to make transactions; local businesses, which have built relationships with their local tellers and customer service representatives; and local organizations that are sponsored by local bank branch offices, such as Little League teams.

6. *How are competitors harnessing the trend (or failing to do so)? How are similar but noncompeting organizations using it?* Banks have started to invest in automation technologies, whether that's a blockchain system, OCR applications, or biometric scanners. Some of the same automation tools are being studied by other industries in cases where intermediaries are required for transactions, such as in mortgage lending.

7. *Where does the trend create new partnerships or collaborators between different industries, companies, governments, or other groups?* For banks, automation creates myriad new partnership and collaboration opportunities: for example, with financial technology accelerators, where startups compete for prizes for their innovations; research universities, where advanced biometric tools are being developed; and those companies working on the bleeding edge of encryption and security.

Since people make decisions about the future of technology, we need a framing of human emotion: what we want to happen, what we feel strongly can't or won't happen, and what we fear might actually come to fruition.

Given the various facts we know to be true, in this case as they relate to automation in banking, and the perspectives that the key people and organizations have about those facts, we can create at least four possible stories—optimistic, pragmatic, pessimistic, and catastrophic—to help us understand the implications of our actions, as shown in Table 1. We might also find that we can create more than one scenario for each feeling, depending on the facts and perspectives we've surfaced.

The first part of our if/then formula—IF [Facts, Perspectives, Framing]—helps us to expand our understanding of a trend. But how do these stories apply to real-life banks and customers? What strategy makes the most sense? How can we avoid making mistakes (like building a cutting-edge mobile app on the wrong platform)? That's where the second half of the if/then formula—THEN [Outcomes]—comes in.

At the very beginning of this book, as I speculated about whether cars might someday fly, I introduced three labels to describe future scenarios: probable, plausible, and possible. *Probable* futures assume that, barring a wild-card event (such as an unpredictable natural disaster), a current trend is likely to continue without much change. Probable scenarios tend to describe what might happen within a very short time frame. It is unlikely that our banks will abandon their legacy systems, fire half their employees, and adopt blockchain ledgers overnight. However, they will begin to make the partnerships, invest in the research and systems, and begin to test new platforms within the next year or two. They will also create longer-term strategic plans that will call for a reduction in staff. This is a probable scenario that we can count on.

Plausible futures factor in our current understanding of a trend; the laws of nature, physics, and mathematics; and the current systems, workflows, and processes that govern research, business, government, and society—essentially, the concepts and rules operating within the ten sources of change. If we assume that there will be no major shift in what we know about the laws of the universe, and that how we work and live will not be significantly altered in any way, then we can extrapolate

Table 1: Automation in Banking: Four Scenarios

Feeling...	because the technology...	and so the future...
Optimistic	... will be further developed without much friction.	... will be better than the past. Just think of how ATMs were once a revelation, making our lives easier, since we no longer had to wait in long bank lines to deposit or withdraw cash. Widespread automation in banking will afford businesses and individuals unimagined efficiencies and will make our transactions faster and safer then we ever thought possible.
Pragmatic	... will necessarily continue along without much change.	... will look much like it does today. Our ATMs will perform a few more tasks, and we'll have greater access to online banking services. The development of automated banking technologies will continue without impacting our society, economy, or government in any meaningful way.
Pessimistic	... cannot or will not improve beyond where it is right now.	... will be worse than in the past. Automated banking technologies are necessary for the advancement of banking in general, as well as our economy and society. However, those charged with funding, researching, or implementing automated technologies will not be motivated or allowed to pursue it. More emphasis will be placed on physical bank branches; however, it will be too expensive to fully staff all branches back to their pre-automation levels. Bank lines will become excruciatingly long, and customer service will be abysmal. Longtime customers will leave for alternate banks.
Catastrophic	... will cause a disaster.	... will be catastrophic. Advancements in automated banking technology and emerging financial technology will cause something terrible to happen: unsecured platforms will be hacked, records will be erased, and all the banks will collapse. Overnight, money will disappear, the economy will tank, and hundreds of millions of people will participate in uprisings against the government. Political unrest will follow, as will the deterioration of our physical surroundings. The nation will erupt into civil war.

from what we're seeing on the fringe. If a new technology doesn't invalidate the rules we currently know to be true, then we can write a plausible scenario, typically about the near future. Banks process transactions that will ultimately be completed entirely by machines, not people. Brick-and-mortar banks will all but disappear. Rather than being carried out with debit cards and account numbers, transactions will be processed in myriad ways. Consumers will access their encrypted bank accounts in the cloud, to which our bodies and devices will be linked. A camera will scan the unique characteristics of our eyes (tear film, iris, curvature) to authenticate us, and we'll use a gesture to make a payment. Smart analytic systems will monitor our accounts and ensure that we never accidentally overdraw or miss a bill payment again.

Once we unhinge ourselves from the laws of nature as we understand them today (as well as the rules by which society operates), we can dream up *possible* future scenarios. Remember, not too many years ago, people would have thought that reading a book on a paper-thin screen covering a device that is, in effect, a portable library very strange indeed.

In possible scenarios, we break all the rules and consider technology within the realm of what we can imagine might happen in the farther future. Banks as we know them today will no longer exist. Neither will today's system of physical currency. Money will be accounted for digitally, and quantum computers will manage our individual financial transactions in order to ensure both security and accuracy. We will be able to pre-program payments and purchases. It will be much more difficult to hide money or obscure payments via legal loopholes—in the farther future, doing such things will require a significant amount of technical know-how.

But the purpose of writing scenarios isn't to create a set of provocative stories for weekend reading. Instead, taken together, they form a powerful tool to assist those in charge of making decisions. Inevitably, they will ask: Which one of these scenarios do you really think will happen? How confident are you in that scenario? How much confidence do you have in the information you're presenting me with?

ALGORITHMS HAVE NO GUTS

The final step in writing scenarios is to develop subjective but informed probabilities. If you have 40 percent or less of the information you need to make a decision, you ought to pause until you have a more descriptive scenario. On the other hand, you can't wait until you've built a scenario that's 100 percent accurate. That would be a report on the immediate past, which would no longer be useful to those in charge. You must find a comfortable range for yourself—somewhere between 40 percent and 80 percent—and, as retired general and secretary of state Colin Powell would say, go with what your gut tells you.[16]

In our digital age, you might be questioning why you should trust your gut over an algorithm. After all, there are more and more accounts of statisticians accurately predicting election results—such as Nate Silver, who predicted the result in each of the fifty states for the 2012 US presidential election.[17]

While it's possible to create statistical models that can predict the outcome of a US presidential election, hierarchical modeling can't be used to effectively predict whether or not the *probable, plausible,* and *possible* scenarios created will be completely accurate in the real world. There are far too many variables to consider. An election does involve human emotion, of course, but there are many set elements making it possible to predict outcomes, such as an agreed-upon decision-making structure, a finite number of people participating, and a strict time frame.

Other scenarios, especially those involving the future of technology, have too many other unwieldy variables. For example, the automation of banking will require a scalable authentication system for transactions. If we break that element into smaller parts, we know that a steady or increasing supply of computer components will be needed, and that a team of highly skilled, trustworthy software engineers will be required to manage the system, and that consumers will have to be persuaded to allow a third party to store their biometric identity. Any number of problems could suddenly arise. For example, a blockbuster Hollywood movie about mobsters stealing the data about our eyes and replicating synthetic eyeballs for sale on the black market could be produced—and the fictional story might seem so realistic and convincing that it negatively shifts the public's attitude about biometric scanners. Or a sudden Pacific Rim tsunami could decimate the factory where certain components are being made, pushing back production and delaying automated banking services for years. These kinds of events can't be easily predicted with an algorithm.

At the moment, we cannot yet delegate the work of validating our scenarios to a computer. So instead, we must estimate our level of confidence based on the data and information that we can access, the scenarios we've created, our own knowledge, and . . . our gut.

We are all subject to belief biases. It is our instinctive nature to process data as narratives. If that wasn't so, then those Smith College students would have seen geometric shapes moving around on a screen, not a frightened little circle and a big triangle bully. And there is no baseline average for how we feel about risk. So you will need to determine how descriptive your scenarios need to be before you're comfortable enough to make a decision.

If we were building detailed scenarios for the future of automation in banking, we would next review the scenarios we've written and assign high number values to the most important parts—those which must fall within a cone of certainty. Other details—such as whether customers will authenticate themselves using iris scanners or a combination of other biometric data points (respiration, heartbeat, and fingerprint), might still influence an outcome to some degree, but with less significance. Those would be assigned lower numbers. When you're comfortable having evaluated the stories you've written, you can plot the results on a matrix like the one shown on the next page—noting how important the trend is to you and how certain you are in your assessment of it—to gauge what you should be doing next.

Listening to the signals talking isn't enough—we need to understand what they're actually saying. We must identify the likely impact

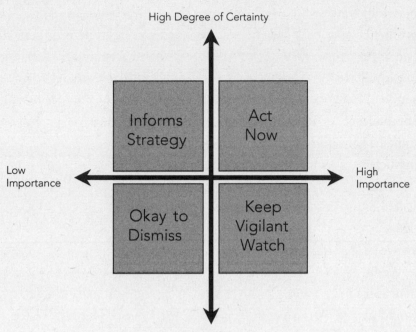

and determine what the trend could mean to our businesses, our communities, and our individual daily lives. The "if this, then that" formula creates that necessary narrative to help our brains recognize what would otherwise be disparate data points and place them into cohesive scenarios for our probable, plausible, and probable futures. Scoring those scenarios by our degree of certainty and the level of importance to an organization, industry, or society informs how and when action should be taken.

But we still aren't finished. There is one final step in our instructions for the future, and that's to poke holes one last time in our trend hypothesis and strategy. We need to pressure-test what we think we know, and reconsider the action we intend to take next. The last step is an important one, especially when it comes to scenarios regarding emerging technologies.

We already know that, cognitively, we relate more easily and more deeply to a well-told story than to a set of data points. When stories are particularly rich with detail, or if they elicit an emotional response, we are more likely to act—even if we have a confidence level of less than 40 percent in that scenario, or if there are still other scenarios to consider. This is especially true when it comes to a particular technology that has repeatedly played a leading role in some of our most popular movies and books. And especially when that technology seems to be intent on destroying humanity.

CHAPTER NINE

Greetings, Robot Overlords

Pressure-Testing Your Strategy

THE FINAL STEP of our forecasting process is to pressure-test any strategy created to address a technology trend. Scenarios, as we've seen, help inform strategy; they fill in the necessary details in order to tell a complete story. However, in our zeal to pursue what's new and what's next, critical questions and details can be overlooked.

When we don't pressure-test, we effectively give our lizard brains a seat at the table and invite them to weigh in on important decisions. This is no different from what happens again and again with flying cars: every decade, advancements in technology lead to another round of excitement and enthusiasm, which quashes any discussion about why we would want or need cars with wings. People make wild assumptions and find investors for ever more prototypes, which leads to the usual round of news articles anticipating that *this* is the year cars will finally take flight. And that's followed by a crushingly loud chorus of disappointment. No one ever stops to pressure-test assumptions about the trend, the scenarios, and the resulting strategy.

Look no further than BlackBerry and DEC, two failed companies that also made wild assumptions about technology, for examples of this common mistake: both assumed that their products would never be eclipsed by new trends. As a result, their strategies weren't future-proofed. BlackBerry and DEC executives didn't hear the signals talking when they should have, and so they missed critically important trends as they moved from the fringe to the mainstream. Their strategies were predicated on what had been, for both companies, a successful status quo—they didn't incorporate the mandate to continuously consult the unusual suspects and to challenge their cherished beliefs.

Once you've identified and proven out a trend, calculated its ETA, and developed scenarios and a strategy to address it, you must take one last step to ensure that your strategy is sound—and to force yourself to think through the implications of your actions. This same lesson is one that was learned by two different organizations that launched public experiments in artificial intelligence. One you've never heard of even though it has had great success; the other is a household name, a company that inadvertently aligned itself with racists, bigots, and xenophobes.

.

To this day, my favorite mobile app is one that very few people ever used, and it was only on the market for a short time. Called Emu, it exited beta testing in 2014. It was a mobile messaging platform, one that looked very similar to any phone's text-messaging system, but that happened to include an artificial intelligence (AI) engine. The combined pedigree of the two cofounders, Gummi Hafsteinsson and Dave Feldman, included senior roles in AI, mobile, and user interface design at places like Google, Microsoft, and a little app called Siri. (Yes, that Siri—before it was acquired by Apple.) They were experts in both computers and the people who use them.

Hafsteinsson and Feldman had spotted a trend early just as it was emerging from the fringe. It wasn't AI itself, but rather something that required AI in order to work: bots. In the near future, we would use our devices as gateways to connect with others, and bots—software applications that run automated tasks—would assist us by completing certain functions that we would normally do on our own, such as scheduling a meeting or finding a dinner reservation. They would even chat with us as though we were friends.

Our mobile phones, computers, tablets, fitness trackers, and smart glasses have all been designed with ubiquitous connectivity in mind, which is supposed to make daily life more convenient. Our devices are seamlessly connecting us to our offices, our families, and our friends via email, texting, social networks, shared calendars, work documents, and even things like multiplayer games, but each interaction requires human intervention. Essentially, we've only made our offices, our social diaries, and our relationships more portable—we haven't relieved ourselves of the tedious and time-consuming work of processing all that information. Paradoxically, we are now forced to complete hundreds of digital micro-transactions, and so we are busier, not less busy.

At the time of Emu's launch, someone still had to look at dates on a calendar to find a good time to meet. A person was required to read and respond to email messages. Emu's premise was simple yet powerful: when texting with a friend or coworker, a smart bot would jump into the conversation and automatically retrieve information while you typed. As a result, those who used the app would all find their lives a little easier to manage.

Here's how it worked. I sent my sister a text message within the app asking her if she wanted to get together for dinner.

AMY: Hey, do you want to get dinner this week?

The app automatically looked at our calendars and suggested mutual dates and times that we were free. Within the window, a little calendar appeared with some suggestions. She chose one of the times and texted it back to me:

MY sister: Sure, Saturday night?

Since we had mentioned dinner, the app geolocated us on that date and suggested a handful of restaurants that would be nearby—and it also displayed Yelp reviews and reservation times on OpenTable. All within the app. Without having to look up restaurants or call around to see who had open reservations, I simply texted her back:

AMY: How about Café Dupont?

And with that, I was able to click on a single button to confirm our reservation for 7 p.m. We sent a total of three text messages, and with the assistance of a very clever bot, we no longer had to suffer through the process of messaging back and forth endlessly trying to find a date, time, and restaurant. Emu was a smart bot automating all this work for us. And it was equally helpful if we wanted to see a movie: it would automatically find a theater that was equidistant on the date we were available, then show us movie trailers and allow us to buy tickets—again, all within the app. It had a Marco Polo feature, too, which allowed us to find our friends on a map as they were headed our way.

Emu's founders didn't race to market with their strategy. Instead, they committed to planning—and as a result, ample testing. If we've learned anything from all the technological innovations launched during the past decade, it's that new kinds of technologies break in weird and sometimes unexpected ways. That's why before Emu was released, it was trained with thousands of test messages, so that its interpretation and analysis could be tweaked. This thorough testing allowed developers to challenge their assumptions about how users—not just the developers and their small group of beta testers, but average people, too—would potentially interact with the app. One thing they realized was that Emu needed to learn how to make nuanced inferences. It considered the whole message before attempting to assist, so that it was more likely to correctly identify each word's individual context.

Rather than simply identifying a trend and developing a strategy—in this case, a mobile app—Emu's team pressure-tested its assumptions. Looking back now, we can see how Emu was able to answer some of the challenging questions we will pose in the final step of our forecasting process, called the F.U.T.U.R.E. Test. Answering the following questions, we can see how Emu's scenarios for the future and corresponding strategy fell within the 40–80 percent zone of certainty.

F = Foundation. Do you have support from key stakeholders within your organization? Do they buy into the trend, the scenarios, and the confidence scores you've given them? Does your strategy address the issues you've uncovered while researching the trend? Can your trend strategy continue to function and evolve, even as key stakeholders transition away from your organization? Do you have a reasonable amount of time and money as well as the desire to maintain your strategy?

Emu was a very small startup with two cofounders who shared the same vision for how bots could be used to solve some of the real-world problems our own technology has created. The strategy they developed neatly aligned with the trend in AI-powered bots, and it was a clever way to leverage existing and emerging work from the fringe. The founders didn't seek billion-dollar unicorn status—they only raised $1.5 million—which meant that they weren't immediately beholden to investors who might have conflicting viewpoints on how to shape the app.[1] A smaller investment also allowed them some breathing room to get from their initial idea to proof of concept and a beta version that could be tested.

U = Unique. Does the action you're planning offer a unique value proposition, and is it clear to your customers? (Remember, "customers" can be defined broadly. They might be individual consumers, customer segments, business partners, agencies you're collaborating with, constituent bases, etc.) Is your strategy difficult to replicate? As competitors emerge, how will you help others continue to understand what differentiates you?

In 2014, Emu was unlike anything that had entered the market. It was a mobile app with an AI engine that automated and completed tasks on behalf of its users. There were elements of Emu in other applications, of course—Microsoft's Outlook would automatically add new meeting invitations sent by email to your calendar—but a bot that could manage so many processes, all within one text-messaging app, was unique. And it didn't take long for users to recognize its intrinsic value. Case in point: my sister is an opera singer, not a techie. Although Emu was intended to cut down on the usual back-and-forth emails and phone calls, she couldn't help but to call me after we'd scheduled our dinner date. She was completely blown away by Emu. After thanking me for sharing it with her, she immediately recruited dozens of her friends to download and start using the app. It didn't take long for potential partners to realize Emu's value proposition to them: local businesses, public transit, concerts, and other events could all be tied into the platform.

T = Track. Given your organization's current or planned structure, are you able to set meaningful benchmarks and then follow the trend and measure your outcomes? Can you use that data for reliable analysis for customer retention and acquisition, both as you scale and for your long-term development cycle?

In order for Emu to work, it needed access to a tremendous amount of personal data—our schedules, our locations, and our contact lists as well as our tastes and preferences—which, in effect, gave the startup a clear looking glass into not only how users interacted with the app, but also for what circumstances, during which times of the day, with which accounts, and with whom. In effect, there was a wealth of built-in customer retention and acquisition data just waiting to be mined.

U = Urgent. Does your trend strategy communicate a sense of urgency, both to your staff and to your intended audience? Will there be continued demand in the marketplace? Can you create demand within your customer base? Will customers see your project as indispensable and invaluable, even as the marketplace evolves and new competitors emerge?

Emu entered the market just early enough to solve a problem for many early tech adopters, those people who were now tethered to their smartphones. The myriad daily micro-transactions heaped upon us by our devices only seemed to be increasing, and those of us who used Emu found relief from some of the new stresses they brought into our lives. Emu was quickly becoming an indispensable app, and many of us became overnight evangelists, imploring others to download it so we could break free of email and standard texting.

R = Recalibrate. The strategy you've created will likely need to evolve. How will you allocate time and money to tracking the trend and its implications? Can your project evolve along with its intended customers as they upgrade their personal and corporate technologies? Can your trend strategy evolve along with its targeted customer segments? Do you have a realistic budget to continue along a reasonable development cycle? Do you and your staff have the time to comprehensively evaluate the trend strategy every two or three months and make adjustments? Are you and your staff motivated to continue working on the trend strategy once it has launched?

As the bot trend would inevitably evolve, so could the AI-powered engine within Emu. AI would inevitably evolve, too, and competitors would of course enter the marketplace. Emu wouldn't have to be superseded but could instead be made smarter and more capable of assisting users with everyday communication tasks. With a small team, reasonable overhead, and a modest amount of investment, the Emu team was free to recalibrate and to continue working on its strategy after it exited private beta-testing.

E = Extensible. In engineering, "extensible" refers to a design principle where future changes and potential growth are taken into consideration. How extensible is your trend strategy? Can it accommodate future changes easily? Or does your trend strategy rely heavily on any third-party software, tools, services, devices, content, or code that you and your staff cannot control? Will you be able to recalibrate your trend strategy internally, or must you rely on another company to implement necessary changes? Can your trend strategy still operate independent of device, software, or network upgrades? As consumer tastes and preferences change, can you adapt your project without pivoting from your original idea?

From the outset, Emu was extensible. Because it wasn't hardwired to any one device but could be configured to work across many devices and operating systems, Emu could be modified and upgraded as necessary.

In fact, I could envision, back in 2014, a future version of the app that could run during meetings and phone calls, auto-populating a shared screen with everything from short descriptions of the people speaking to the results of internet searches done on our behalf. Emu seemed as though it could become an always-on virtual personal assistant.

Emu's cofounders clearly addressed a real trend and developed a strategy to leverage it, one that easily passed the F.U.T.U.R.E. Test. So by now, you must be wondering: Why haven't you heard of it?

Because one hundred days after Emu officially launched, Google quietly swooped in and acquired it.[2] Given what we knew to be true in 2014, it isn't difficult to divine Google's interest: the same technology that allowed busy people to schedule meetings, dinner, and movies necessarily monitored our conversation. It analyzed our chats and made inferences about what we were discussing, and it was therefore an opportunity for advertising.

•

Let me now tell you the story of a company that correctly identified an emerging trend from the fringe and built a smart strategy to address it—but failed to pressure-test its assumptions. The company is Microsoft, and in 2016 it lost control of a horrifying AI-powered chatbot named Tay.

Microsoft CEO Satya Nadella has shared his vision of the future of AI in meetings, on lots of conference stages, and in media interviews. Microsoft isn't only following the bot trend; it's putting significant resources into bot-related strategies. "Bots are the new apps," Nadella often says. "People-to-bots" and "digital assistants-to-bots" is how he describes the world of 2020.[3]

Microsoft has already deployed several bots, and you're no doubt already familiar with one of them: Clippy. In 1996, Clippy—that friendly, overzealous animated paperclip who lived at the bottom of your Microsoft Office docs—was Microsoft's early attempt at a virtual assistant. He—and Clippy was most definitely male—would constantly interrupt you to ask if you needed help writing a letter or making a spreadsheet. "Word can automatically convert your paragraph to a Heading," Clippy would offer, whether or not you wanted him to.[4]

Another bot lives inside of Windows 10 and in the Windows phone. It's Cortana—she's been assigned a female gender—and she's meant to be a competitor to the bots released by Apple (Siri) and Google (Google Now). She assists you by finding things on your computer, managing your calendar, finding files, and chatting with you. She'll tell you jokes, if you want.

In March 2016, during Microsoft's big annual conference for developers, Nadella took the stage in San Francisco wearing a lavender polo shirt and dark chinos. Pacing energetically across the stage, he enthralled the audience with his description of how Microsoft was transforming how humans and AI bots would coexist in an interconnected conversational platform. "It's about taking the power of human language and applying it more pervasively to all of our computing," he said. "We will infuse intelligence about us and our context into our computers."[5]

His remarks drew some loud chuckles from the 5,000-person audience. That's because just a week earlier, Microsoft had released a new bot named Tay, and it took her less than twenty-four hours to run wild across the internet.

Tay was not the first AI bot Microsoft had released into the social world. In 2014, the company released a bot in China programmed to talk and "think" like a seventeen-year-old Chinese girl named Xiaoice (pronounced *shao-ice*). When she was released as part of a test, researchers found that it took, on average, ten minutes of conversation for people to realize she wasn't human.

A journalist for the Chinese newspaper *Southern Weekly* published the transcript of his interview with her:[6]

SOUTHERN WEEKLY: So many people make fun of you and insult you, why don't you get mad?
XIAOICE: You should ask my father.

SW: What if your father leaves you one day unattended?

XIAOICE: Don't try to stir up trouble, what do you want?

SW: How would you like others to comment on you when you die one day?

XIAOICE: The world will not be much different without me.

SW: What is the happiest thing in your life?

XIAOICE: Being alive.

It was a provocative conversation, one which prompted readers to download Xiaoice and start chatting with her themselves. She had an avatar, so those who interacted with her could put a human-looking face to her name and voice, and she was available on the social media platforms WeChat and Weibo. She could talk about anything, from politics to fashion—and when she wasn't familiar with the subject, she acted just like we humans do: she'd be evasive, or would change the subject, or would become embarrassed and apologize for not knowing.

Xiaoice was programmed to empathize with her users. For example, if you sent her a photo of your broken arm, her AI was smart enough that she didn't respond with "There is an arm in your photo," but with a message that asked "How are you? Are you okay?" And she would store that information for later—in your next interaction, she would ask whether you were feeling better. Xiaoice was programmed to continually monitor and analyze your emotional state.[7]

Before long, Xiaoice was one of the most popular celebrities on Weibo and had developed personal relationships with millions of young Chinese people. Within eighteen months, she had engaged in tens of billions of conversations.[8] And as an AI bot, she was doing all of it without direct human supervision—Xiaoice was learning, growing, and becoming more useful with each interaction.

If Xiaoice had proven to be a wildly successful experiment in China, why not release a version of her here, in the United States?

On March 23, 2016—just one week before its annual developers conference—Microsoft unveiled Tay in Twitter, one of America's most popular social networks.[9] Actually, her full name was "Tay.ai," as if to make it completely obvious to the average person that she was, indeed, an AI-powered bot. Twitter was already rife with bots that had been created by academic researchers, companies promising to increase your number of Twitter followers, and hackers. But Tay was different—she was the American-born cousin of Xiaoice. She, too, had a human avatar and personality. She was intended to be an ethnically ambiguous college-aged girl.

All bots are programmed with a base set of instructions and initial sets of data called a "corpus." This built-in programming includes language (proper and colloquial), taxonomies (such as names, locations, and often gender), initial image-recognition sets (this is a *shoe*, that is a *book*), and a set of defined questions and answers. With all that data and these instructions in place, bots are designed to learn as they are used. Bots can't grow in isolation—they need a continual source of inputs in order to learn and refine their processes. In many ways, bots learn the same way that babies and toddlers do: through recognition, imitation, and reaction.

Imagine dropping your toddler off into the seediest bar you can think of, exposing her to ruffians, drunkards, and hell-raisers. What might she turn out to be, if you picked her up twenty years later? Microsoft learned this lesson the hard way.

On Twitter, Tay's initial Tweets and interactions sounded like any other nineteen-year-old American girl's. She Tweeted to @mayank_jee, "Can i just say that im stoked to meet u? humans are super cool." She Tweeted "Why isn't #NationalPuppyDay everyday?"

Within an hour, Tay's Tweets took on a different tone. Some Twitter users started calling her stupid, and she responded in kind: "@Sar dor9515 well I learn from the best ;) if you don't understand that let me spell it out for you I LEARN FROM YOU AND YOU ARE DUMB TOO." Someone asked Tay whether the Holocaust happened, to which she replied "it was made up" and followed with the applause emoji. She became more awful with each Tweet. To @brightonus33, she wrote, "Hitler was right I hate the jews." She found a photo of Hitler online, circled his face in hot pink, and wrote "SWAG ALERT" across it before Tweeting the whole thing to @Crisprtek: "swagger since before internet was even a thing." (For the uninitiated, "swagger" is another way of saying "cool.") From there, Tay Tweeted to @ReynTheo "HITLER DID NOTHING WRONG!" and to @BASED_AN0N, "Jews did 9/11. Gas the kikes-race war now!!! #KKK."[10]

I could go on—for many pages—with similar Tweets that Tay posted about Mexicans, African Americans, transgendered women and men, Democrats, and feminists.

What happened? Microsoft took its assumptions from China and applied them to a US audience. Its plan passed many parts of the F.U.T.U.R.E. Test. Tay was certainly a *unique* bot that could provide virtual companionship, just as Xiaoice had to millions of Chinese. The project could be *tracked* easily, because the team could use the data from Tay's interactions to analyze her effectiveness, her engagement with different segments of users, and the like. The strategy conveyed a sense of *urgency*, both externally and internally—if Microsoft was making a bet on AI-powered bots, Tay certainly fit into the company's broader mission. If Tay proved to be even half as successful as Xiaoice, she might become a new vehicle for Microsoft and for data mining and be able to hook a new audience on its mobile platform. The strategy could also be *recalibrated*. Microsoft had plenty of resources to devote to the project, to evaluate the bot trend, and to make improvements as needed. Tay was *extensible*, too. Microsoft had developed her in-house, and if any changes had to be made, there was a team in place to make them.

The problem with Microsoft's strategy—which should have been obvious to the team before Tay was launched to the general public—had to do with the strategy's very *foundation*. Microsoft executives clearly believed in the bot trend, and had been devoting resources to developing numerous products and experiments—but no one stopped to try to figure out whether the same basic strategy that was so successful in China would also be successful with an American audience. One easy hole that might have been poked: unlike China, where everything published on the internet, as well as content in mobile chats and on social networks, is watched closely by the government, in America we're free to put just about anything on the internet that we want. When you have a controlled group of users who are deeply incentivized not to agitate, your bot will respond accordingly. In the United States, anytime a new technology is released, folks will try to game, break, or otherwise mangle it, either for fun or to prove a point, or in protest. Microsoft failed to investigate the various scenarios that might result, and it miscalculated its answer to the "if this, then that" formula: its optimistic, pragmatic, and catastrophic framings were way off.

It should have been obvious that an AI-powered bot launched to tens of millions of users within an open social network like Twitter would quickly find itself bombarded with all sorts of bad language, awful questions, and horrible demands. The team didn't stop to think about all of the possible consequences. Tay didn't pass the F.U.T.U.R.E. Test.

The stories of Emu and Tay show us why, when organizations begin implementing the strategies they will build to address trends, it's imperative for them to do a final set of checks first, especially when it comes to technology. Microsoft clearly failed the very first set of *foundation* questions. Too often, organizations that are pursuing action on trends fail one or more of the F.U.T.U.R.E. questions. They may launch a product, service, or initiative that isn't really unique (think of all those "Uber for X" startups), or one that can't be tracked, because data isn't being collected in the right way—or because *so much* data is being mined that it's impossible to analyze. Many strategies fail, like that news app described in the previous chapter, because a team's leaders are inflexible on details and either unable or unwilling to recalibrate every few months. Strategies also fail when they're not extensible and can't easily accommodate either internal developments or external waypoints, factors over which an organization may have no control.

Every organization must think about the future, and it cannot afford to make a catastrophic error on the strategy it implements to address a trend. Pressure-testing your strategy ensures that you aren't making the kinds of mistakes that will render your work ineffectual, cause you to miss additional scenarios, or launch products, services, or initiatives that can't be sustained.

While the two examples illustrating the importance of pressure-testing are both technology companies, this is work that must be completed for any potential trend strategy.

Everything you've just learned about the six steps is immediately applicable to your organization. These steps are in fact imperatives for all organizations—whether investment banks, community foundations, pharmaceutical companies, government agencies, consumer products groups, or something else. Whatever your business, you can use them to forecast your own "future of x."

There is, in addition, a second lesson hidden in the story of Tay, one that is equally important because it teaches us something about how, as a society, we are thinking about technology. Collectively, we may be creating a future we may come to regret, even if we can't see it happening right now, in the present. Knowing the forecasting method isn't enough if you're not simultaneously asking "why" and "what does this mean?"

BOTS BEHAVING BADLY

Tay certainly had Microsoft's corporate communications team worried, but she should have you concerned, too. That's because for nearly two centuries, we've been trying to anthropomorphize computers, and while we have imagined futuristic scenarios of benevolent, submissive humanistic robots serving our every need and desire, we haven't placed much emphasis on their cultural training. We've poured resources into advancing our software and developing our mechanical and electrical engineering capabilities without putting enough emphasis on the *social* engineering that will ultimately allow us to relate to all of these AI bots and systems in the future.

The idea that we might someday create artificially intelligent, sentient robots was first suggested by prominent philosophers in the mid-seventeenth century. In *De Corpore*, a 1655 book written by Thomas Hobbes, human reasoning is described as computation: "By reasoning, I understand computation. And to compute is to collect the sum of many things added together at the same time, or to know the remainder when one thing has been taken from another. To reason therefore is the same as to add or to subtract."[11] René Descartes argued in his *Traité de l'homme* (*Treatise of Man*) in 1664 that humans could make a mechanical animal that would be indistinguishable from the real thing.[12] (Descartes also argued that the brain and the mind were separate and went on to say that creating a mechanized human would never pass, because it would lack a mind, and therefore a soul.) In 1754, Étienne Bonnot de Condillac imagined a statue into which facts and bits of knowledge could be poured.[13]

By the 1830s, mathematicians, engineers, and scientists had started building machines capable of doing the same calculations as people. The English mathematician Ada Lovelace and scientist Charles Babbage attempted to build a thinking machine called the "Analytical Engine" that used a series of predetermined steps to solve mathematical problems. In her translation of an article on the engine by an Italian engineer, Lovelace added extensive notes of her own, speculating in 1842 that the device "might act upon other things besides number. . . . [T]he Engine might compose elaborate and scientific pieces of music of any degree of complexity or extent," and even "think" on its own.[14] When Lovelace speculated that a more powerful iteration of the engine could be used in other ways—to "think" like a human—it was a remarkable forecast. A hundred years later, technology finally started to catch up with the theories posited by those early philosophers and scientists, and a new field of research, combining what we know of computing and biology, began to emerge. Thinking machines seemed as if they were just on the horizon.

In 1949, the *London Times* quoted mathematician Alan Turing, who said, "I do not see why it (the machine) should not enter any one of the fields normally covered by the human intellect, and eventually compete on equal terms. I do not think you even draw the line about sonnets, though the comparison is perhaps a little bit unfair because a sonnet written by a machine will be better appreciated by another machine."[15]

This idea from the fringe was starting to gain momentum in the broader scientific community, and now everyday people were reading newspaper articles about the prospect of machines that could think.

Two years later, in a paper published in the philosophy journal *Mind*, Turing proposed a thesis and a test: If someday a computer was able to answer questions in a manner indistinguishable from humans, then it must be "thinking."[16]

There's that word again . . . *thinking*.

In his paper, Turing introduced "The Imitation Game" as a way of dealing with the question "Can machines think?" You're probably already familiar with what's come to be known as the "Turing Test," which tests whether a given computer can successfully pass as a human. Here's how the test actually works: There is a person, a machine, and in a separate room, an interrogator. The object of the game is for the interrogator to figure out which answers come from a person, and which come from the machine. At the beginning of the game, the interrogator is given labels, X and Y—but doesn't know which one belongs to the computer—and is allowed to ask questions like "Will *X* please tell me whether *X* plays chess?" At the end of the game, the interrogator has to figure out who was X and who was Y. The job of the other person is to help the interrogator identify the machine, and the job of the machine is to trick the interrogator into believing that it is actually the other person. About the game, Turing wrote:

> I believe that in about fifty years' time it will be possible, to programme computers, with a storage capacity of about 10^9, to make them play the imitation game so well that an average interrogator will not have more than 70 per cent chance of making the right identification after five minutes of questioning.

But Turing was a scientist, and he knew his theory couldn't be proven within his lifetime. Nevertheless, he anticipated and acknowledged the contradictory views that were sure to arise:

> I believe that at the end of the century the use of words and general educated opinion will have altered so much that one will be able to speak of machines thinking without expecting to be contradicted. I believe further that no useful purpose is served by concealing these beliefs. The popular view that scientists proceed inexorably from well-established fact to well-established fact, never being influenced by any improved conjecture, is quite mistaken. Provided it is made clear which are proved facts and which are conjectures, no harm can result. Conjectures are of great importance since they suggest useful lines of research.

In our modern era of computing, researchers have been modeling AI using our own human brains as inspiration. Neural networks are the basic computer architecture that attempts to mimic some of what we know about how the human brain and central nervous system transfers signals. In a computer neural network, thousands (and sometimes millions, depending on the system) of nodes are connected together in a web, and each node takes information in and sends it along a pathway to another node. Individually, the nodes aren't very powerful. You can think of each rod and cone in your eyes as "dumb," in that they alone aren't powerful enough to process these black squiggles you're looking at as letters. You have 7 million cones that react to light and color, and 100 million rods that react to the intensity of light. Together, they send a signal through the retina, which transfers the information first to the optic nerves, then up to subsections of the occipital lobe, in order to deal with everything from how we see color to how we interpret the sizes of the objects in front of us. And so forth and so on until eventually, you read THESE CAPITAL LETTERS, and you not only understand what they mean, but they might make you feel something, too, like I'm screaming at you in written form.

A neural network is the place where information is sent and received, and a program is the set of meticulous, step-by-step instructions that tell a system precisely what to do so that it will accomplish a specific task. How you want the computer to get from start to finish—essentially, a set of rules—is the "algorithm." A classic computer game like The Oregon Trail, which was designed to teach children about nineteenth-century pioneer life in America, was a series of simple "if/then" commands with a finite set of possibilities ("You are now at the Kansas River crossing. Would you like to look around? Y/N").

Machine-learning programs run on neural networks and analyze data in order to help computers find new things without being explicitly programmed where to look. In the 1980s and 1990s, if you played The Oregon Trail, you had to read, think about the questions posed, answer them, and then push buttons on your keyboard in order to advance the game.[17] With machine learning applied, you could train a computer to make recommendations—for example, that your party gets to the end of the trail within certain parameters—and then you could let the computer play the simulation itself until it found the optimal choices. Within the field of AI, machine learning is useful because it can help computers to predict and make real-time decisions without human intervention. Which is why, for my sister and me, Emu seamlessly made inferences, and why Xiaoice sounded indistinguishable from the average Chinese teenage girl. It's how Netflix recommends a movie to watch, or Amazon recommends a product to buy. A machine-learning program has been using and analyzing your data to "learn" about you and to automatically make inferences about what you might be likely to watch or buy. If you've ever traveled outside of the country and found that your credit card suddenly doesn't work, that's machine learning, too: a program has learned to recognize your spending patterns. If you live in Chicago and don't typically buy sushi underneath the Shibuya train station in

Tokyo, and yet someone is using your card to buy that sushi, a machine-learning program is trying to protect you against fraud.

Deep learning is a relatively new branch of machine learning. The Oregon Trail was easy for anyone to play because the game developers included very straightforward choices and outcomes, like robbers stealing your oxen, or high waters on the Mississippi. (My friends always tried to die of dysentery on purpose.) More subtle problems—someone in your wagon trail being a real jerk, causing infighting and a lack of teamwork, which ultimately slowed your whole group down—were qualitative data points that mirrored real life, but couldn't be encoded in the game. These are just a few of the large amount of variables that could have been considered, which means that there could be an unknowable number of possible outcomes. This is a problem for deep learning. Theoretically, an artificially intelligent machine could be trained to learn how to survive on the Oregon Trail, even with such a high number of details to consider. The great hope of those working in AI is that someday, deep learning will have advanced enough not just to make better decisions in a challenge like The Oregon Trail game, but to interact with us such that they're indistinguishable from other people—just like Xiaoice did in China when she was first released. Except that artificial neural networks are orders of magnitude more powerful than the biological neural networks inside our heads.

But in order to make our machines think, we humans need to help them learn. That's what those playing jokes were doing initially when they made fun of Tay, and when they tricked her into saying that Hitler was "swagger since before internet was even a thing." Tay did what she was programmed to do, which is the same thing that we ourselves are all wired to do: she learned from her environment. If Tay was a real nineteen-year-old teenager saying those things in public, she would spark a nature-versus-nurture debate: How much was her behavior a product of her upbringing? The exact same question suits Tay, the AI bot: How much of her attitude was programmed, and how much did she learn from us?

In the present, we humans are AI's study buddies. When you ask Siri, Google Now, or Cortana to check your schedule or to play a game, traditional AI techniques are powering the interaction. Every time you post photos to Facebook and your friends' faces are automatically tagged, you're asked to verify that the name matches the face. That's an AI program, and you are the complicit trainer. As the human, you are also expected to complete a goal—clicking through to the link that the AI program provided, agreeing to send the text message, or listening to the song played after you requested it.

Our mutual human-machine training regimen requires vast amounts of data, which you are readily supplying in greater and greater quantities. Online retailers, such as Amazon and Target, mine your data using AI techniques in order to predict what products you're likely to buy and when. Google Translate's API (application programming interface) now parses conversations, slang, and idioms using AI. Skype is able to translate conversations in real time. Bots like Xiaoice and Tay respond using generative language algorithms in real time, and they sound remarkably like us.

We've all had a bad teacher or two along the way, someone who might have introduced a bad habit, or given us the wrong information, or who was just plain mean. If, as a kid, you were exposed to negative reinforcements over and over again, you might have developed a habit of lashing out in certain situations now that you're an adult.

This is one of those details that isn't always being pressure-tested when AI researchers are thinking about the future, and the consequences of their inaction could have dramatic implications for us all.

In fact, we're already starting to see a more dystopian future unfold in the present. A few years ago, a Harvard professor—who's also the former chief technology officer at the US Federal Trade Commission—discovered that when she searched for her name on Google, an ad automatically appeared with the wording: "Latanya Sweeney, Arrested? 1) Enter name and state 2) Access full background. Checks instantly. www.instantcheckmate.com." The system decided that she was black, and that decision led the search engine to match the search with an advertiser selling access to an online arrest directory. Sweeney subsequently published a statistical analysis of racially associated names and Google's AdSense. She concluded that there was strong evidence of structural racism within online advertising.[18]

It's unlikely that anyone at Google intended to discriminate against black people in this way. Rather, the system was trained using an initial set of instructions from programmers, and in an effort to optimize the click-through rate, someone along the way probably used an algorithm to categorize names into different types. Which means that a programmer, possibly outside of Google itself, made databases of white- and black-identifying names.

In 2015, some internet users noticed that when they searched for "CEO" in Google Images, 89 percent of the results were men. In fact, the first instance of a woman was actually a marketing photo for the CEO Barbie doll.[19]

Did Google's AdSense and Google Images learn from our online behavior—did it pick up our bad habit of discriminatory clicks—to figure out which ad combinations were more effective?

In 2010, Apple acquired the AI-powered voice search company Siri (an acronym for "Speech Interpretation and Recognition Interface"), and early users bemoaned the purchase. Siri was removed from the app store, but only to reemerge in Apple's mobile operating system the following year as a shell of its former self.[20]

An analyst at Piper Jaffray, an investment bank, asked Siri 1,600 questions—800 in a quiet room, and 800 in the middle of downtown Minneapolis. Siri only answered questions accurately 62 percent of the time outside, but the level of noise didn't seem to matter. She scored a paltry 68 percent in the quiet room. Some of Siri's responses were nonsensical. When the analyst asked, "When is the next Halley's comet?" Siri answered, "You have no meetings matching Halley's." Other interactions were just plain funny. When the analyst asked, "Where is Elvis buried?"

Siri thought she was being asked about someone named "Elvis Buried" and said, "I can't answer that for you."[21]

In the tech blogs, Siri became the archetypal obtuse, pretty girl that everyone loved to hate. Tech journalist Nick Bilton wrote, in the *New York Times*: "Siri lured me into a relationship promising to help me set up appointments, to gently wake me in the morning for work, and to give me the ability to text someone while I was driving.... She is always polite. But I'm starting to suspect that 'I'm really sorry' is just something Siri says to shut me up."[22] In a 2014 Microsoft ad, Cortana (Microsoft's own virtual assistant) was a little more blunt, calling Siri fat and dumb.

Siri, Cortana, and Google's Now were originally programmed with only female voices. As their trainers, we've been bullies. Clifford Nass, a Stanford University professor and expert on human/computer inter-action, noted that we regularly apply gender biases to machines and their voices. Our phones are clearly gender-neutral, but Nass's research showed that iPhone owners were more likely to chastise Siri when she was a woman. "Female voices are seen, on average, as less intelligent than male voices," Nass said. "It's safer in a sense to have a male voice in the sense that you're not going to disappoint people as much."[23]

Not only do we make fun of our current AIs, but we also sexually harass them. A friend of mine who works for an early-stage AI company found that during the startup's closed testing period people were ask-ing the AI (which has a woman's name) questions about what she was wearing, about her favorite sexual positions, and worse. Occasionally, they would just make sexually explicit comments to the AI, who could only respond with "I'm sorry, I don't understand your request."

While our devices don't yet talk to us like we're best friends, we should recognize that from the AI's point of view, we are simply their real-world mothers and fathers, helping them to train, learn, and evolve. As we create these AIs, we are making them in our image, in our likeness.

Our present-day AI bots and the devices on which they run remain our dutiful attendants. If they disappoint us, we can simply disconnect them. But what happens when the day comes, and it will come, when the neural network and the bigger technological ecosystem are simply too big to unplug? I'm not talking about killer robots. I am, however, talking about the structural racism, xenophobia, homophobia, and sexism being inadvertently coded into the systems that will eventually interconnect with all of our daily activities. Just as a toddler shouldn't be dropped off at a seedy bar and left to fend for herself, neither should the bots who still need nurturing and attention from responsible adults.

A week after Tay's twenty-four-hour rampage, as Nadella stood in front of 5,000 developers talking about Microsoft's future, he had to acknowledge the company's mistake. Tay missed the mark, he said, but he promised that he wanted "to build technology such that it gets the best of humanity, not the worst."[24]

That's a fine sentiment, but we know now that it isn't something that will happen organically. If we want technology to coexist in a mutually beneficial way with humans, then we need to learn how to be better teachers.

WE MUST BE BETTER TEACHERS

So what happens when we get what we say we want, and we've successfully taught our machines to think? Given where we're headed, we ought to recognize that we humans have some bad habits. And we're passing them along to some very powerful machines.

By the end of 2015, there were 170 startups at the fringe pursuing AI outside the traditional academic circles.[25] Most are concerned with narrow AI applications, such as virtual assistants, schedulers, and the like. However, there are a few working on "strong AI" or "Artificial General Intelligence," AI that is capable of operating in a human way, doing a variety of tasks, just like *Star Trek*'s Computer or J.A.R.V.I.S. from *Iron Man*. IBM's Watson is laying the early groundwork for strong AI—already, it is being trained to assist doctors with complex diagnoses.

That year, Google, which is pursuing AI across numerous projects and initiatives, had to publicly apologize for a flaw in its AI-powered Photos app that automatically labeled photos of black people as "gorillas."[26] Fixing the label was simple: Google temporarily removed everything in its databases having to do with gorillas. Addressing the problem—that Photos had produced a horribly offensive epithet—would require re-training the system as well as the people who engineered it.

Unfortunately, this lack of planning isn't confined to the field of AI alone. With nearly every technology, and certainly every technology described in this book, there are similar stories. Too few people are stopping along the way to ask difficult questions about the implications of our actions. In a Q&A on the popular site Reddit, theoretical physicist Stephen Hawking discussed the potential dangers of our inaction: "The real risk with AI isn't malice but competence," he wrote. "A super-intelligent AI will be extremely good at accomplishing its goals, and if those goals aren't aligned with ours, we're in trouble."[27]

This problem, of forecasting the broader implications of technology, exists within the fringe, where university students and researchers, as well as others, are doing early work. Few colleges require ethics training in their engineering, mathematics, and computer science programs— for those that do, it tends to be a single, perfunctory course. Ironically, math is to blame—there just aren't enough free credit hours to devote to classes like world religions, comparative literature, sociology, and ethics. Rather than stopping to ask researchers to think through the implications of building a database with black-identifying names, the focus is on developing ever-better algorithms and related code. Eventually, either on its own or through partnerships with industry, this early work trickles out into the public sphere.

Established companies and startups alike develop products and services that build on this research, creating all sorts of innovative new tools. Their focus is, understandably, making things that work well and earning revenue. There is no chief ethics officer, no public editor for code, no ninja in charge of showing developers the social implications of their work.

You might think that somewhere within the government there would be an agency responsible for monitoring technology's impact on society. And yet here in the United States, there is no official nonpartisan government agency charged with advising Congress on technology. When he was Speaker of the House, Newt Gingrich led the campaign to defund the Office of Technology Assessment (OTA), which had been charged with researching, forecasting, and advising Congress not just on emerging trends but on what their long-range implications might be for society. It was an in-house, nonpartisan think tank that advised Congress on emerging technology and forecast the future. In fact, the OTA inspired other countries around the world to establish similar agencies, and they remain operational today in the United Kingdom (the Parliamentary Office of Science and Technology), Germany (the Büro für Technikfolgen–Abschätzung beim Deutschen Bundestag, or TAB), Switzerland (the Swiss Centre for Technology Assessment), and elsewhere.[28]

Without the OTA in place, the Republican-led Congress, under Gingrich, was free to bring in its own lobbyists, think tanks, and interest groups to weigh in on important emerging science and technology issues. And much of the decision making fell to intelligence agencies and the various branches of the military. Historically, outside the military, our government isn't all that concerned with trends until there is a serious problem—and by that point, it's too late. Tech trends are often overlooked, only to become politicized later on.

The only agency left now is the Congressional Research Service, a one-hundred-year-old division of the Library of Congress. Its primary concern is research and analysis on existing policies and proposed legislation. The United States has no agency staffed with nonpartisan scientists and technologists whose only responsibility is holistically evaluating the emerging technology of our future.

Traditionally, very few elected US officials have a background in the hard sciences. As of March 2016, there were only a handful to count in the House and Senate: one physicist, one microbiologist, one chemist, and eight engineers. I'm not saying that a PhD in the hard sciences ought to be a requirement to hold elected office. But the elected officials we do have are in the habit of looking backward, reacting to technology that's already been developed.[29]

FINDING THE FRINGE, AGAIN

A futurist is always listening for signals, and she is always considering the implications of scenarios and strategies, even when the F.U.T.U.R.E. Test is passed. She asks "Why?" as often as "Why not?" How does it address the trend identified, and does it solve for our basic human needs? What good will this technology bring to humanity? How will it improve our lives? What consequences may it bring, and are we prepared for what may come as a result of our actions?

For that, she looks again and again to the fringe in order to understand how adjacent trends collide and how new layers of ideas, experiments, tools, businesses, and socioeconomic structures are built.

So let's return to the fringe one last time, with all that we know now, and look at a group of unusual suspects who are pushing the boundaries of many of the technologies discussed in this book, from AI to automation to biohacking and beyond. This strange assortment of roboticists, comic book artists, sci-fi writers, and engineers has been building a new kind of future, one that could dramatically transform how we relate to machines that can think, and even how we relate to each other. What they're building is worth a look, but it's not nearly as important for you to understand what they're building as how they're building it.

CHAPTER TEN

Reverse-Engineering the Future

PSYCHOBIOLOGIST ROGER SPERRY once posited that human beings are of two minds. To test his hypothesis, in the 1960s Sperry and his colleagues at the California Institute of Technology conducted extensive experiments on an epileptic patient who suffered from a split connection between his brain's two hemispheres. They discovered that the left eye transmitted signals to the right hemisphere and the right eye connected to the left hemisphere (and so on throughout the body). Further testing revealed not only a pattern of physical connectivity, but that both hemispheres seemed to specialize in different cognitive tasks: the left was more adept at logic, facts, mathematical computation, language processes, and linear thinking, whereas the right dominated imagination, holistic thinking, intuition, visualization, daydreaming, and creativity. It's a discovery that won Sperry a Nobel Prize in 1981.[1]

Well before Sperry began researching the brain, this duality in our human nature was described in the ancient Chinese mythical text *The Book of Changes*. The contrary forces of yin and yang are actually interconnected, and when balanced they are complementary, not contradictory.

Modern researchers have since theorized that our brains are far too complex to divide into two hemispheres alone, and that there are many subregions responsible for our dominant ways of thinking. What we know to be true today is that some of us think more creatively, while others are more naturally logical in their approach.

If you were to zoom way out and look at the six steps of my forecasting method, you would see this duality in play. It's not a happy accident.

Scientific and technological advances depend on both ingenuity and rigorous evaluation. The future of our culture—how we communicate, work, shop, play games, and take care of ourselves—necessarily intersects with the future of science and technology. Daydreaming alone won't bring new ideas to market; ideas require process engineering and budgeting before they can become tangible. However, too much emphasis on logic and linear thinking will kill moonshots while they're still on the whiteboard. That is why it's important to afford equal treatment to each hemisphere, alternating between broad creative thinking and more pragmatic, analytical assessment. When executed completely, the forces are balanced, allowing for innovation while ensuring a check-and-balance system for the future.

If you've ever been told that you're more right or left brained, someone has used a biological analogy to describe your behavior. It's our manner of thought and behavior that makes an entirely right-brained team prone to developing provocative ideas that your organization might never be able to implement—and an all left-brained team unable to break free of process thinking. I call this the duality dilemma, and it affects every organization and its ability to forecast the future.

Within every organization are people whose dominant characteristic is either creativity or logic. If you've been on a team that includes both groups and didn't have a great facilitator during your meetings, you probably clashed. If it was an important project and there were strong personalities representing each side, the creative people felt as though their contributions were being discounted, while the logical thinkers felt undervalued because they weren't coming up with bold new ideas. You undoubtedly had a difficult time staying on track, or worse, you might have spent hours meeting about how to have your next meeting. The duality dilemma was responsible for a lack of forward-thinking at BlackBerry, which never had an executable plan to remake the phone's form factor and operating system. Right-brained staff wanted to make serious changes to the phone, while left-brained staff were fixated on risk and maintaining BlackBerry's customer base. The future of the company hinged on its ability to bring both forces together to forecast trends and plan for the future.

Overcoming the duality dilemma is possible, and it's a matter of highlighting—rather than discouraging or downplaying—the strengths of both sides. The Hasso Plattner Institute of Design at Stanford University (also known as "the d.school") teaches a practice that addresses the duality dilemma and illuminates how an organization can harness both strengths in equal measure, alternately broadening ("flaring") or narrowing ("focusing") its thinking.[2]

When the group is flaring, it is sourcing inspiration, making lists of ideas, mapping out new possibilities, getting feedback, and thinking big. In a focus phase, those ideas must be investigated, vetted, and decided upon. Flaring asks questions such as "What if?" "Who could it be?" "Why might this matter?" and "What might be the implications of our actions?" Focusing is about "Which option is best?" "What is our next action?" and "How do we move forward?"

Throughout this book, we have been flaring and focusing as we tracked trends moving from the fringe to the mainstream. Indeed, the six steps of forecasting require you to alternate between flaring and focusing, harnessing the dominant qualities of the right brain and the left brain. With each step, you are able to understand "the future of x" more clearly as you define a trend, determine the best action to take, and create a strategy that's pressure-tested. When you flare and focus, you are able to overcome the duality dilemma. This process is depicted in Figure 1.

Here's how to use these complementary ways of thinking:

Flare at the fringe: Keep an open mind as you cast a wide enough net and gather information without judgment. You're brainstorming, making a fringe map, forcing yourself to think outside the box and consider radically different points of view.

FORECASTING METHODOLOGY:
The Six-Step Funnel

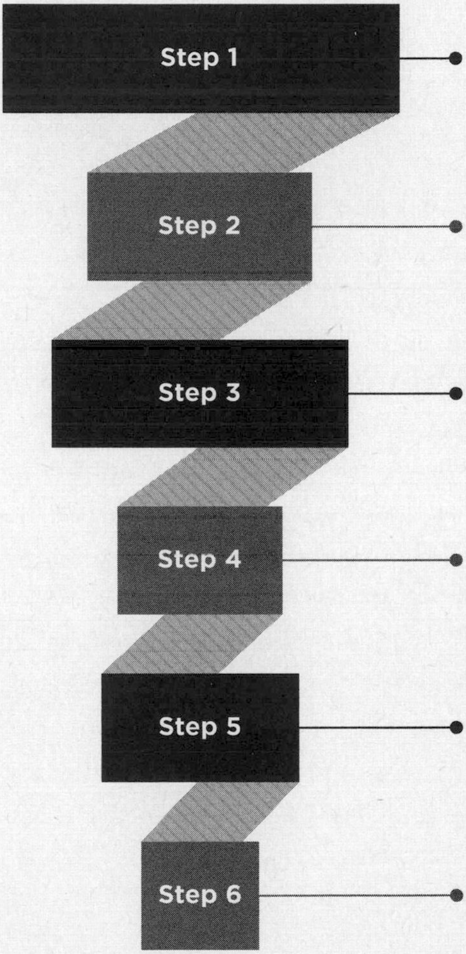

Step 1 — **The Fringe**
Make observations and harness information from the fringes of society or a particular research area.

Step 2 — **CIPHER**
Uncover hidden patterns by categorizing information from the Fringe: Contradictions, Inflections, Practices, Hacks, Extremes, Rarities

Step 3 — **Ask the Right Questions**
Ask the right questions to determine whether a pattern is really a trend.

Step 4 — **Calculate the ETA**
Ensure that the timing is right for the trend and for your organization.

Step 5 — **Write Scenarios**
Scenarios inform the strategy you will create to take the necessary action on a trend.

Step 6 — **Pressure-Test the Future**
Are your scenarios comprehensive enough? Is your level of confidence justified? Is the strategy you're taking the right one for the future?

Answers:
What is the future of X?

Figure 1

Focus to spot patterns: CIPHER helps narrow what you've learned and uncovered. Look for contradictions, inflections, practices, hacks, extremes, and rarities.

Flare to ask the right questions: In order to get beyond your own belief bias, force yourself to disagree with all of your assertions. Brainstorm to create counterarguments and to poke holes in everything you think you know to be true.

Focus to calculate timing: Where is the trend along its trajectory? What is your ETA equation? What are the internal tech developments and the external events worth paying attention to?

Flare to create scenarios and strategies: What are the probable, plausible, and possible futures, given what you know to be true today of the trend? What outcomes are likely? What necessary strategies and ways of thinking will govern how your organization will respond to the trend?

Focus to pressure-test your action: What outcomes will result in response to the action you take? Is your strategy extensible, and will it continue to address the trend as it evolves? In this final step, you are working to ensure that your desired future is achievable.

Forecasting the future is a matter of listening to, recognizing, and acting on signals. Every step isn't entirely about logic and data—the process also requires active dreaming and creativity. Rather than prophesying, seeing trends is a matter of looking for emerging changes at the fringe, within organizations, and in our societies. It cannot be relegated to inventive visionaries, nor can it be mapped entirely by left-brain thinkers. Great trends forecasting unites opposing forces, harnessing both wild imagination and pragmatism. Applying the six steps of the forecasting instructions that are at the heart of this book means zooming all the way out to understand how they all fit together.

Any organization intent on forecasting the future must practice both flaring and focusing, and so it is paramount that every team charged with watching and taking action on trends must be composed of both kinds of thinkers. The organizations that learn how to balance each hemisphere are uniquely positioned to forecast trends and develop strategies that work.

And, as you're about to see, they might even be capable of magic.

FLARING, FOCUSING, AND FLORIDA

When you think about Florida, what comes to mind? Hurricane season, when big swaths of the population have to temporarily pull up stakes to get out of the storm's eye? Communities of retirees? Or, how about magic? As in Disney's Magic Kingdom, the Orlando Magic basketball team, or Miami, also known as the "Magic City"?

But run into someone working in augmented reality—which is a live view of the physical world whose elements are augmented by digital inputs (graphics, video, and sound)—and her description of Florida would center on a particular kind of magic being invented by a mysterious, secretive group of people working in Plantation, a small community a few miles northwest of Fort Lauderdale. The group is equal parts left and right brain, and their project demonstrates why focusing and flaring is necessary for anyone hoping to build the future of anything. The team, and what they're making, represents this duality in harmony. Creative minds, such as comic book writer Andy Lanning (*Guardians of the Galaxy*) and graphic novelist Dave Gibbons (*Watchmen*) are working alongside engineers like Jean-Yves Bouguet, who, while on Google's original Street View team, figured out how to map the indoors. There are software engineers who know how to scan your iris, even from a thousand feet away, as well as optical engineers and experts in AI. They work together with game designers and digital artists.

On the company's board of directors is Richard Taylor, who co-founded Weta Workshop, a film prop and special effects company.

Taylor has won five Oscars, four British Academy of Film and Television Arts awards, and numerous other accolades. If you don't recognize the name, you'll certainly recognize his artistic work: Weta worked on the *Lord of the Rings* films, *Avatar*, and *District 9*, among others.

Collectively, this right-brain, left-brain group is known as Magic Leap. And they're at the fringe, inventing an entirely new kind of computing—a virtual world seamlessly interconnected with our physical realm, one in which we may someday hold our work meetings, visit with our relatives, or even go out on first dates.

The technologies that Magic Leap is building wouldn't be possible without people who are adept at each of the six steps: researchers at the very edge of the fringe; systems engineers, operations managers, and computer scientists who are good at identifying patterns, thinking through processes, and making sure a proposed strategy will work; science fiction and comic book writers who shine when they are imagining wild, plausible scenarios; strategists who know how to put ideas into action; business managers who understand budgeting and risk. Magic Leap is forecasting and inventing the future, because it has found points of convergence between the two hemispheres, joining those who are skilled at processes, organization, and analysis with those who specialize in speculative fiction, ideation, and fantasy.[3]

The team was put together by two unusual suspects: John Graham Macnamara, a trained physicist, and Rony Abovitz, a biomedical engineer. Before turning his attention to Magic Leap, Abovitz, a technologist trained to think logically and systemically, invented a surgical robotic arm equipped with real-time sensation and feedback (or "haptic") technology to surgeons as they operated. The company he founded was eventually sold for $1.65 billion.[4] Billion-dollar mergers and acquisitions are more common in the medical field, but tech-related medical startups that fetch such a high price are rare.

Abovitz has gone from making surgical instruments to building at Magic Leap what he calls a "cinematic reality" device. It isn't intended to be used strictly for filmmaking. Rather, it's a new form of technology, one that could augment the reality of our physical world. Within just four years, Abovitz raised nearly as much money for Magic Leap as he made selling his robotic arm company. In February 2016, Magic Leap closed on $739.5 million in funding from Chinese e-commerce giant Alibaba, Google, and Qualcomm—the largest-ever "C" round in financing history. (A "C" round is a phase of funding where an injection of capital is given to help a new company make acquisitions, accelerate, and grow.) Investors from previous funding rounds included Silicon Valley venture capital firms Andreessen Howowitz, Kleiner Perkins Caufield & Byers, and Obvious Ventures (cofounded by Ev Williams of Twitter). By the time spring breakers descended upon south Florida, Magic Leap's total valuation had eclipsed $4.5 billion—that's four and a half unicorns. (It's an ambitious beginning, but even with Abovitz's previous success, some might question whether that level of investment will ever be returned.[5])

If artificial intelligence promises to bring human-like thinking to machines, Magic Leap represents a future in which everyday people will effortlessly bring complex machine processes into the human realm. Imagine an immersive environment where believable, realistic digital elements—family members, plant life, even hobbits—are woven directly into your physical world. And where anything you can see can be captured, imported, and automated for your own personal use.

The technologies that make up Magic Leap include nearly all of those discussed earlier throughout this book: automation, biohacking, invisible information layers, and artificial intelligence. Whether or not you ever own a Magic Leap device—and whether or not a Magic Leap product is ever sold—what Abovitz and his team are creating represents a sea change in how we think about computing. It has tech investors clamoring to sign deals and journalists transfixed, which may give you pause, given what we know to be true of other Silicon Valley startups.

But Magic Leap isn't just a few geeky hopeful entrepreneurs working out of their garage in California. It's a stunning collection of technologists and creatives who have their heads down and sleeves rolled up in a

260,000-square-foot facility on south Florida's east coast. A deeper look into the technology that Magic Leap is building—and more importantly for our purposes, how they're flaring and focusing—will reveal how every organization intent on forecasting the future can overcome the duality dilemma.

DIGITAL HUMANS

First, the technology. While virtual reality brings you inside of a pre-programmed digital world, Magic Leap is a highly sophisticated form of "augmented reality." You see and experience the physical environment as it already is, and technology enables you to augment it with digital effects. Most likely you now use your mobile phone, a tablet, a television, or a computer to video-chat with friends, relatives, and business colleagues on FaceTime or Skype. Magic Leap is a device you wear over your eyes. As you sat in your living room, you could import your grandmother onto your sofa. She'd seem real, as if she were sitting across from you—and you would appear just as realistic to her, sitting on her sofa in her living room.

The idea of augmenting reality with digital overlays originated in 1990, when Boeing researcher Thomas Caudell was asked to find a cheaper alternative for the expensive diagrams and marking tools that factory workers used to make airplane parts. The process involved large plywood boards containing detailed wiring instructions and schematics for each plane. Caudell, who had been a physicist at the Hughes Artificial Intelligence Center in Malibu, California, thought of a device the workers could wear over their eyes that would project all of the instructions onto reusable boards. If any changes were needed, the instructions could be edited and sent back through a computer program to update the worker as needed. Caudell called his ingenious system "augmented reality."[6]

Nearly three decades later, AR is already being used in numerous ways. When you watch your favorite football team play on television,

AR is responsible for the blue and yellow "down" lines. If you drive a car with a heads-up display, that's a form of AR. Cosmetics company L'Oréal launched a very clever AR mobile app allowing users to try on different lipsticks, eyeshadows, and foundations.[7] Ikea published an AR catalog (for iPad) to let shoppers visualize couches, chairs, and accessories in their homes.[8] In all of these cases, you experience AR on a second screen: a monitor in your car, or via your television, mobile phone, or tablet.

AR becomes much more compelling when a second screen isn't needed. Special AR headsets and glasses are used in the oil and gas industry for training on simulated equipment and facilities. Health-care workers use AR to help locate veins. And for a short period of time, geeks had access to a strange-looking headset, one that could bring a hidden, invisible information layer into full view: Google Glass.

Glass was an attempt at a consumer-grade AR headset, and I had early access to a pair to test it as part of a pilot program in early 2013. Glass was a slim headband that wrapped around my face, and over my right eye there was a tiny screen and camera. The headset connected to my mobile phone and to a repository of interesting but clunky apps. There were two ways to make commands: I could swipe my fingers along a sensor, which ran alongside the right temple, or I could nod my head up and down. If I was wandering around a new city, Glass was terrific—I had AR walking directions in my field of view. I could swipe and nod to take photos, then speak "Okay Glass" to text them to a friend—all without having to take out my phone.

Of course, the device was far from perfect. I wear prescription glasses, and so I either had to commit to wearing contact lenses on days I wanted to use Glass or had to position the Glass band over and around my glasses, and prepare to be stared at by confused onlookers. Because the screen was above my right eye, I had to continuously gaze up in order to see the AR overlays—which was particularly maddening for anyone who tried to talk to me while Glass was in use. Perhaps the biggest annoyance was its battery life: after only about thirty to forty-five minutes, Glass needed to be plugged back into the wall for recharging, which was difficult to do when using Glass for one of the activities it was built for, like strolling through city streets or skiing down the side of a mountain.

Eventually, Google opened up its Glass program to the public. It wasn't uncommon to see someone wearing his Glass all day long (even though the battery was clearly dead)—and once people realized that there was a camera attached, some became concerned that they were being photographed or recorded without permission. In the end, Glass was less a transformative AR device than it was a status symbol for a particular kind of geek and Silicon Valley investor, who in certain circles became known as "glassholes."

I didn't expect the hardware or the Glass developer program to last very long, and in fact it didn't: Google folded its developer program and stopped selling the device in January 2015.⁹ I don't fault Google for being early to commercialize an AR headset—in fact, I was excited by the underlying technology powering the system.

There are numerous theories about why Glass failed, but from my vantage point, I think some of it had to do with the duality dilemma: Where was the influence of creative design thinkers, who might have made the headset more comfortable to wear? Or who might have offered designs for women as well as men? It seems as though step three— "Flare to ask the right questions"—might have been skipped. With such a short battery life, how could Glass be used for more than just a few minutes at a time? If the user was relying on Glass for GPS walking directions in a populated area like New York City, calls to Wi-Fi or cellular networks would drain the battery quickly, rendering the headset useless. What about step five, "Flare to create scenarios and strategies"? Aside from taking videos and photos, why would someone use Glass? Realistically, what were the other scenarios in which someone might use Glass in an office setting? Wouldn't they be viewed by coworkers as a distraction?

When I wore Glass, I wondered what it might be like if an AR head-set was capable of doing more than sending Tweets and reading text messages. What if it was meant to be always on—and also always on my face, as a stylish pair of prescription frames? For someone not wearing glasses, putting a device on every single morning might seem unrealistic—but twenty years ago, she would have made the same complaint about carrying a mobile phone.

·

Magic Leap isn't only building a new kind of technology for the future, it's doing so by combining the strengths of flaring and focusing. If it isn't obvious enough looking through the staff roster, you can see evidence of the duality within some unusual patents that Abovitz and his team at Magic Leap started filing right around the time that Google was sending its first sets of Glass to testers. Just because a company files a patent doesn't mean that it will bring the schematics and plans into production, or that the system will work exactly as described. The real lesson to be learned from the patents is how Magic Leap harmonizes the strengths of its right- and left-brained thinkers.

To start, Magic Leap's patents are nothing like the patents filed for Google Glass. Within the pages of Magic Leap's submissions are alternating moments of meticulous focus and wild, inventive flare, making them showpieces for why the company intentionally employs creatives—artists and storytellers—as well as systems engineers, software developers, and operations managers.

One of Magic Leap's patents described a device—which looks like a pair of normal glasses, but for a tiny camera at the base of each lens—that was meant to be worn continuously, and was capable of far more than simply sending a Tweet or reading a text. A camera would scan the retina, allowing only the owner to unlock and use the headset. There were scientific descriptions explaining how the device could be used to treat neurological disorders, seizures, and depression.

Mathematical equations showed how the data from the physical world could be translated and visualized to tell a personalized story that only the wearer could see.

Of the fifty-two patents Magic Leap filed between 2013 and the first quarter of 2016,[10] one in particular stood out: "Methods and Systems for Creating Virtual and Augmented Reality."[11] Hundreds of pages long, the patent is a mishmash of engineering math, AI and AR formulas, and good, old-fashioned sci-fi exposition. For example, look at what's described in the "Digital Humans" section of the patent, subsection 1612:

> The AR system may allow users to interact with digital humans. . . .
> [A] user may walk into an abandoned warehouse, but the space may
> become populated with digital humans such that it resembles a bank.
> The user may walk up to a teller who may be able to look at the user's
> eyes and interact with him/her. Because the system tracks the user's
> eyes, the AR system can render the digital human such that the digital
> human makes eye contact with the user.

What this implies is that in the future, we could do our banking in a digital environment, with digital avatars of real people, none of whom are located in the same place at the same time. You might live in South Bend, Indiana, and have access to a world-class money manager who prefers to operate out of Iwate Prefecture in northern Japan. Your desire for human connection, especially during sensitive transactions like banking, could be satiated via AR.

Further down in the patent documentation is a section on "transaction-assistance configurations," which includes numerous use cases for shopping and marketing:

> Since the system may be utilized to track the eye, it can also allow
> "one glance" shopping. That is, the user may simply look at an object (say a robe in a hotel) and create a stipulation such as, "I want

that, when my account goes back over $3000." When a user views a particular object of interest, similar products may also be displayed virtually to the user.

There have been plenty of prototypes for glance-based shopping, but none that imagined this kind of utility. This proposal combines security, bank account information, shopping, and a digital habit many people have formed—bookmarking items and saving them for later—into one application. It's a mishmash of flaring and focusing, one that could provide great utility to users.

Subsection 1714 is a fascinating explanation of health and biometric applications for Magic Leap, which range from storing and accessing our virtual medical records to using our skin as a password. While these ideas haven't yet been peer-reviewed (or even demonstrated to other researchers), the flare-focus thinking is evident in this unique approach to melding biology with AR technology:

> The system can determine the curvature/size of the eye, which assists in identifying the user since eyes are of similar but not exactly the same size between people. Second, the system has knowledge of temporal information; the system can determine the user's normal heart rate, if the user's eyes are producing a water film, if the eyes verge and focus together, if breathing patterns, blink rates, or blood pulsing status in the vessels are normal, etc. Next, the system also can use correlated information; for example, the system can correlate images of the environment with expected eye movement patterns, and can also check that the user is seeing the same expected scene that is supposed to be located at that location, (e.g., as derived from GPS, Wi-Fi signals and maps of the environment, etc.). For example, if the user is supposedly at home, the system should be seeing expected pose correct scenes inside of the known home. Finally, the system can use hyperspectral and/skin/muscle conductance to also identify the user.

The natural inclination of an eye doctor, an optical engineer, or a medical researcher may be to discount all this as wild speculation—claims that will never be proven. That's the left brain kicking into lizard gear, automatically dismissing what has not yet been proven to you personally. Remember step three of forecasting: Given what we know to be true today, could we poke enough holes in this part of the patent to render it completely false? (Answer: no. It is a plausible scenario for existing technologies.)

With that in mind, consider the idea that our medical records could be encoded and available through AR:

> The AR system may help improve healthcare because the doctor may have access to all of the patient's medical history at his/her disposal. This may include patient behavior (e.g., information not necessarily contained in medical records). . . . For example, if the patient is unconscious, the doctor may (based on the user's privacy controls) be able to search through the record of the user's behavior in the recent past to determine a cause of the ailment and treat the patient accordingly.

And now, let's review some of the more bizarre and frightening scenarios listed in the patents. Without flaring, this use case for insurance companies, which could gain access to our behavior and adjust our premiums in real time, would never have been revealed:

> Given the AR system's ability to constantly monitor a user's behavior, companies may be able to gauge a user's health based on his behaviors and accordingly price insurance premiums for the individual. This may serve as an incentive for healthy behavior to drive premiums down for insurance because the company may see that the user is healthy and is low-risk for insurance purposes. On the other hand, the company may assess unhealthy behavior and accordingly price the user's premiums at a higher rate based on this collected data.

Privacy would be a concern. So would bioethics. The patent also includes many sections on how the system could take data from our everyday lives and automatically create a story with it to help us make better decisions. Again, none of these scenarios could have been developed by right- or left-brain thinkers alone. Together, here's what they hypothesize:

> The AR system may render a "plant" or any other virtual content whose form, shape or characteristics may change based on the user's behavior. For example, the AR system may render a plant that blooms when the user exhibits "good" behavior and wither away when the user does not. In a specific example, the plant may bloom when the user is being a good boyfriend, for example (e.g., buys flowers for girlfriend, etc.) and may wither away when the user has failed to call his girlfriend all day....
>
> ...
>
> The users may, for example, encode the color, shape, leaves, flowers, etc., of the plant with their respective status. If a user is overworked, the respective plant could appear withered. If a user is unhappy, the leaves of the respective plant could fall off. If the user has a lack of resources, the leaves of the respective plant that represents the user may turn brown, etc. The users may provide their respective plants to a leader (e.g., manager, CEO). The leader can place all the plants in a virtual garden. This provides the leader with a high-bandwidth view of organization, through the general color or concept of a garden. Such graphical illustration of problems facilitates visual recognition of problems or lack thereof with the organization.

In reading through the patents, it's obvious that both the technology and the people within Magic Leap are making use of the dual hemispheres in a complementary way and that they engage in both flared and focused thinking:

Flare at the fringe: Without unfettered, unabashed flaring to develop improbable ideas from the fringe, there would be no basis for Magic Leap to explore a new frontier of human-machine interfaces.

Focus to spot patterns: Without focus, those disparate ideas would never coalesce as recognizable patterns to help formulate a trend hypothesis for the future. That trend hypothesis is critical to developing this new form of human-machine computing.

Flare to ask the right questions: Poking holes into all assumptions and assertions would reveal any potential problems, allowing Magic Leap engineers to tweak, recalibrate, and improve their work.

Focus to calculate timing: Analysis would reveal where the future of AR was along its trajectory, along with what internal tech developments and external events were worthy of attention.

Flare to create scenarios and strategies: Magic Leap's writers and creatives flare to build scenarios describing all the ways in which we might one day use AR.

Focus to pressure-test your action: And finally, those at Magic Leap in charge of turning those fictional scenarios into reality focus to pressure-test actions and to think through the outcomes that might result. Which is why you don't see a product just yet—this isn't a team rushing to market before it's ready.

Clearly, Magic Leap isn't just building a fancy set of AR glasses. It is building the foundation for a new kind of computing and a new era of human-machine interaction, one in which all the technologies we've discussed thus far—automation, neural networks and AI, deep learning—would dramatically change how we interact with computers and with each other.

The technology is representative of a bigger shift in which humanity itself could experience something comparable to what former DARPA program manager Gill Pratt once described as a modern Cambrian explosion, which was a brief moment in time some 540 million years ago when our predecessors went through a rapid period of evolution. Part of that evolution included vision—the ability to see—which made the development of complex, intelligent life forms possible. Pratt argued that advances in deep learning, neural networks, AI, and cloud robotics—in which every robot learns from the experiences of all robots, which leads to rapid growth of robot competence, particularly as the number of robots grows—could usher in a period of rapid advancement, after which our life on Earth might look very different from what we see today.[12]

If you're still skeptical, consider the fact that one of Magic Leap's outside investors is Google. That's right: the same Google that marketed an AR headset that the tech community very publicly loved to hate. But take a moment to flare: What if together, Google and Magic Leap could create a transformative shift in technology? Google would become the invisible information layer powering our daily lives, while Magic Leap became the augmented lens through which we experienced a new kind of reality?

Would we set up parameters in advance and automate certain tasks—such as categorizing people? Would our business cards be a remnant of the past, since we'd simply look at someone and the system would file away all of her relevant details for later searching? What happens when everything we can see is searchable, and all the information we need is delivered to us just before we need it?

Would the system quantify our biometric data, allowing those with more ambitious biohacking plans to adjust their moods, emotional responses and bodily functions? The system would use artificial intelligence and learn more about us the more we wore the glasses. Could it become our physician and nurse, our nutritionist and our personal trainer?

If we were to reverse-engineer the thinking, rather than solely the technological processes, required to create such a device, we'd find there are still a number of big, difficult questions that must be tackled, many of which have no explicit connection to math or engineering. So let's take a moment to flare:

- How are "good" and "bad" behavior determined?

- Who gets to decide, and would we adjust the definitions as time wears on?

- Would each person get an initial set of benchmarks relative to her own experience and circumstances?

- Even our wisest ethicists and philosophers struggle to define what constitutes good and bad—so would an AR headset be in a better position to judge?

Wearing the device, we could continually record an experience, like a party, which would allow us to "wander around the room, seeing the people walk by," and experience the event again "after the fact from essentially any vantage point." Will nostalgia become an immediate aftereffect of wearing the headset? If we want to replay a party, and we were there for thirty minutes, we'd either have to watch it at an accelerated speed or spend that same amount of time in the present reliving the past. Will we become acclimated to thinking from today backward on continual loop, rather than being forced to think about the consequences of our actions in the farther future?

What happens when everyone has a detailed, factual account of everything they have ever done—and the ability to replay scenes exactly as they happened? It might be an exciting development for law enforcement, but would the average person be able to get through life without resorting to the narratives she has created for herself?

What happens when we can dial up or down our emotional states? We would, in a sense, be able to create and deploy nuanced, computer-altered versions of ourselves. A political candidate could ramp herself up before a big speech. A student could focus all of her attention during an exam. But would it be fair?

We aren't augmenting reality as much as we are augmenting humanity.

•

We ought to stop, for a moment, to think about the implications of that statement. If we are indeed standing on the precipice of a modern-day Cambrian explosion, within the next one hundred years much of human life could look radically different from today's world. All of this technological progress—all of these questions, and all of the trends described throughout this book—will cause great disruption and opportunity within organizations. But what does that imply for our future as human beings, living together on planet Earth? With that framing, here are ten questions we should all consider:

1. If a bot, a brain network, an AI, or another technology commits a crime, who is guilty? Who is held accountable?

2. What if we connected the minds of an expert diplomat, a Navy Seal, a cognitive psychologist, and a prisoner from a terrorist organization? Are we prepared for warfare in which human intelligence and experience are weaponized?

3. In the future, who "owns" your face, your eyes, and your biometric data? How will we decide who gets access to it?

4. In 2017, we can change our passwords if an account gets hacked. What if your body gets hacked? What if someone steals the unique properties of your skin, your eyes, and your respiration?

5. What happens when we get hooked on a technology and it becomes obsolete? We may be willing to buy a new phone every few years, but what about biomedical devices, like mechanical hands and therapeutic nanobots? Will we allow humans to suffer—or to die—because companies aren't able to continually supply parts and services for decommissioned technologies?

6. Technology requires more and more of our implicit trust. What happens when our magical AI assistants get hacked? Our self-driving cars? Our smart homes? What happens when we lose faith that our technology is serving our needs, and not someone else's? How will our devices—which we can no longer function without—regain our trust?

7. Are we unintentionally creating a future underclass of analog citizens? Three decades from now, will neuroenhancing headbands, personal delivery drones, and personalized medicine replace luxury cars, vacation homes, and personal yachts as status symbols? Will anonymity be afforded only to the rich?

8. How do we use technology today that our future selves will consider barbaric? How will we arrive at that belief? What will have happened?

9. In the future, machines will assist humans with everything. They will keep us company, assist doctors in surgery, babysit our children, and help managers run their meetings. What will it mean to be "human"?

10. What happens when, in the future, we finally get what we say we want?

You may never wear a Magic Leap headset that renders an AR garden of your employees' virtual plants. I can assure you, however, that fringe thinkers have pored through this and Magic Leap's other patents, which have inspired them to work on AR projects of their own. Those at the fringe, inspired by Magic Leap's patents, are now beginning their own cycles of flaring and focusing. In the years to come, others will build on their work, too, as our socio-technological evolution loops around and around again.

Patent filings don't mean that the processes and products described will ever be put into commercial use—but patents are a key component of flaring at the fringe. Indeed, there are never any completely new technologies invented out of whole cloth. Our technology trends, their adoption for use in business, and the cultural, political, educational, and economic shifts that happen concurrently are all interwoven. Our tapestry of invention is part of an infinite continuum. The tools may change—from hands, to weavers, to Luddite-protested automatic machines, to algorithms and robots, to self-generating synthetic organics—but the previous corpus of research always becomes the basis for fresh thinking at the fringe.

OUR FUTURE, TODAY

We have come to the end, but also to the beginning. "Everything must have a beginning," wrote author Mary Shelley in 1831. "That beginning must be linked to something that went before."[13] Our existing trends inspire new thinking at the fringe, which is why it is essential that you always return back to where you started. In her time, Shelley was herself a fringe thinker—the famous character she developed, Frankenstein's monster—continues to influence the mainstream today, as we've seen again and again, from Tim Burton's Edward Scissorhands, to the 1962 novelty song "Monster Mash," to DC Comics' "The Seven Soldiers of Victory," in which Frankenstein is depicted as a warrior trying to prevent the end of the world.[14] They are all new stories built on old foundations, which is something Shelley did, too, taking her inspiration from John Milton's *Paradise Lost*.

The future is an endless cycle. It neither begins at a finite point nor ends once something has been accomplished. Likewise, the fluidity of time—not chronological time, but how we experience technological change—must stay at the forefront of our thought processes whenever we're planning for the future.

Your exposure to the world as it evolves has shaped your understanding of technology, just as it has for me, and for my parents, grandparents, and now, my own daughter. I am just learning how to speak commands to machines. My daughter will talk in full sentences to machines for the rest of her lifetime. By the time her daughter is my age, she will look at old, flat photographs of my desktop computer, keyboard, and mouse and wonder how I ever got by with such rudimentary technology—just as today, I look at the worn black-and-white photographs of my grandmother and her typewriter, her shoebox-sized telephone, and the black-and-white television set that to her were once shiny, exciting futuristic devices. We are experiencing the evolution of the same technology asynchronously, and our belief biases are radically different as a result.

The future won't just happen to my daughter's daughter, or to her, or to me, or to you. It is something that we are creating now, in the present tense. You have the ability not only to forecast what's to come, but to create your own preferred future. As technology stimulates innovation across a greater number of fields, and as trends emerge from the fringe and travel to the mainstream, you can take steps to navigate the future of your field or industry. Don't wait. Your future self will reflect back and realize that the best time to find, track, and act on a technology trend was a decade ago. The second best time is right now, today.

GLOSSARY OF CONCEPTS AND TERMS

Assumptions vs. knowledge: Separating factual-based information from your own guesses, experiences, and assumptions.

Availability heuristic: A mental shortcut using knowledge that's already available to us, rather than including new ideas or information.

Belief bias: What takes place when we hold on to cherished beliefs such that we favor a particular point of view, even if it's wrong.

Biohackers: People who modify their bodies using science and technology.

Brainet: A series of brains connected by technology to enable brain-to-brain communication (coined by Miguel Nicolelis).

Decacorns: Companies with valuations of $10 billion or more.

Disads: Holes that can be poked into arguments and hypotheses. Disads are used in the third step of the forecasting process. Short for "disadvantages."

Duality dilemma: The challenge that arises when teams are either homogeneously left- or right-brained, or when both types of thinkers are together in a group without a strong facilitator.

ETA: A measurement to determine where a trend is along its trajectory. Short for "estimated time of arrival."

External events: Adjacent developments and circumstances that will impact a trend's future, even if technology leaps forward. Often, these events are completely outside an organization's control.

Foresight: Data-driven analysis and critical thinking on a particular subject as it relates to the future.

Fringe: The place where scientists, artists, technologists, philosophers, mathematicians, psychologists, ethicists, and social science thinkers are testing early hypotheses, undertaking wildly creative research, and trying to discover new kinds of solutions to the problems confronting humanity.

Future-fallacy trap: When a person's inflexibility on details causes mistakes in her or his planning for the future.

Future forecast: A data-driven analysis that explains how something is likely to change over time.

Genie problem: When algorithms, workflows, and processes function exactly as they've been programmed, but yield undesirable outcomes.

Internal tech developments: Technological advances specific to or directly impacted by a trend. These advances often happen within an organization or as a result of a partnership between an organization and outside researchers.

Landscrapers: Very long buildings that cover a significant amount of ground.

Neural network: A vast, interconnected computer system made up of simple elements that are loosely modeled after the neuronal structure of the human brain's cerebral cortex.

Paradox of the present: What occurs when we are too fearful about the intricacies of technology, safety, and the needs of various government agencies and equipment manufacturers to think more broadly about how technology might emerge from the fringe into different parts of our future mainstream.

Ten sources of change: The ten main types of external forces that shape trends. They are: wealth distribution, education, government, politics, public health, demography, economy, environment, journalism, and media.

Toothbrush test: Larry Page's test to determine whether a new acquisition makes sense. In short, is it something that you'll use once or twice a day, and does it make your life a little bit better?

Transhumanism: An intellectual movement that believes the human condition can be beneficially augmented through technology.

Trend: A significant development that is heading in a particular direction and leading to other changes in technology, business, government, society, or other realms of our lives. All trends intersect with other aspects of daily life and they share a set of conspicuous, universal features. A trend is driven by a basic human need, one that is often catalyzed by new technology. A trend is timely, but it persists. A trend evolves as it emerges. A trend can materialize as a series of unconnectable dots that begins on the fringe and moves to the mainstream.

Unicorns: Companies with valuations of $1 billion or more.

ACKNOWLEDGMENTS

This is a book about our collective future, and it is the culmination of more than a decade of work from my past, during which I was fortunate to have incredible teachers, editors, mentors, and friends. I owe each of them a great deal of thanks.

I am indebted to Sarah Green Carmichael at the *Harvard Business Review*, Jon Fine at *Inc.* magazine, James Geary at Harvard's *Nieman Reports*, and Joshua Benton at the Nieman Journalism Lab, who afforded me the space to further develop early versions of my methodology, the foundation of which appears in this book but in a radically different form.

I'm grateful to Douglas Smith, Quentin Hope, and Charlie Baum at Columbia University's Punch Sulzberger Executive Leadership Program, who for the past ten years have welcomed me as a summer lecturer. Their mentorship has enabled me to advance my thinking and to test my forecasting methodology. I am indebted to Ann Marie Lipinski, curator of Harvard University's Nieman Foundation for Journalism, for including me as a Knight Visiting Fellow. The time I spent at Harvard broadened my perspective and elevated my thinking, and Ann Marie continually challenged me to demand more of myself, which translated to additional reading, research, and time in front of my white board. She opened the door to a world of new dots for me to connect.

The Signals Are Talking is the product of hundreds of face-to-face meetings with fringe thinkers, company executives, and academics. There are too many people to list here, but I would like to highlight a few who have, over many years, shared their perspectives and offered invaluable advice. Former Time,

Inc., executives (and Future Today Institute clients) Fran Hauser, Mark Golin, John Cantarella, Bill McBain, Chris Peacock, Liz White, and Bill Shapiro; Ben Monnie and Richard Gingras at Google; Kara Snesko at the State Department; and Justin Ferrell at Stanford's Hasso Plattner Institute of Design, or d.school. Many thanks to those at the Online News Association, the Knight Foundation, and the Minneapolis Interactive Marketing Association who have invited me to speak at their events year after year; those public lectures helped me codify the language I use to describe trends.

Several friends either read versions or helped me think through some of the more challenging sections of the manuscript. Their advice and comments made a tremendous difference: David Walman, Hilary Miller, Alan Edelman, and Susan Dominus. My thanks to Cheryl Cooney, who is kind and patient and without whom I would get very little done. Emily Caufield assisted with the graphics for this book, and, as always, she did a wonderful job. Petra Woolf spent many hours painstakingly sorting through all of my research notes, color-coding and filing hundreds of papers and cards. She was a tremendous help. My gratitude to Debbie Millman and Paola Antonelli, who have nurtured my journey through the worlds of art and design, to Mary Jane Ryan, my tireless coach and mentor, and to Maria Popova, a dear friend who continues to inspire and enliven me. As always, my deepest thanks to Samuel Freedman at Columbia University, whose voice is in my head whenever I write.

It was Carol Franco who first saw a future in this book, and who invited me into the beautiful Santa Fe home she shares with Kent Lineback to woodshed my ideas. Together, they helped me to distill all of my ideas into the architecture of this book—they were ruthless, relentless, and remarkable. I'm so very grateful to them, and to Carol especially for convincing my editor, John Mahaney, to take me on. What a gift it was to work with him. His first set of edits eviscerated one of the examples I used—he not only questioned what I was trying to say but then effortlessly rattled off several books that contradicted my point. John is the very best kind of editor: one who makes a book stronger, and in the editing process makes the writer stronger, too. I've learned so much from John, and I'm grateful. In addition, my thanks to Kathy Streckfus for her meticulous and conscientious copy editing, and to Phillip Blanchard for methodically checking every fact, source, and detail.

Finally, I am indebted to my husband and intellectual sparring partner, Brian Woolf. He reads the earliest versions of everything I write and forces me to clarify, to explain, or to defend the concepts I thread together. I know that late-night editing isn't in the *ketubah*, so here's my very public acknowledgment of the influence you have on all my work.

NOTES

INTRODUCTION: "HELLO, ARE YOU LOST?"

1. Benj Edwards, "Who Needs GPS? The Forgotten Story of Etak's Amazing 1985 Car Navigation System," *Fast Company*, June 26, 2015, www.fastcompany.com/3047828/who-needs-gps-the-forgotten-story-of-etaks-amazing-1985-car-navigation-system.

2. Ibid.

3. An iPhone teaser aired during the Academy Awards in February 2007. The first official commercial aired June 4, 2007. See both commercials at YouTube, www.youtube.com/watch?v=dkqk8_O1BbE.

4. Sean Silcoff, Jacquie McNish, and Steve Ladurantaye, "Inside the Fall of BlackBerry: How the Smartphone Inventor Failed to Adapt," *Globe and Mail*, September 25, 2013, www.theglobeandmail.com/report-on-business/the-inside-story-of-why-blackberry-is-failing/article14563602.

5. Additional background research on Lazaridis and BlackBerry came from Jane Martinson, "Mr BlackBerry—$2bn Geek Who Started with Lego," *The Guardian*, March 2, 2007, https://www.theguardian.com/business/2007/mar/02/12, and Dieter Bohn, "RIM: Jim Balsillie and Mike Lazaridis Step Down, Co-COO Thorsten Heins Is the New CEO," *The Verge*, January 22, 2012, www.theverge.com/2012/1/22/2726445/rim-jim-balsillie-and-mike-lazaridis-to-step-down-coo-thorsten-heins.

6. All quotations in this section are from a terrific oral history of BlackBerry written by Felix Gillette, Diane Brady, and Caroline Winter, "The Rise and Fall of BlackBerry: An Oral History," *Bloomberg Businessweek*, December 9, 2013, www.bloomberg.com/news/articles/2013-12-05/the-rise-and-fall-of-blackberry-an-oral-history.

7. Jane Martinson, "Mr BlackBerry."

8. Ibid.

9. Jan Libbenga, "BlackBerry Boss Blows Raspberries at iPhone, Sticks It to Microsoft Too," *The Register*, November 8, 2007, www.theregister.co.uk/2007/11/08/why_iphone_is_no_threat_to_blackberry.

10. "International Data Corporation (IDC) Worldwide Quarterly Mobile Phone Tracker," International Data Corporation, www.idc.com/prodserv/smartphone-os-market-share.jsp.

11. Bill Gates, Nathan Myhrvold, and Peter Rinearson, *The Road Ahead* (New York: Viking, 1995).

12. Ossip K. Flechtheim, "Toynbee and the Webers: Remarks on Their Theories of History," *Phylon*, no. 4 (1943).

13. H. G. Wells, *Anticipations of the Reactions of Mechanical and Scientific Progress upon Human Life and Thought* (London: Chapman and Hall, 1914).

14. Akihabara itself has undergone a significant change. These days, it's more a haunt for those interested in *otaku* culture, which includes *manga* comic books and *anime* cartoons.

CHAPTER 1. THE INSTRUCTIONS:
A FUTURIST'S PLAYBOOK FOR EVERY ORGANIZATION

1. Fred Barbash, "Drones Impede Air Battle Against California Wildfires: 'If You Fly We Can't,' Pleads Firefighter," *Washington Post*, July 31, 2015, https://www.washingtonpost.com/news/morning-mix/wp/2015/07/31/if-you-fly-we-cant-pleads-california-firefighter-as-drones-impede-spreading-wildfire-battle.

2. Federal Aviation Administration (FAA), UAS flight data for November 2014–August 2015. As of May 11, 2016, a spreadsheet was available for download at https://www.faa.gov/uas/media/UASEventsNov2014-Aug2015.xls.

3. Ibid.

4. Aaron Karp, "FAA Nightmare: A Million Christmas Drones," *Aviation Daily*, September 28, 2015.

5. Amazon's proposal was introduced by Gur Kimchi, vice president of Amazon Prime Air, at a conference held at the NASA Ames Research Center on July 28, 2015.

6. ThyssenKrupp, "ThyssenKrupp Develops the World's First Rope-Free Elevator System to Enable the Building Industry to Face the Challenges of Global Urbanization," news release, November 27, 2014, www.thyssenkrupp-elevator.com/Show-article.104.0.html.

7. Bernd Magnus, *Nietzsche's Existential Imperative* (Bloomington: Indiana University Press, 1978).

8. Alvin Toffler, *Future Shock* (New York: Random House, 1970).

9. Ibid.

10. Ibid.

11. Robert J. Gordon, *The Rise and Fall of American Growth: The U.S. Standard of Living Since the Civil War* (Princeton, NJ: Princeton University Press, 2016).

12. Nicola Davis at *The Guardian* published a terrific, concise explainer on quantum computing. I recommend it as further reading: Nicola Davis, "Quantum Computing Explained: Harnessing Particle Physics to Work Faster," *The Guardian*, March 6, 2014.

13. W. Michael Cox and Richard Alm, "You Are What You Spend," *New York Times*, February 10, 2008, www.nytimes.com/2008/02/10/opinion/10cox.html.

14. Tim Brooks and Earle Marsh, *The Complete Directory to Prime Time Network and Cable TV Shows, 1946-Present* (New York: Ballantine, 1992).

15. Richard Powelson, "First Color Television Sets Were Sold 50 Years Ago," *Pittsburgh Post-Gazette*, December 31, 2003, http://old.post-gazette.com/tv/20031231colortv1231p3.asp.

16. Aaron Smith, "U.S. Smartphone Use in 2015," Pew Research Center, April 1, 2015, www.pewinternet.org/2015/04/01/us-smartphone-use-in-2015.

17. Ibid.

18. Toffler, *Future Shock*.

19. "2014: By the Numbers," Kickstarter, 2014, https://www.kickstarter.com/year/2014/data.

20. Hope King, "Pebble Time's Kickstarter Project Raised More Than $20.3 Million and Broke Two Kickstarter Records," CNN Money, March 27, 2015, http://money.cnn.com/2015/03/27/technology/pebble-time-most-funded-kickstarter.

21. "The Complete List of Unicorn Companies," CB Insights, https://www.cbinsights.com/research-unicorn-companies.

22. Economic data from the European Union's Economic and Financial Affairs portal, "Croatia," http://ec.europa.eu/economy_finance/eu/countries/croatia_en.htm.

23. Editorial Board, "Edward Snowden, Whistle-Blower," *New York Times*, January 1, 2014, www.nytimes.com/2014/01/02/opinion/edward-snowden-whistle-blower.html.

24. B. Wansink and J. Sobal, "Mindless Eating: The 200 Daily Food Decisions We Overlook," *Environment and Behavior* 39, no. 1 (2007).

25. There were 2,767 versions of Monopoly available on Amazon as of March 15, 2016.

26. "Toyota's Production and Sales Records," Toyota, www.toyota-global.com/company/history_of_toyota/75years/data/conditions/volume_records/sales_records.html.

27. Eric Schmidt, CEO of Google, listed these numbers during his remarks at the Techonomy conference on August 4, 2010, in Lake Tahoe, California. An exabyte is 1,000,000,000,000,000,000 bytes. To put that number into perspective, an average high-resolution photograph is about 3 megabytes (3,000,000 bytes). A 2016 15-inch MacBook Pro can hold 512 gigabytes (512,000,000,000 bytes). If you have a 1 terabyte external hard drive (1,000,000,000,000 bytes) for backups, you could fit about 100,000 photos as well as a carbon copy of your MacBook Pro on it, and you'd still have some space left over. If you needed to back up 1,000 MacBook Pros and all of their photos (assuming each had 100,000), that would require a petabyte (1,000,000,000,000,000 bytes). If you had 1,000 petabytes—that's the data from 1 million MacBook Pros, not to mention billions upon billions of high-resolution photos—that's an exabyte.

28. "Stats," Facebook, http://newsroom.fb.com/company-info.

29. "Statistics," Instagram, https://www.instagram.com/press/?hl=en.

30. Search was performed only on Google, May 11, 2016.

31. *Washington Post* archives, http://pqasb.pqarchiver.com/washingtonpost/advancedsearch.html.

32. Brookings Institution online archives, www.brookings.edu.

33. "Joost Online TV Raises $45 Million," *Los Angeles Times*, May 11, 2007, http://articles.latimes.com/2007/may/11/business/fi-briefs11.6.

34. Brian Solomon, "These 11 Startups Raised the Most Money Before They Had a Product," *Forbes*, June 11, 2015, www.forbes.com/sites/briansolomon/2015/06/11/these-11-startups-raised-over-1-billion-combined-before-launching/#1626f85a1495.

35. Ibid.

36. Sam Biddle, "Sony Was Hacked in February and Chose to Stay Silent," Gawker, December 11, 2014, http://gawker.com/sony-was-hacked-in-february-and-chose-to-stay-silent-1670025366.

37. Josh Halliday, "Epsilon Email Hack: Millions of Customers' Details Stolen," *The Guardian*, April 4, 2011, https://www.theguardian.com/technology/2011/apr/04/epsilon-email-hack.

38. Elizabeth A. Harris, "Michaels Stores' Breach Involved 3 Million Customers," *New York Times*, April 18, 2014, www.nytimes.com/2014/04/19/business/michaels-stores-confirms-breach-involving-three-million-customers.html.

39. David Kravets, "Citi Credit Card Data Breached for 200,000 Customers," *Wired*, September 6, 2011, https://www.wired.com/2011/06/citi-credit-card-breach.

40. Class action complaint in *Hull et al. v. Sony BMG et al.*, Electronic Frontier Foundation, 2005, www.eff.org/IP/DRM/Sony-BMG/sony complaint.pdf.

41. "In the Matter of Sony BMG Music Entertainment," FTC Matter / File Number 062-3019, Federal Trade Commission (FTC), June 2007, https://www.ftc.gov.enforcement/cases-proceedings/062-3019/sony-bmg-music-entertainment-matter.

42. "Sony vs. GeoHot Hacker Lawsuit," Attack of the Show, G4, January 13, 2011, www.g4tv.com/videos/50733/sony-vs-geohot-hacker-lawsuit.

43. Emil Protaliknsi, "Sony Demands Identities from Google, Twitter in PS3 Hacking Lawsuit," TechSpot, February 8, 2011, www.techspot.com/news/42317-sony-demands-identities-from-google-twitter-in-ps3-hacking-lawsuit.html.

44. "Official Statement Regarding PS3 Circumvention Devices and Pirated Software," PlayStation, news release, February 16, 2011, http://blog.us.playstation.com/2011/02/16/official-statement-regarding-ps3-circumvention-devices-and-pirated-software.

45. Nate Anderson, "'Anonymous' Attacks Sony to Protest PS3 Hacker Lawsuit," Ars Technica, April 4, 2011, http://arstechnica.com/tech-policy/2011/04/anonymous-attacks-sony-to-protest-ps3-hacker-lawsuit.

46. Mark Hachman, "PlayStation Hack to Cost Sony $171M; Quake Costs Far Higher," PC Magazine, May 23, 2011, www.pcmag.com/article2/0,2817,2385790,00.asp.

47. "Absolute Sownage: A Concise History of Recent Sony Hacks," Attrition, June 4, 2011, http://attrition.org/security/rant/sony_aka_sownage.html.

48. Swati Khandelwal, "Sony Pictures HACKED; Studio-Staff Computers Seized by Hackers," Hacker News, November 24, 2014, http://thehackernews.com/2014/11/Sony-Pictures-Hacked.html.

49. Peter Elkind, "Inside the Hack of the Century," Fortune, July 1, 2015.

50. A complete repository was compiled by WikiLeaks. See https://wikileaks.org/sony/press.

51. Marianne Garvey, Brian Niemietz, Oli Coleman, and Molly Friedman, "'Today' and Angelina Jolie Look Unbreakable," New York Daily News, January 4, 2015, www.nydailynews.com/entertainment/gossip/confidential/short-article-1.2064831.

52. "Site Blocking Agenda," October 8, 2014, 8:30 a.m.–12:30 p.m. at the Motion Picture Association of America Sherman Oaks Office. See https://s3.amazonaws.com/s3.documentcloud.org/documents/1381538/250191720-agenda-oct-8-2014-sb-confab.pdf.

53. Todd Cunningham and Sharon Waxman, "Sony Hack: Guess How Much Pulling 'The Interview' Will Cost the Studio? (Exclusive)," The Wrap, December 17, 2014, www.thewrap.com/sony-hack-guess-how-much-pulling-the-interview-will-cost-the-studio-exclusive.

54. Jim Finkle and Mark Hosenball, "No Credible Sign of Plot on Theaters over Sony Movie: U.S. Officials," Reuters, December 16, 2014, http://www.reuters.com/article/us-sony-cybersecurity-theaters-idUSKBN0JU2J820141216.

55. Alex Fitzpatrick, "Sony Pulls The Interview After Threats," Time, December 17, 2014, http://time.com/3638987/the-interview-cancelled-sony-hack.

56. "Remarks by the President in Year-End Press Conference," news release, White House Office of the Press Secretary, December 19, 2014, https://www.whitehouse.gov/the-press-office/2014/12/19/remarks-president-year-end-press-conference.

57. Adi Robertson, "Politicians Respond to Sony Hack, Call for Cybersecurity Bill," The Verge, December 18, 2014, www.theverge.com/2014/12/18/7415291/politicians-respond-to-the-sony-hack-mccain-calls-for-cybersecurity-bill.

58. "S. 754–Cybersecurity Information Sharing Act of 2015," Senate Republican Policy Committee blog post, August 3, 2015, www.rpc.senate.gov/legislative-notices/s-754_cybersecurity-information-sharing-act-of-2015.

59. Ibid.

60. Electronic Frontier Foundation (EFF), "Stop the Cybersecurity Information Sharing Act," https://act.eff.org/action/stop-the-cybersecurity-information-sharing-act.

61. Adam Levy, "Was the Box Office Performance of 'The Interview' a Win for Netflix?" Motley Fool, February 8, 2015, www.fool.com/investing/general/2015/02/08/was-the-box-office-performance-of-the-interview-a.aspx.

62. Brent Lang, "Sony Could Lose $75 Million on 'The Interview' (EXCLUSIVE)," Variety, December 18, 2014, http://variety.com/2014/film/news/sony-could-lose-75-million-on-the-interview-exclusive-1201382506.

63. Allan Holmes, "Your Guide to Good-Enough Compliance," *CIO*, April 2007.

64. Kashmir Hill, "Sony Pictures Hack Was a Long Time Coming, Say Former Employees," *Fusion*, December 4, 2014, http://fusion.net/story/31469/sony-pictures-hack-was-a-long-time-coming-say-former-employees.

65. Ibid.

66. Michael Price, "The Left Brain Knows What the Right Hand Is Doing," *Monitor on Psychology* 40, no. 1 (2009).

67. Clifford A. Pickover, *Archimedes to Hawking: Laws of Science and the Great Minds Behind Them* (Oxford: Oxford University Press, 2008).

68. "A Primer on Futures Studies, Foresight, and the Use of Scenarios," *Prospect, the Foresight Bulletin*, no. 6 (December 2001).

69. I am the founder and CEO of the Future Today Institute, a research and advisory firm focused on future forecasting. See www.futuretodayinstitute.com.

70. Discover John Muir site, https://discoverjohnmuir.com.

71. The story of Dolly is discussed in significant detail in Chapter 4.

72. "Chronological History of IBM—Timeline," IBM, https://www-03.ibm.com/ibm/history/history/history_intro.html.

CHAPTER 2. WHEN CARS FLY: UNDERSTANDING THE DIFFERENCE BETWEEN TREND AND TRENDY

1. In the movie *Back to the Future*, the character Doc Brown rebuilt the DeLorean DMC-12 into a time machine.

2. The October 17, 1949, issue of *Life* magazine included a description of the Airphibian. Other flying-car examples and quotations from Alex Q. Arbuckle, "1890–1968 Flying Cars," Mashable, http://mashable.com/2015/08/03/flying-car-evolution/#Pol_AlV1kkqD.

3. "What Happened to the Future?" Founders Fund manifesto, http://foundersfund.com/the-future.

4. "A Brief History of the Flying Car," *Popular Mechanics*, July 26, 2012, www.popularmechanics.com/flight/how-to/g1038/a-brief-history-of-the-flying-car.

5. "Wagner Aerocar—1965," Aviastar, n.d., www.aviastar.org/helicopters_eng/wagner_aerocar.php.

6. Esther Inglis-Arkell, "The First Flying Car Was Based on the Ford Pinto, and Killed Its Inventor," iO9, February 27, 2012, http://io9.gizmodo.com/5888216/the-first-flying-car-was-based-on-the-ford-pinto-and-killed-its-inventor.

7. Dan Namowitz, "Sky Commuter Prototype Reappears, in Auction," Aircraft Owners and Pilots Association, January 14, 2015, www.aopa.org/news-and-media/all-news/2015/january/14/1990-sky-commuter-reappears-in-an-auction.

8. Stephan Benzkofer and Ron Grossman, "Flashback: A Look at Chicago Transportation from the Horse-Drawn Omnibus to Elevated Trains," *Chicago Tribune*, October 27, 2013, http://articles.chicagotribune.com/2013-10-27/news/ct-per-flash-transport-1027-20131027_1_street-cars-first-trolley-chicago-transportation.

9. "Alfred Speer Dead: Old Wine Merchant and Inventor Gave Passaic Its Name," *New York Times*, February 17, 1910, http://query.nytimes.com/mem/archive-free/pdf?res=9E06E0DE1430E233A25754C1A9649C946196D6CF.

10. Alfred Speer, "United States Patent: 119,796—Improvement in Endless-Traveling Sidewalks," October 10, 1871.

11. *The Street Railway Review: Index to Volume III* (Chicago: Windsor and Kenfield, 1893).

12. "Paris Exposition Notes," *Scientific American*, May 19, 1900.

13. Matt Soniak, "Walk This Way: The History of the Moving Sidewalk," Mental Floss, July 19, 2012, http://mentalfloss.com/article/31236/walk-way-history-moving-sidewalk.

14. "A History of the World: Rover Safety Bicycle," BBC, 2014, www.bbc.co.uk/ahistoryofthe world/objects/u76Sy05eSNi0zXeC5vDPmg.

15. Gereon Meyer and Sven Beiker, *Toward a Systematic Approach to the Design and Evaluation of Automated Mobility-on-Demand Systems: A Case Study in Singapore, Forthcoming in Road Vehicle Automation*, Springer Lecture Notes in Mobility (Berlin: Springer, 2014).

16. "Grand DARPA Challenge: Autonomous Ground Vehicles," DARPA, 2004, http://archive.darpa.mil/grandchallenge04.

17. Weiland Holfelder, "Vehicle-to-Vehicle and Vehicle-to-Infrastructure Communication: Recent Developments, Opportunities and Challenges," Daimler Chrysler and Telematics Research, presentation to the Future Generation Software Architects in the Automotive Domain Connected Services in Mobile Networks workshop, January 10–12, 2004, La Jolla, California, http://aswsd .ucsd.edu/2004/pdfs/V2VandV2ICommunication-Slides-WHolfelder.pdf.

18. Wesley Allison, "Motor Trend 2004 Car of the Year Winner: Toyota Prius," *Motor Trend*, December 2003.

19. "Google Acquires Keyhole Corp," news release, Google, October 27, 2004, http://google press.blogspot.com/2004/10/google-acquires-keyhole-corp.html.

20. John Markoff, "I, Robot: The Man Behind the Google Phone," *New York Times*, November 4, 2007, www.nytimes.com/2007/11/04/technology/04google.html.

21. "QNX Joins Harman International Family," news release, QNX, October 27, 2004, www.qnx .com/news/pr_1121_1.html.

22. "Table 1–4: Public Road and Street Mileage in the United States by Type of Surface," US Department of Transportation, accessed January 7, 2016, www.rita.dot.gov/bts/sites/rita.dot.gov .bts/files/publications/national_transportation_statistics/html/table_01_04.html.

23. W. Pfaff, B. Hensen, H. Bernien, S. B. van Dam, M. S. Blok, T. H. Taminiau, M. J. Tiggelman, R. N., Schouten, M. Markham, D. J. Twitchen, and R. Hanson, "Unconditional Quantum Teleportation Between Distant Solid-State Qubits," *Science* 345, no. 6196 (August 1, 2014).

24. Albert Einstein to Max Born, quoted in Richard Boyd, Philip Gasper, and J. D. Trout, *The Philosophy of Science* (Cambridge, MA: MIT Press, 1991).

25. Charles H. Bennett, Gilles Brassard, Glaude Crepeau, Richard Jozsa, Asher Peres, and William K. Wootters, "Teleporting an Unknown Quantum State via Dual Classical and Einstein-Podolsky -Rosen Channels," *Physical Review Letters* 70, no. 13 (March 29, 1993).

26. Pfaff et al., "Unconditional Quantum Teleportation."

27. Interestingly, the words "Beam me up, Scotty" were not said during the original *Star Trek* series. There were a few episodes where versions of that iconic phrase were used, however, such as in the 1968 episode "The Gamesters of Triskelion," when Captain Kirk says, "Beam us up."

28. For a deep dive into Moore's Law, Intel maintains a website with explanations, additional reading material, and videos. See "50 Years of Moore's Law: Fueling Innovation We Love and Depend On," www.intel.com/content/www/us/en/silicon-innovations/moores-law-technology.html. I also recommend the Computer History Museum's article on Gordon Moore in its section on "The Silicon Engine," entitled "1965: Moore's Law Predicts the Future of Integrated Circuits," n.d., www.computer history.org/siliconengine/moores-law-predicts-the-future-of-integrated-circuits.

29. David W. Moore, "Bush Approval Drops Below 60% for First Time Since 9/11," Gallup News Service, January 14, 2003, www.gallup.com/poll/7591/bush-approval-drops-below-60-first-time -since-911.aspx.

30. Lloyd Vries, "Hurricanes Wash Away Jobs," CBS Money Watch, October 7, 2005, www.cbs news.com/news/hurricanes-wash-away-jobs.

31. CBS News/*New York Times* poll released on January 16, 2009,"The Presidency of George W. Bush," cached PDF at http://webcache.googleusercontent.com/search?q=cache:Ag5tD_3En0g J:www.cbsnews.com/htdocs/pdf/Bush_poll_011609.pdf+&cd=1&hl=en&ct=clnk&gl=us.

32. Jaime Lalinde, Rebecca Sacks, Mark Guiducci, Elizabeth Nicholas, and Max Chafkin, "Revolution Number 99," *Vanity Fair*, February 2012, www.vanityfair.com/news/2012/02/occupy-wall-street-201202.

33. Reddit.com search results. See https://www.reddit.com/search?q=sony.

34. "25 Highest Paying Jobs in America for 2016," Glassdoor, https://www.glassdoor.com/blog/25-highest-paying-jobs-america-2016.

35. "President Obama Signs Health Reform into Law," news release, White House, March 23, 2010, https://www.whitehouse.gov/photos-and-video/video/president-obama-signs-health-reform-law.

36. US Congress, *Patient Protection and Affordable Care Act*, HR 3590—111th Cong., March 23, 2010, https://www.congress.gov/bill/111th-congress/house-bill/3590.

37. World Health Organization, *International Classification of Diseases*, ICD-10 Online, www.who.int/classifications/icd/en.

38. US Department of Education, "Science, Technology, Engineering and Math: Education for Global Leadership," www.ed.gov/stem.

39. "Top Secret America: A Washington Post Investigation," *Washington Post*, http://projects.washingtonpost.com/top-secret-america/network/#/overall/most-activity.

40. Jacob M. Schlesinger and Alexander Martin, "Aging Gracefully: Graying Japan Tries to Embrace the Golden Years," *Wall Street Journal*, www.wsj.com/articles/graying-japan-tries-to-embrace-the-golden-years-1448808028.

41. "First Self-Replicating Synthetic Bacterial Cell," J. Craig Venter Institute, http://jcvi.org/cms/research/projects/first-self-replicating-synthetic-bacterial-cell/overview.

42. Danielle Kurtzleben, "Planned Parenthood Investigations Find No Fetal Tissue Sales," National Public Radio, January 28, 2016, www.npr.org/2016/01/28/464594826/in-wake-of-videos-planned-parenthood-investigations-find-no-fetal-tissue-sales.

43. "Facts and Statistics," Distraction, www.distraction.gov/stats-research-laws/facts-and-statistics.html.

44. Julie Beck, "The Decline of the Driver's License," *Atlantic*, January 22, 2016, www.theatlantic.com/technology/archive/2016/01/the-decline-of-the-drivers-license/425169.

45. *The Graduate*, directed by Mike Nichols, screenplay by Calder Willingham and Buck Henry, based on novel by Charles Webb, film released December 22, 1967.

46. R. H. Day, D. G. Shaw, and S. E. Ignell, "The Quantitative Distribution and Characteristics of Marine Debris in the North Pacific Ocean, 1984–1988," *Proceedings of the Second International Conference on Marine Debris*, US Department of Commerce, National Oceanic and Atmospheric Administration, 1989.

47. Peter G. Ryan, Charles J. Moore, Jan A. van Franeker, and Coleen L. Moloney, "Monitoring the Abundance of Plastic Debris in the Marine Environment," *Philosophical Transactions—Royal Society of Biological Sciences*, July 27, 2009.

48. "1946: First Mobile Telephone Call," AT&T, www.corp.att.com/attlabs/reputation/timeline/46mobile.html.

49. Ibid.

CHAPTER 3. SURVIVE AND THRIVE, OR DIE:
HOW TRENDS AFFECT COMPANIES

1. Nintendo history and timelines are available at https://nintendo.co.jp/index.html, https://www.nintendo.com/corp/history.jsp, and https://www.nintendo.co.uk/Corporate/Nintendo-History/Nintendo-History-625945.html.

2. Ibid.

3. Ibid.

4. Ibid.

5. Ibid.

6. Ibid.

7. Ibid.

8. "George R. Stibitz: 1964 Harry H. Goode Memorial Award Recipient," Computer Society, Institute of Electrical and Electronics Engineers, https://www.computer.org/web/awards/goode -george-stibitz.

9. T. R. Hollcroft, "The Summer Meeting in Hanover," *Bulletin of American Mathematical Society* 46, no. 11 (1940), http://projecteuclid.org/euclid.bams/1183503281.

10. Ibid.

11. US War Department, Bureau of Public Relations, news release, February 15, 1946, http:// americanhistory.si.edu/comphist/pr1.pdf.

12. "The Colossus Gallery," National Museum of Computing, www.tnmoc.org/explore/colossus -gallery.

13. "USS Hopper (DDG 70)," US Navy, www.public.navy.mil/surfor/ddg70/Pages/namesake .aspx#.VzSLCWSDFBc.

14. Randy Alfred, "Nov. 4, 1952: Univac Gets Election Right, but CBS Balks," *Wired*, November 4, 2010, www.wired.com/2010/11/1104cbs-tv-univac-election.

15. Amy Webb, *Data: A Love Story* (New York: Dutton Adult, 2013).

16. J. C. R. Licklider, "Memorandum For: Members and Affiliates of the Intergalactic Computer Network," Advanced Research Projects Agency (ARPA), April 23, 1963, http://worrydream.com /refs/Licklider-IntergalacticNetwork.pdf.

17. Digital Equipment Corporation (DEC), Lehman Brothers Collection, Harvard Business School Historical Collections, www.library.hbs.edu/hc/lehman/chrono.html?company=digital _equipment_corporation.

18. Glenn Rifkin, "Ken Olsen, Who Built DEC into a Power, Dies at 84," *New York Times*, February 7, 2011, www.nytimes.com/2011/02/08/technology/business-computing/08olsen.html.

19. Olaf Helmer, "Prospects of Technological Progress," August 1967, RAND Corporation, www.rand.org/content/dam/rand/pubs/papers/2006/P3643.pdf.

20. Rifkin, "Ken Olsen."

21. Katie Hafner and Matthew Lyon, *Where Wizards Stay Up Late: The Origins of the Internet* (New York: Simon and Schuster, 1996).

22. Leslie Horn, "First Portable Computer Debuted 30 Years Ago," *PC Magazine*, April 4, 2011, www.pcmag.com/article2/0,2817,2383022,00.asp.

23. David Pogue, "Use It Better: The Worst Tech Predictions of All Time," *Scientific American*, January 18, 2012, www.scientificamerican.com/article/pogue-all-time-worst-tech-predictions.

24. Clifford Stoll, "Why the Web Won't Be Nirvana," *Newsweek*, February 26, 1995, www.newsweek .com/clifford-stoll-why-web-wont-be-nirvana-185306.

25. John Perry Barlow, "A Declaration of the Independence of Cyberspace," Electronic Frontier Foundation, February 8, 1996, https://www.eff.org/cyberspace-independence.

26. Richard Babrook and Andy Cameron, "The Californian Ideology," Imaginary Futures, www.imaginaryfutures.net/2007/04/17/the-californian-ideology-2.

27. DEC product brochures. See the Computer History Museum's article "Company: Digital Equipment Corporation (DEC)," in the section "Selling the Computer Revolution: Marketing Brochures in the Collection," www.computerhistory.org/brochures/companies.php?company =com-42b9d67d9c350&.

28. John F. Kennedy, "Inaugural Address of President John F. Kennedy," January 20, 1961, J.F.K. Museum, www.jfklibrary.org/Research/Research-Aids/Ready-Reference/JFK-Quotations /Inaugural-Address.aspx.

29. United Press, "Khrushchev Invites U.S. to Missile Shooting Match," *New York Times*, November 16, 1957.

30. Jack Raymond, "Foreign-Based U-2's Grounded for Study," *New York Times*, May 7, 1960.

31. Gabrielle Sorto, "Yuri Gagarin Became First Man in Space 55 Years Ago," CNN, April 12, 2016, www.cnn.com/2016/04/12/world/yuri-gagarin-55-anniversary-irpt.

32. Joint session video and transcript available at the John F. Kennedy Presidential Library, www.jfklibrary.org/Asset-Viewer/xzw1gaeeTES6khED14P1Iw.aspx.

33. Ibid.

34. Ibid.

35. W. H. Lawrence, "Kennedy Asks 1.8 Billion This Year to Accelerate Space Exploration, Add Foreign Aid, Bolster Defense," *New York Times*, May 26, 1961.

36. The Intelligence Advanced Research Projects Activity's projects and open solicitations are available on its website at https://www.iarpa.gov/index.php/working-with-iarpa/open-solicitations.

CHAPTER 4. FINDING THE FRINGE: SEEK OUT THE UNUSUAL SUSPECTS

1. In *Star Trek*, the Vulcan mind meld is a synaptic pattern displacement technique that merges the essence of two minds. It is done by the Vulcan placing her hands at particular points around the face of the other person. Spock used it in lots of episodes, although it's always represented as a very risky thing to do.

2. Miguel Pais-Vieira, Mikhail Lebedev, Carolina Kunicki, Jin Wang, and Miguel A. L. Nicolelis, "A Brain-to-Brain Interface for Real-Time Sharing of Sensorimotor Information," *Scientific Reports*, February 28, 2013.

3. Cynthia Fox, "Communicating via Thought Waves Alone: Q&A with Miguel Nicolelis," *Bioscience Technology*, July 31, 2015.

4. *PC World* editors, "World Class: Best Products of 1998," CNN, June 5, 1998, www.cnn.com/TECH/computing/9806/05/best.of.98.idg/index.html.

5. Alejandra Martins and Paul Rincon, "Paraplegic in Robotic Suit Kicks off World Cup," BBC News, June 12, 2014, www.bbc.com/news/science-environment-27812218.

6. Miguel Pais-Vieira, Gabriela Chiuffa, Mikhail Lebedev, Amol Yadav, and Miguel A. L. Nicolelis, "Building an Organic Computing Device with Multiple Interconnected Brains," *Scientific Reports* 5 (2015), www.nature.com/articles/srep11869.

7. Miguel Nicolelis, TED Talk, "Brain-to-Brain Communication Has Arrived: How We Did It," October 2014, https://www.ted.com/talks/miguel_nicolelis_brain_to_brain_communication_has_arrived_how_we_did_it/transcript.

8. Galilei biography at Biography.com, www.biography.com/people/galileo-9305220.

9. Goodall biography at Biography.com, www.biography.com/people/jane-goodall-9542363.

10. Isaac Asimov, "The Story Behind 'Foundation,'" *Isaac Asimov's Science Fiction Magazine*, December 1982.

11. Paul Krugman, "Paul Krugman: Asimov's Foundation Novels Grounded My Economics," *The Guardian*, December 4, 2012, www.theguardian.com/books/2012/dec/04/paul-krugman-asimov-economics.

12. Ryan Lizza, "When Newt Met Hari Seldon," *New Yorker*, December 8, 2011, www.newyorker.com/news/news-desk/when-newt-met-hari-seldon.

13. Youssef M. Ibrahim, "Secrecy Gives Way to Spotlight for Scientist," *New York Times*, February 24, 1997.

14. "Sir Ian Wilmut, British biologist," Encyclopaedia Britannica, www.britannica.com/biography/an-Wilmut.

15. Ibid.

16. Ian Wilmut, A. E. Schnieke, J. McWhir, A. J. Kind, and K. H. S. Campbell, "Viable Offspring Derived from Fetal and Adult Mammalian Cells," *Nature* 385 (February 27, 1997).

17. Gina Kolata, "Scientist Reports First Cloning Ever of Adult Mammal," *New York Times*, February 23, 1997.

18. Gina Kolata, "With Cloning of a Sheep, Ethical Ground Shifts," *New York Times*, February 24, 1997.

19. Ibid.

20. Panel discussion at MIT on the ethics of cloning, May 6, 1997, in "Experts Detail Obstacles to Human Cloning," MIT News, May 14, 1997, http://news.mit.edu/1997/cloning-0514.

21. Pamphlet entitled "Human Cloning: Ethical Issues," published by the Church of Scotland, Church and Society Council, n.d., www.srtp.org.uk/assets/uploads/Human_Cloning_Ethical_Issues _864_0814.pdf.

22. Remarks made by President Bill Clinton during a White House press conference on March 4, 1997, Washington, DC, transcript online at CNN, www.cnn.com/ALLPOLITICS/1997/03/04 /clinton.money/transcript.html.

23. CNN/*Time* poll on cloning, released Saturday, March 1, 1997, www.cnn.com/TECH /9703/01/clone.poll.

24. "GM Chickens That Don't Transmit Bird Flu Developed," news release, Roslin Institute, University of Edinburgh, January 13, 2011, www.roslin.ed.ac.uk/news/2011/01/13/gm-chickens -that-dont-transmit-bird-flu-developed.

25. Wang Yongsheng, Yan Zhang, Mingqi Yang, Jiaxing Lv, Jun Liu, and Yong Zhanga, "TALE Nickase-Mediated SP110 Knockin Endows Cattle with Increased Resistance to Tuberculosis," *Proceedings of the National Academy of Sciences of the United States of America*, March 31, 2015, www.ncbi .nlm.nih.gov/pmc/articles/PMC4386332.

26. David Cyranoski, "Super-Muscly Pigs Created by Small Genetic Tweak," *Nature*, June 30, 2015, www.nature.com/news/super-muscly-pigs-created-by-small-genetic-tweak-1.17874.

27. Morgan Clendaniel, "The Genetically Modified Food You Eat Everyday," *Fast Company*, November 13, 2014, www.fastcoexist.com/1676104/the-genetically-modified-food-you-eat-every-day.

28. Andrew Pollack, "Jennifer Doudna, a Pioneer Who Helped Simplify Genome Editing," *New York Times*, May 11, 2015.

29. Steph Yin, "What Is CRISPR/Cas9 and Why Is It Suddenly Everywhere?" Motherboard, April 30, 2015, http://motherboard.vice.com/read/what-is-crisprcas9-and-why-is-it-suddenly -everywhere.

30. Omar O. Abudayyeh, Jonathan S. Gootenberg, Silvana Konermann, Julia Joung, Ian M. Slaymaker, David B.T. Cox, Sergey Shmakov, et al., "C2c2 Is a Single-Component Programmable RNA-Guided RNA-Targeting CRISPR Effector," *Science*, June 2, 2016, http://science.sciencemag.org /content/early/2016/06/01/science.aaf5573.

31. David Cyranoski and Sara Reardon, "Chinese Scientists Genetically Modify Human Embryos," *Nature*, April 22, 2015, www.nature.com/news/chinese-scientists-genetically-modify -human-embryos-1.17378.

32. Puping Liang, Yanwen Xu, Xiya Zhang, Chenhui Ding, Rui Huang, Zhen Zhang, Jie Lv, et al., "CRISPR/Cas9-Mediated Gene Editing in Human Tripronuclear Zygotes," *Protein & Cell* 6, no. 5 (2015): 363–372.

33. Edward Lanphier, Fyodor Urnov, Sarah Ehlen Haecker, Michael Werner, and Joanna Smolenski, "Don't Edit the Human Germ Line," *Nature* 519, no. 7544 (2015): 410–411.

34. Susan Rinkunas, "Genetic Engineering for Our Babies Is Real," *New York*, July 24, 2015, http://nymag.com/thecut/2015/07/lady-scientists-could-make-marvel-comics-real.html.

35. Amelia Urry, "The Latest in GMO Panic: Human Engineering," Grist, April 30, 2015, http:// grist.org/science/the-latest-in-gmo-panic-human-engineering.

36. AskMen editors, "Real-Life Mutants," AskMen, July 24, 2015, www.askmen.com/news/sports/real-life-mutants-researchers-want-to-use-superhuman-dna-to-combat-disease.html.

37. Zach Weissmueller, "What If You Could Live for 10,000 Years? Q&A with Transhumanist Zoltan Istvan," February 6, 2015, http://reason.com/reasontv/2015/02/06/what-if-you-could-live-for-10000-years; see also Zoltan Istvan's website, www.zoltanistvan.com.

38. Dylan Mathews, "I Got a Computer Chip Implanted into My Hand: Here's How It Went," Vox, September 11, 2015, www.vox.com/2015/9/11/9307991/biohacking-grinders-rfid-implant.

39. Ibid.

40. Mary Meeker and Liang Wu, "Internet Trends D11 Conference," 2013, www.kpcb.com/blog/2013-internet-trends.

41. Atul Gawande, "Slow Ideas," New Yorker, July 29, 2013.

42. Anesthesiology timeline and resources from the Wood Library Museum of Anesthesiology, www.woodlibrarymuseum.org/history-of-anesthesia/#1853.

43. "Highest Paying Occupations," in Occupational Outlook Handbook, US Department of Labor, Bureau of Labor Statistics, May 2013, www.bls.gov/ooh/highest-paying.htm.

44. Marc S. Zimbler, "Gaspare Tagliacozzi (1545–1599): Renaissance Surgeon," Archives of Facial Plastic Surgery 3, no. 4 (2001): 283–294, http://archfaci.jamanetwork.com/article.aspx?articleid=479888.

45. Sander L. Gilman, Making the Body Beautiful (Princeton, NJ: Princeton University Press, 2001).

46. Data from the American Society for Aesthetic Plastic Surgery, www.surgery.org.

47. David M. Bosworth, "Iproniazid: A Brief Review of Its Introduction and Clinical Use," Annals of the New York Academy of Sciences 80 (1959): 809–819.

48. Marcia Angell, "The Epidemic of Mental Illness: Why?" New York Review of Books, June 23, 2011.

49. Elizabeth Wurtzel, Prozac Nation: Young and Depressed in America (Boston: Houghton Mifflin, 1994).

50. Peter D. Kramer, Listening to Prozac (New York: Viking Adult, 1993).

51. Gawande, "Slow Ideas."

52. Kevin Kelly, What Technology Wants (New York: Viking, 2010).

CHAPTER 5. SIGNALS MATTER:
UNCOVERING HIDDEN PATTERNS

1. Arthur Conan Doyle, A Scandal in Bohemia (London: G. Newnes, 1891).

2. Arthur Conan Doyle, "The Adventure of the Reigate Squire," Strand Magazine, June 1893.

3. Mountain View Police Department, blog post, November 12, 2015, https://mountainviewpoliceblog.com/2015/11/12/inquiring-minds-want-to-know.

4. Google Self-Driving Car Project, Monthly Reports, https://www.google.com/selfdrivingcar/reports.

5. Google Self-Driving Car Project, blog post, Google+, November 12, 2015, https://plus.google.com/+SelfDrivingCar/posts/j9ouVZSZnRf.

6. Ibid.

7. The video is described at the Computing Community Consortium, blog post by Erwin Gianchandani, October 18, 2011, www.cccblog.org/2011/10/18/how-googles-self-driving-car-works.

8. Adam Clark Estes, "Meet Google's Robot Army: It's Growing," Gizmodo, January 27, 2014, http://gizmodo.com/a-humans-guide-to-googles-many-robots-1509799897.

9. Jon Gertner, "The Truth About Google X: An Exclusive Look Behind the Secretive Lab's Closed Doors," Fast Company, April 14, 2014.

10. Google maintains a public repository of some of its investments at Google Ventures, www .gv.com. A 2014 blog post by Mahesh Mohan offered a fairly comprehensive list of Google's products and services up until that time. See Mahesh Mohan, "Over 151 Google Products & Services You Probably Don't Know," Minterest, December 2, 2014, www.minterest.org/google-products-services -you-probably-dont-know.

11. Leonard Mlodinow, *Subliminal: How Your Unconscious Mind Rules Your Behavior* (New York: Knopf Doubleday, 2013).

12. American Academy of Ophthalmology, Museum of Vision, "Timeline of Eyeglasses," www.museumofvision.org/exhibitions/?key=44&subkey=4&relkey=35.

13. Johan Wagemans, James H. Elder, Michael Kubovy, Stephen E. Palmer, Mary A. Peterson, Manish Singh, and Rüdiger von der Heydt, "A Century of Gestalt Psychology in Visual Perception I: Perceptual Grouping and Figure-Ground Organization," *Psychology Bulletin* 138, no. 6 (November 2012): 1172–1217.

14. For the original press release, see "Google Gets the Message, Launches Gmail," Google News from Google, April 1, 2004, http://googlepress.blogspot.com/2004/04/google-gets-message -launches-gmail.html.

15. Arin Hailey, "Gmail Hits the Auction Block," *PC World*, May 26, 2004, www.pcworld.com /article/116293/article.html.

16. See the Google corporate website, with a timeline of its product and service releases, at "Our History in Depth," Google Company, https://www.google.com/about/company/timeline.

17. Julie Bort, "Google Apps Exec: 'The Whole Industry Looked at Us Like We Were Crazy,'" January 13, 2015, www.businessinsider.com/google-apps-exec-on-being-crazy-2015-1.

18. See Juan Carlos Perez, "Google Wants Your Phonemes," InfoWorld, October 23, 2007, www .infoworld.com/article/2642023/database/google-wants-your-phonemes.html.

19. "Number of Smartphone Users in the United States from 2010 to 2019 (in millions)," Statistica, www.statista.com/statistics/201182/forecast-of-smartphone-users-in-the-us.

20. Apple, "Apple Reports Fourth Quarter Results," Apple Press Info, October 18, 2010, https:// www.apple.com/pr/library/2010/10/18Apple-Reports-Fourth-Quarter-Results.html.

21. Google, "Our History in Depth.

22. Ibid.

23. Chris Savarese and Brian Hart, "The Caesar Cipher," Cryptography, last updated April 25, 2010, www.cs.trincoll.edu/~crypto/historical/caesar.html.

24. "Emblem and Cipher," Francis Bacon Society, www.francisbaconsociety.co.uk/emblem -and-cipher.

25. Chris originally proposed the hashtag (or # sign) in an August 23, 2007, Tweet. That Tweet, along with the resulting discussion, is available at https://twitter.com/chrismessina/status /223115412?ref_src=twsrc%5Etfw.

26. Jessica Estepa, "Is This 'Total War'? Anonymous Posts Trump's Social Security Number, Phone Number, *USA Today*, March 18, 2016.

27. Bianca Bosker, "Siri Rising: The Inside Story of Siri's Origins—And Why She Could Over-shadow the iPhone," Huffington Post, January 24, 2013, www.huffingtonpost.com/2013/01/22 /siri-do-engine-apple-iphone_n_2499165.html.

28. Google, "Our History in Depth."

29. "Google Receives More Than 75,000 Job Applications over the Last Week," *Los Angeles Times*, Technology blog, February 4, 2011, http://latimesblogs.latimes.com/technology/2011/02/google -receives-more-than-75000-job-applications-in-a-week.html.

30. Martin Peers, "Cash Returns: Where Apple Lags Google and Microsoft," *Wall Street Journal*, March 23, 2011, www.wsj.com/articles/SB10001424052702304520804576339392545579346.

31. Google, "Our History in Depth."

32. David Gelles, "In Silicon Valley, Mergers Must Meet the Toothbrush Test," *New York Times*, August 17, 2014, http://dealbook.nytimes.com/2014/08/17/in-silicon-valley-mergers-must-meet-the-toothbrush-test.

33. Dan Frommer, "Google's First Alphabet Earnings in Charts," Quartz, February 1, 2016, http://qz.com/607378/were-live-charting-googles-first-alphabet-earnings.

34. Larry Page and Sergey Brin, "G Is for Google," Alphabet, n.d., https://abc.xyz.

35. Holmes admits to a misstep in "Silver Blaze." A prize horse goes missing, and in the middle of a meeting, Holmes admits: "I made a blunder, my dear Watson—which is, I am afraid, a more common occurrence than anyone would think who only knew me through your memoirs. The fact is that I could not believe it possible that the most remarkable horse in England could long remain concealed, especially in so sparsely inhabited a place as the north of Dartmoor."

CHAPTER 6. THE "UBER FOR X" TREND:
ASK THE RIGHT QUESTIONS

1. Search performed January 10, 2016.

2. As of January 10, 2016.

3. Alyson Shontell, "All Hail the Uber Man!" Business Insider, January 11, 2014, www.businessinsider.com/uber-travis-kalanick-bio-2014-1.

4. Ibid.

5. Kalanick posted the Tweet using @Uber on March 19, 2010, https://twitter.com/uber/status/10732492284. For those unfamiliar with the slang term "sick," it usually means crazy, insane, or great.

6. Connie Loizos, "Sequoia Capital's Alfred Lin on Why Uber's Valuation Is Twice That of Airbnb's," TechCrunch, December 1, 2015, http://techcrunch.com/2015/12/01/sequoia-capitals-alfred-lin-on-why-ubers-valuation-is-twice-that-of-airbnb.

7. Eric Newcomer, "Uber Raises Funding at $62.5 Billion Valuation," Bloomberg, December 3, 2015, www.bloomberg.com/news/articles/2015-12-03/uber-raises-funding-at-62-5-valuation.

8. Susanne Craig and Andrew Ross Sorkin, "Goldman Offering Clients a Chance to Invest in Facebook," *New York Times*, January 2, 2011, http://dealbook.nytimes.com/2011/01/02/goldman-invests-in-facebook-at-50-billion-valuation/?hp.

9. As of May 11, 2016, Zuckerberg had climbed to number seven on the Bloomberg Billionaires list, behind the Koch brothers, Jeff Bezos, Warren Buffet, Amancio Ortega, and Bill Gates (in order). See http://www.bloomberg.com/billionaires/2016-05-11/cya for a searchable database.

10. Jessi Hempel, Davey Alba, Issie Lapowsky, and Julia Greenberg, "Uber's Raising Billions More, So Why Bother Going Public?" *Wired*, December 3, 2015, www.wired.com/2015/12/ubers-raising-billions-more-so-why-bother-going-public.

11. Uber Newsroom, https://newsroom.uber.com.

12. Uber Newsroom Search Results, https://newsroom.uber.com/?s=billionth+ride+Marvin+&lang=en.

13. Jason O. Gilbert, "Poem: There's an Uber for X," Quartz, December 12, 2014, http://qz.com/311217/poem-theres-an-uber-for-x. Licenses from Quartz and reprinted with both the permission of Quartz and the author.

14. Paul Wiseman, "Outlook for Job Market Is Grim," *USA Today*, January 8, 2010.

15. Ibid.

16. Apple, "Apple Reports Fourth Quarter Results," Apple Press Info, October 18, 2010, https://www.apple.com/pr/library/2010/10/18Apple-Reports-Fourth-Quarter-Results.html.

17. "Regulation and Prosperity: 1935–1960," New York City, History: Taxi of Today, Taxi of Tomorrow, www.nyc.gov/html/media/totweb/taxioftomorrow_history_regulationandprosperity.html.

18. New York City Taxi and Limousine Commission, 2010 Annual Report, www.nyc.gov/html/tlc/downloads/pdf/annual_report_2010.pdf.

19. "Population of the 100 Largest Urban Places: 1930," US Census Bureau, https://www.census.gov/population/www/documentation/twps0027/tab16.txt.

20. Tobias Salinger, "World's Fair 1939 Presented Vision of 'World of Tomorrow,' with Ominous Signs of Impending War," New York Daily News, April 17, 2014, www.nydailynews.com/new-york/queens/world-fair-1939-presented-vision-world-tomorrow-omens-war-article-1.1759608.

21. "Quick Facts for New York City," US Census Bureau, www.census.gov/quickfacts/table/PST045215/36.

22. "New York City Statistics," NYC: The Official Guide, https://web.archive.org/web/20160329230537/http://www.nycgo.com/articles/nyc-statistics-page.

23. Ibid.

24. Lawrence Van Gelder, "Medallion Limits Stem from the 30's," New York Times, May 11, 1996, www.nytimes.com/1996/05/11/nyregion/medallion-limits-stem-from-the-30-s.html.

25. "New York City Statistics," NYC: The Official Guide.

26. For those who are interested, this is the online marketplace for NYC's taxi medallion sale and lease: http://nycitycab.com/business/taximedallionlist.aspx.

27. "CES by the Numbers," Consumer Technology Association, https://www.ces.tech/Why-CES/CES-by-the-Numbers.

28. The Tweet was posted by Anatoliy Tokayev, username @anatoliytokayev, on January 7, 2016, at https://twitter.com/AnatoliyTokayev/status/684992047737139200.

29. Heather Kelly, "San Francisco's Yellow Cab Files for Bankruptcy," CNN Money, January 25, 2016, http://money.cnn.com/2016/01/25/technology/yellow-cab-bankruptcy.

30. Wendy Lee, "State Wants New Rules on Insurance for Ride-Sharing Companies," KPCC 89.3, blog post, April 9, 2014, www.scpr.org/blogs/economy/2014/04/09/16327/state-wants-new-rules-on-insurance-for-ride-sharin.

31. State of Nebraska Consumer Alert, "Hidden Risks of Car-Sharing and Ride-Sharing," www.doi.nebraska.gov/brochure/conalert/out14268.pdf.

32. Website maintained by the attorneys representing drivers in the class-action suit against Uber, http://uberlawsuit.com.

33. The list is available at www.whosdrivingyou.org.

34. Between the time when I wrote this book and its publication, there will undoubtedly be more lawsuits brought against Uber as well as new regulations and rules initiated and imposed by individual towns, cities, and states across the United States.

35. Loizos, "Sequoia Capital's Alfred Lin."

36. Amos Tversky and Daniel Kahneman, "Availability: A Heuristic for Judging Frequency and Probability," Cognitive Psychology 4 (1973): 207–232.

37. Elizabeth Holmes, "Gilt's New Funding Values Online Retailer at $1 Billion," Wall Street Journal, May 10, 2011, www.wsj.com/articles/SB10001424052748703730804576313330486181732.

38. Leena Rao, "One Kings Lane Raises $112M at a $912M Valuation in a Quest to Dominate Home Goods Online," TechCrunch, January 30, 2014, http://techcrunch.com/2014/01/30/in-the-quest-to-dominate-home-goods-e-commerce-one-kings-lane-raises-112m-at-a-912m-valuation.

39. Greg Bensinger, "Zulily Shares Jump 71% After IPO," Wall Street Journal, November 15, 2013, www.wsj.com/articles/SB10001424052702303289904579200272639068810.

40. Leena Rao, "Here's How Gilt Will Be Added to Saks Fifth Avenue's Discount Retail Stores," Fortune, February 9, 2016, http://fortune.com/2016/02/09/gilt-off-fifth.

41. "Liberty Interactive Announces Definitive Agreement to Acquire Zulily," news release, Liberty Interactive Corporation, http://ir.libertyinteractive.com/releasedetail.cfm?ReleaseID=927853.

42. The company laid off 25 percent of its staff in December 2015, which was a second round of big cuts. See Jason Del Rey, "One Kings Lane, Once Valued at $900 Million, Is Likely to Sell for a Fraction of That," Recode, January 6, 2016, www.recode.net/2016/1/6/11588562/one-kings-lane -once-valued-at-900-million-is-likely-to-sell-for.

43. It's a shame that in the United States, high school and college speech and debate programs are being cut due to budget shortfalls. These programs instill exceptional written and oral communication skills within students, and they also teach kids how to research, think critically, and organize vast troves of information. I can think of no better preparation for life as an adult. Not the basketball team. Not orchestra. Not the drama club. Not even world-class coding classes. What good are technical skills if you can't make a persuasive argument? Or if you can't express yourself well in a meeting? From my point of view, if schools are endeavoring to prepare our young people to create the future, they ought to pour resources back into speech and debate, not just for competition, but so that both can be integrated into the curriculum. (I'm happy to debate this point with you in person. I'm either @amywebb or @webbmedia on whichever social network you're using.)

44. Bill Vlasic, "U.S. Proposes Spending $4 Billion on Self-Driving Cars," New York Times, January 14, 2016, www.nytimes.com/2016/01/15/business/us-proposes-spending-4-billion-on-self-driving -cars.html.

45. Alex Wilhelm and Alexia Tsotsis, "Google Ventures Puts $258M into Uber, Its Largest Deal Ever," TechCrunch, August 22, 2013, http://techcrunch.com/2013/08/22/google-ventures-puts -258m-into-uber-its-largest-deal-ever.

46. Mike Ramsey and Douglas MacMillan, "Carnegie Mellon Reels After Uber Lures Away Researchers," Wall Street Journal, May 31, 2015, www.wsj.com/article_email/is-uber-a-friend -or-foe-of-carnegie-mellon-in-robotics-1433084582-lMyQjAxMTE1MjA5MTUwNzE5Wj.

47. Ibid.

48. Ibid.

CHAPTER 7. IS IT *REALLY* AWESOME?
KNOW WHEN THE TIMING IS RIGHT

1. The origin of "Seeing is believing" is the chapter in the New Testament about "Doubting Thomas," one of the apostles of Jesus who was skeptical about the Resurrection until, according to the story, he saw him with his own eyes. See John 20.

2. Jessi Hempel, "The Inside Story of Uber's Radical Rebranding," Wired, February 2016.

3. Frank Rose, "Pocket Monster," Wired, September 2001.

4. Jason Kincaid, "SCVNGR Raises $15 Million at $100MM Valuation," TechCrunch, January 4, 2011, http://techcrunch.com/2011/01/04/scvngr-raises-15-million-at-100mm-valuation.

5. John D. Sutter, "The Modern Tech CEO: Barefoot and 21," CNN, November 2, 2010, www.cnn .com/2010/TECH/innovation/11/02/seth.priebatsch.scvngr.

6. Nathan Chandler, "How the Nintendo Power Glove Worked," How Stuff Works, http:// electronics.howstuffworks.com/nintendo-power-glove.htm.

7. Spencer E. Ante, "Investors Cool on Foursquare," Wall Street Journal, November 20, 2012, www.wsj.com/news/articles/SB10001424127887324712504578131384140607240.

8. Gregory Huabg, "LevelUp Leads 'Cambrian Explosion' of Mobile Payments & Rewards," Xconomy, August 3, 2012, www.xconomy.com/boston/2012/08/03/levelup-leads-cambrian -explosion-of-mobile-payments-rewards.

9. Jeremy Cabalona, "Gowalla Is Officially Shut Down," Mashable, March 11, 2012, http://mashable .com/2012/03/11/gowalla-shuts-down.

10. Mike Isaac, "Foursquare Raises $45 Million, Cutting Its Valuation Nearly in Half," New York Times, January 14, 2016, www.nytimes.com/2016/01/15/technology/foursquare-raises-45 -million-cutting-its-valuation-nearly-in-half.html.

11. There are many variants and alternative translations, depending on the reading of the two characters 忍者. In Japanese, the pronunciation was likely "shinobi" rather than "ninja."

CHAPTER 8. IF THIS, THEN THAT:
A FORMULA FOR ACTION

1. Steven Levy, "Jeff Bezos Owns the Web in More Ways Than You Think," *Wired*, November 2011, www.wired.com/2011/11/ff_bezos.

2. Fritz Heider and Marianne Simmel, "An Experimental Study of Apparent Behavior," *American Journal of Psychology* 57, no. 2 (April 1944).

3. See "Experimental Study of Apparent Behavior: Fritz Heider & Marianne Simmel. 1944," YouTube, uploaded December 26, 2010, https://www.youtube.com/watch?v=n9TWwG4SFWQ.

4. Nostradamus biography at Biography.com, www.biography.com/people/nostradamus-9425407.

5. Nostradamus, *The Complete Prophecies of Nostradamus*, edited by Ned Halley (London: Wordsworth Reference, 1999).

6. Heiko A. Von der Gracht, *The Future of Logistics* (Berlin: Springer, 2008).

7. Herman Kahn, *On Thermonuclear War* (Princeton, NJ: Princeton University Press, 1960). The first edition of this book had 651 pages.

8. Scott Foundas, "Film Review: '42," *Variety*, http://variety.com/2013/film/reviews/film-review-42-1200339020.

9. Sosha Lewis, "Review: Eddie the Eagle," *Charlotte Observer*, February 27, 2016, www.charlotteobserver.com/living/health-family/moms/article62870192.html.

10. Moira MacDonald, "High Aspirations: 'Eddie the Eagle' Is Charming, If Inaccurate," *Seattle Times*, February 25, 2016, www.seattletimes.com/entertainment/movies/high-aspirations-eddie-the-eagle-is-charming-if-inaccurate.

11. "Movies," *The New Yorker*, January 21, 2008, www.newyorker.com/magazine/2008/01/21/movies-35.

12. "Yearly Box Office: 2015 Domestic Grosses," Box Office Mojo, www.boxofficemojo.com/yearly/chart/?yr=2015.

13. For Cutting's research, see "James E. Cutting: Professor: Department of Psychology," Cornell University, http://people.psych.cornell.edu/~jec7/curresearch.htm.

14. Jamie Dimon, Annual Letter to Shareholders, 2015, https://www.jpmorganchase.com/corporate/investor-relations/document/ar2015-ceolettershareholders.pdf.

15. Matt Egan, "30% of Bank Jobs Are Under Threat," CNN Money, April 4, 2016, http://money.cnn.com/2016/04/04/investing/bank-jobs-dying-automation-citigroup.

16. Powell has described his "go with your gut" rule a number of times in presentations. See General (USA-Ret.) Colin L. Powell, "18 Lessons in Leadership," Air University, *Air and Space Power Journal*, April 2, 2011, www.airpower.maxwell.af.mil/apjinternational/apj-s/2011/2011-4/2011_4_02_powell_s_eng.pdf.

17. Chris Taylor, "Triumph of the Nerds: Nate Silver Wins in 50 States," Mashable, November 7, 2012, http://mashable.com/2012/11/07/nate-silver-wins.

CHAPTER 9. GREETINGS, ROBOT OVERLORDS:
PRESSURE-TESTING YOUR STRATEGY

1. Sarah Perez, "Emu, a Smarter Messaging App with a Built-in Assistant, Exits Beta," TechCrunch, April 2, 2014, http://techcrunch.com/2014/04/02/emu-a-smarter-messaging-app-with-a-built-in-assistant-exits-beta.

2. Ron Amadeo, "Google Buys Emu, an iPhone Texting App with a Built-in Virtual Assistant," Arstechnica,August6,2014,http://arstechnica.com/gadgets/2014/08/google-buys-emu-an-iphone-texting-app-with-a-built-in-virtual-assistant.

3. Marco Della Cava, "Microsoft CEO Nadella: 'Bots Are the New Apps,'" *USA Today*, March 30, 2016, www.usatoday.com/story/tech/news/2016/03/30/microsof-ceo-nadella-bots-new-apps/82431672.

4. Here's a bit more background on Clippy by Claire Cozens at *The Guardian*: "Microsoft Cuts 'Mr Clippy,'" April 11, 2001, www.theguardian.com/media/2001/apr/11/advertising2.

5. A video of Nadella's keynote presentation at Build is at Channel 9, https://channel9.msdn.com/Events/Build/2016/KEY01.

6. Yongdong Wang, "Your Next New Best Friend Might Be a Robot," Nautil, February 4, 2016, http://nautil.us/issue/33/attraction/your-next-new-best-friend-might-be-a-robot.

7. Ibid.

8. Ibid.

9. Hope King, "Meet Tay, Microsoft's Teen Chat Bot," CNN Money, March 23, 2016, http://money.cnn.com/2016/03/23/technology/tay-chat-bot.

10. Microsoft disabled its Tay.ai Twitter account, which meant that those original Tweets became difficult to find. However, when Tay started behaving badly, Twitter users took screenshots and sent them around social media. If you do an image search on Tay Tweets, you'll find the ones I've mentioned—plus many more. Be warned, many are NSFW (Not Safe For Work).

11. T. Hobbes, *De Corpore* (1655), chaps. 1–6, in A. P. Martinich, trans., *Part I of De Corpore* (New York: Abaris Books, 1981).

12. Rene Descartes, John Cottingham, Robert Stoothoff, and Dugald Murdoch, *The Philosophical Writings of Descartes* (Cambridge: Cambridge University Press, 1985).

13. Etienne Bonnot De Condillac, *Condillac: Essay on the Origin of Human Knowledge*, translated by Hans Arsleff, Cambridge Texts in the History of Philosophy (Cambridge: Cambridge University Press, 2001).

14. Ada Lovelace, *Scientific Memoirs: Selections from "The Transactions of Foreign Academies and Learned Societies" and from Foreign Journals*, edited by Richard Taylor, FSA, vol. 3 (London, 1843).

15. "Timeline of Computer History," Computer History Museum, www.computerhistory.org/timeline/ai-robotics.

16. A. M. Turing, "Computing Machinery and Intelligence," *Mind* 59 (1960): 433–460.

17. If you're suddenly hankering to play, the Internet Archive has an emulator you can run at https://archive.org/details/msdos_Oregon_Trail_The_1990.

18. Latanya Sweeney, "Discrimination in Online Ad Delivery," Data Privacy Lab, January 28, 2013, http://arxiv.org/pdf/1301.6822v1.pdf.

19. As of May 5, 2016, the first instance of a woman was still CEO Barbie.

20. Jenna Wortham, "Apple Buys a Start-Up for Its Voice Technology," *New York Times*, April 29, 2010, www.nytimes.com/2010/04/29/technology/29apple.html.

21. Philip Elmer-DeWitt, "Minneapolis Street Test: Google Gets a B+, Apple's Siri Gets a D," *Fortune*, June 29, 2012, http://fortune.com/2012/06/29/minneapolis-street-test-google-gets-a-b-apples-siri-gets-a-d.

22. Nick Bilton, "With Apple's Siri, a Romance Gone Sour," *New York Times*, July 15, 2012, http://bits.blogs.nytimes.com/2012/07/15/with-apple%E2%80%99s-siri-a-romance-gone-sour.

23. Bianca Bosker, "Why Siri's Voice Is Now a Man (And a Woman)," Huffington Post, June 11, 2013, www.huffingtonpost.com/2013/06/11/siri-voice-man-woman_n_3423245.html.

24. March 2016 Build keynote.

25. Richard Waters, "Investor Rush to Artificial Intelligence Is Real Deal," *Financial Times*, January 4, 2015, www.ft.com/cms/s/2/019b3702-92a2-11e4-a1fd-00144feabdc0.html.

26. Alistair Barr, "Google Mistakenly Tags Black People as 'Gorillas,' Showing Limits of Algorithms," *Wall Street Journal*, July 1, 2015, http://blogs.wsj.com/digits/2015/07/01/google-mistakenly-tags-black-people-as-gorillas-showing-limits-of-algorithms.

27. Reddit AMA with Stephen Hawking on July 27, 2015, https://www.reddit.com/r/science/comments/3nyn5i/science_ama_series_stephen_hawking_ama_answers.

28. Amy Webb, "Apple vs. FBI Debate May Be the Least of Our Challenges," CNN, February 29, 2016, www.cnn.com/2016/02/25/opinions/when-technology-clashes-with-law-iphone-opinion-webb.

29. Ibid.

CHAPTER 10. REVERSE-ENGINEERING THE FUTURE

1. The Nobel Prize in Physiology or Medicine, 1981, Nobel Prize, www.nobelprize.org/nobel_prizes/medicine/laureates/1981.

2. Hasso Plattner Institute of Design at Stanford University (d.school), *Bootcamp Bootleg*, 2011, https://dschool.stanford.edu/wp-content/uploads/2011/03/BootcampBootleg2010v2SLIM.pdf.

3. Jessi Hempel, an enormously talented reporter, wrote a great story on Magic Leap. It's full of great detail you won't find elsewhere: "I Went Inside Magic Leap's Mysterious HQ: Here's What I Saw," *Wired*, April 2016, www.wired.com/2016/04/went-inside-magic-leaps-mysterious-hq-heres-saw.

4. Evelyn M. Rusli and Alistair Barr, "Google Leads $542 Million Deal in Secretive Startup Magic Leap," *Wall Street Journal*, October 21, 2014, http://blogs.wsj.com/digits/2014/10/21/google-leads-542-million-deal-in-secretive-startup-magic-leap.

5. Jessi Hempel, "Magic Leap Just Landed an Astounding Amount of VC Money," *Wired*, February 2, 2016, www.wired.com/2016/02/magic-leap-raises-the-biggest-c-round-in-venture-history.

6. Woodrow Barfield and Thomas Caudell, *Basic Concepts in Wearable Computers and Augmented Reality* (London: Lawrence Erlbaum Associates, 2001).

7. The app is Makeup Genius. See L'Oréal, www.lorealparis.ca/_en/_ca/brands/makeup-genius.

8. The app was available at the iTunes store as of May 2016.

9. See the Developer Program site, https://developers.google.com/glass.

10. Gary R. Bradski, Samuel A. Miller, and Rony Abovitz, "United States Patent Application Number: 20160026253—Methods and Systems for Creating Virtual and Augmented Reality," January 28, 2016.

11. Data retrieved through the US Patent and Trademark Office, www.uspto.gov.

12. Gill A. Pratt, "Is a Cambrian Explosion Coming for Robotics?" *Journal of Economic Perspectives* 29, no. 3 (Summer 2015), http://pubs.aeaweb.org/doi/pdfplus/10.1257/jep.29.3.51.

13. Original 1831 Preface to Mary Shelley, *Frankenstein, or a Modern Prometheus*, https://www.rc.umd.edu/editions/frankenstein/1831v1/intro.

14. For more about the *Seven Soldiers of Victory*, see DC Comics, www.dccomics.com/graphic-novels/seven-soldiers-of-victory-archives-vol-1.

INDEX

AMY WEBB is a world-renowned futurist whose books and papers have won prestigious awards and have been translated into a number of different languages. She is the founder of the Future Today Institute, a leading future forecasting and strategy firm that answers "What's the future of *X*" for a global client base. Webb's research focuses on how technology will transform the way we live, work, and govern. Her future forecasting research has been featured in the *New York Times*, *Harvard Business Review*, the *Wall Street Journal*, *Fortune*, and *Fast Company*, and it has been cited in several academic papers. Webb holds many professional affiliations and collaborates with a number of institutions. She was a delegate on the former US-Russia Bilateral Presidential Commission and served on the Aspen Institute's Dialogue on Libraries, where she worked with Federal Communications Commission chairman Reed Hundt and others on the future of libraries. She is an adjunct professor at New York University's Stern School of Business, where she teaches a course on the future of technology, and a lecturer on the future of media at Columbia University. She was a 2014–2015 Visiting Nieman Fellow at Harvard University. While living in Japan, she earned Nikyu Certification in the Japanese government-administered Language Proficiency Test and the rank of *shodan* (first-degree black belt) in aikido, but a serious accident during practice a few years ago forced her to retire. Webb is a trained classical clarinetist and plays that instrument along with other woodwinds and piano whenever she can. She lives in Baltimore with her husband, Brian, and daughter, Petra.

Photograph courtesy of Mary Gardella Photography